D0700775

WORLD WAR II
FROM ABOVE

TO SARAH, GUY, AND TOBY AND TO DEE, THE MOST PATIENT EDITOR I KNOW

WORLD WAR II FROM ABOVE
By Jeremy Harwood

First published in North America in 2014 by Zenith Press, an imprint of
Quarto Publishing Group USA Inc., 400 First Avenue North, Suite 400,
Minneapolis, MN 55401 USA, by arrangement with Quid Publishing.

© 2014 Quid Publishing

All rights reserved. With the exception of quoting brief passages for the
purposes of review, no part of this publication may be reproduced
without prior written permission from the Publisher.

The information in this book is true and complete to the best of our
knowledge. All recommendations are made without any guarantee on
the part of the author or Publisher, who also disclaims any liability
incurred in connection with the use of this data or specific details.

We recognize, further, that some words, model names, and designations
mentioned herein are the property of the trademark holder. We use them
for identification purposes only. This is not an official publication.

Zenith Press titles are also available at discounts in bulk quantity for
industrial or sales-promotional use. For details write to Special Sales
Manager at Quarto Publishing Group USA Inc., 400 First Avenue North,
Suite 400, Minneapolis, MN 55401 USA.

To find out more about our books, visit us online at www.zenithpress.com.

ISBN: 978-0-7603-4573-3

Set in Akzidenz Grotesk, New Century Schoolbook, and Trade Gothic

Printed and bound in China

Conceived, designed, and produced by
Quid Publishing
Level 4 Sheridan House
Hove BN3 1DD
England

Design and illustration: Simon Daley

Cover image:
Boeing B-17F formation over Schweinfurt, Germany, on Aug. 17, 1943.
Reprinted by permission from Air Force Magazine, published by
the Air Force Association.

rwood, Jeremy, 1947—
orld War II from above
 an aerial view of the
014.
33305231326277
a   10/16/14

WORLD WAR II FROM ABOVE

AN AERIAL VIEW OF THE GLOBAL CONFLICT

JEREMY HARWOOD

ZENITH PRESS

CONTENTS

◀ A squadron of B-17 Flying Fortresses from the US 8th Army Air Force is captured in the air over Germany on its way to bomb Stuttgart's ball-bearing factories on September 7, 1943. The American high command was wedded to daylight precision bombing, believing that their heavily-armed bombers could fight off Luftwaffe fighter attacks on their own. They were to be proved wrong. Only the eventual arrival of long-range fighter escorts managed to reverse the ever-mounting rate of losses.

INTRODUCTION

Looking at it from a 21st-century perspective, the vital role air power plays on the modern battleground seems self-evident. Looking back into the past, however, it may well seem surprising that it took a relatively long time for this to be fully recognized. As Tami Biddle, a noted historian of air power has written, "virtually every manifestation of 20th-century air power, was envisaged and worked out in at least rudimentary form between 1914–1918"—that is, during World War I.

This is why this book, though primarily concerned with World War II, takes "the war to end war" as its starting point. To quote from Biddle again: "Those who wish to understand the role of aircraft in subsequent conflicts do well to turn back to the experience of the Great War precisely because all the roots of modern practice are there to be explored."

It was as a reconnaissance instrument that the airplane first made its mark. Indeed, the outcomes of the battles of the Marne and Tannenberg at the start of the war might have been very different if first the Allies and then the Germans had not taken advantage of the intelligence provided by the airborne scouts. Aircraft soon became invaluable for artillery spotting; aerial photography also proved vital in building up a comprehensive picture of what was going on in the trenches and behind the lines on "the other side of the hill." The need to achieve dominance in the air led to the birth of the fighter; the development of tactical and long-range strategic bombers was not far behind. By 1918, air power was on the verge of coming of age.

It was not surprising therefore that, in the period between the two world wars, fears about the extraordinary destructive powers of aircraft flourished. "The bomber," people were grimly assured, "will always get through." Apostles of air power, such as the Italian air strategist Giulio Douhet and the American aviator Billy Mitchell, fuelled such fears. In the 1930s, Goering boasted that his newly created Luftwaffe, then the world's most powerful air force, "stood ready to carry out every command of the Fuehrer with lightning speed and undreamed-of might."

The truth was somewhat different. Though air power indeed emerged as a major strategic element during World War II, it could not win wars on its own. What the war showed was that, operating in close collaboration with the other armed forces, it was the vital ingredient in the cocktail that won battlefield victories. On both the Western and Eastern Fronts, air power complemented ground power in bringing about the defeat of Nazi Germany. In the Far East, its collaboration with surface forces was instrumental in achieving the collapse of imperial Japan.

The actual air war, of course, is a fascinating story in itself. Highlights of this book include vivid accounts of the great strategic bombing offensives, from the Luftwaffe's attempt to blitz Britain into submission to the RAF's great area bombing raids that laid waste to Germany's major cities, and the USAAF's precision strikes on key German targets, to the 1945 fire raids on Japan and the atomic bombing of Hiroshima and Nagasaki, which brought the curtain down on the war. The book also places equal emphasis on another important side of the story, which is less familiar than it ought to be. This is the unsung efforts of the "spies in the skies" to obtain accurate air intelligence—a struggle that began even before the outbreak of hostilities.

Arguably, the work of the aerial photographers and photographic interpreters had even more impact on the outcome of the war than that of the Bletchley Park code-breakers. Indeed, some commentators believe that, without it, the Allies might well have lost the war. The detection of Hitler's vaunted "vengeance weapons" is a prime case in point. Had they remained undetected and gone into operation as the Germans had planned, it is an open question as to whether they would have delayed Allied victory in Normandy at the best, or, at the worst, brought about a humiliating Allied defeat.

A US photographer managed to shoot this dramatic picture of bombs falling on the industrial city of Terni, Italy, in late 1943. The bombers involved in the raid came from the US 12th Army Air Force, their targets being the city's steel works and railway marshalling yards. Milan, Foggia, Naples, Palermo, Treviso, and Turin were among other Italian targets that were heavily bombed. Rome was largely spared after Pope Pius XI appealed to President Roosevelt not to attack the capital.

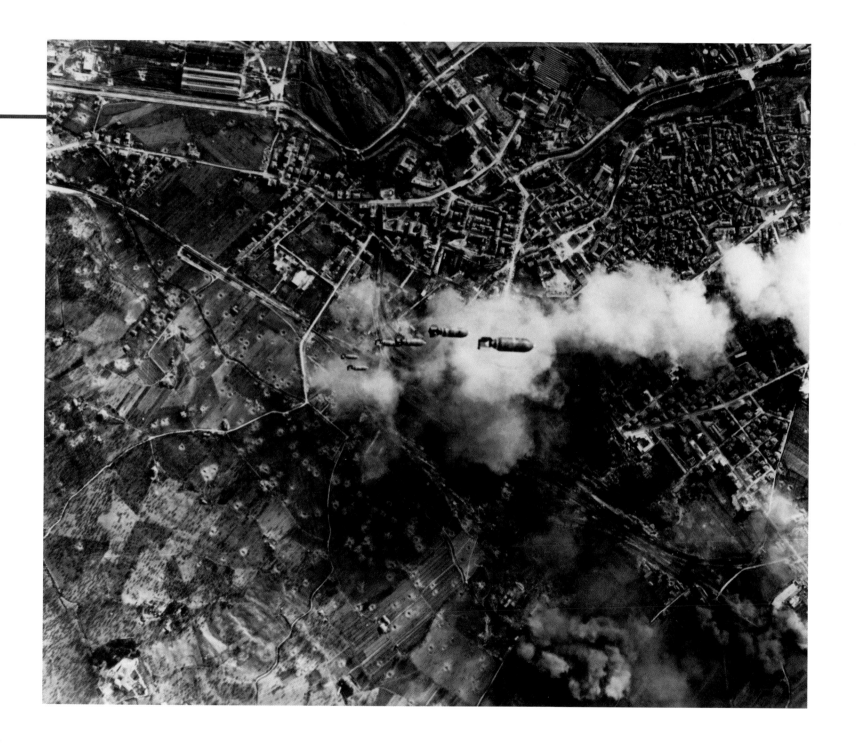

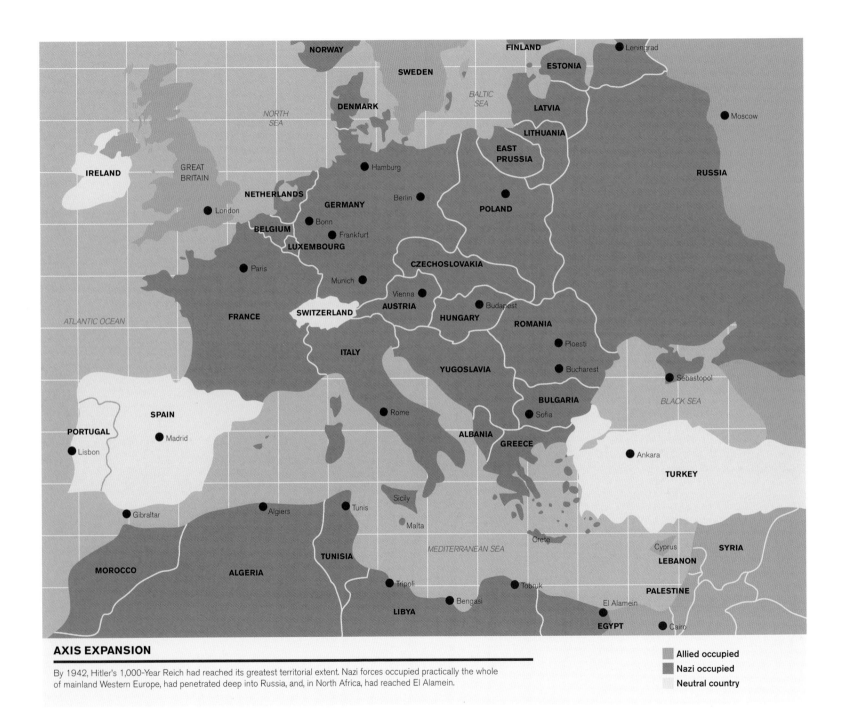

AXIS EXPANSION

By 1942, Hitler's 1,000-Year Reich had reached its greatest territorial extent. Nazi forces occupied practically the whole of mainland Western Europe, had penetrated deep into Russia, and, in North Africa, had reached El Alamein.

Allied occupied

Nazi occupied

Neutral country

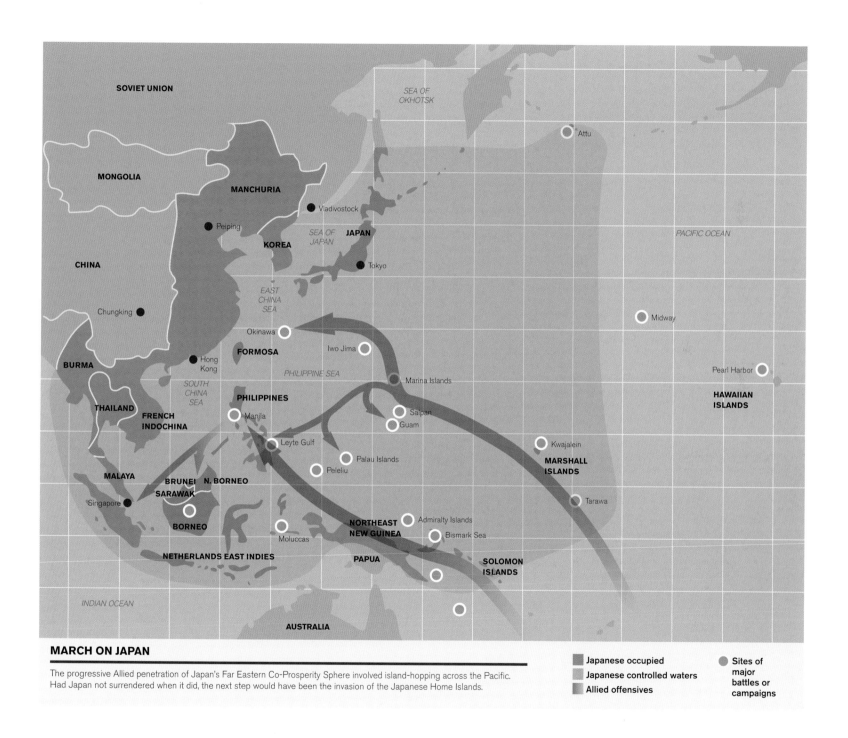

MARCH ON JAPAN

The progressive Allied penetration of Japan's Far Eastern Co-Prosperity Sphere involved island-hopping across the Pacific. Had Japan not surrendered when it did, the next step would have been the invasion of the Japanese Home Islands.

Japanese occupied
Japanese controlled waters
Allied offensives
Sites of major battles or campaigns

BEGINNINGS

From early times, land commanders used cavalry to reconnoiter enemy strength and battlefield intentions. In the 19th century, balloons were deployed as aerial spotting posts to increase artillery accuracy; just before the outbreak of World War I, they were joined by airplanes. By 1918, air reconnaissance had become a highly sophisticated business; in that year alone, Allied aircraft took over 10 million aerial photographs of German positions along the Western Front. The war witnessed other important aerial developments; Germany's Zeppelin airships and Gotha and Giant aircraft were the forerunners of the heavy bombers that were to feature so prominently in the strategic bombing campaigns of World War II.

PIONEER BALLOONISTS

It was France that pioneered balloon flight. Jean-François-Pilâtre de Rozier became the first man to take to the air, when, on October 15, 1783, his tethered balloon soared into the sky over Paris. On December 1 of the same year, two Frenchmen—their names are uncertain—bettered this by flying 27 miles (43.5km); in January 1785, Jean-Pierre Blanchard managed to fly across the English Channel. Britain had witnessed its first successful balloon flight the previous May, when Vincenzo Lunardi, a pioneer Italian balloonist, made a 20-mile (32km) flight, his starting point being the grounds of the Honourable Artillery Company at Moorfields in London.

Though a single 20-mile (32km) military test flight followed that June, the British concluded that ballooning had nothing valuable to contribute to warfare. Many army officers were prejudiced against them, considering the use of balloons for observational purposes to be unfair. It was not, they pontificated, "playing the game."

The French, however, thought differently. During the Revolutionary Wars of the 1790s, they pioneered the use of balloons for aerial military reconnaissance during their campaigns against the Austrians and Prussians. However, Nelson's destruction of a ship carrying a balloon company at Aboukir Bay in 1798 seems to have discouraged French aerial efforts.

THE FIRST PHOTOGRAPHS

Though photography was invented in the late 1830s, it was impossible to use early cameras in the air. They were too big and cumbersome; they relied on fragile glass plates that not only had to be coated with light-sensitive emulsion before exposure, but also had to be developed while the balloon was still in flight. Otherwise the hydrogen gas such balloons employed as their lifting agent spoiled the images.

It was not until 1858 that Gaspard Félix Tournachon, a Parisian photographer, caricaturist, and journalist

▲ Aviation pioneers Jean-François Pilâtre de Rozier and Giroud de Villette take to the skies in a tethered hot-air balloon in Paris on October 19, 1783. They got as high as 330ft (100m) in a flight lasting nine minutes. Later, France became the first nation in the world to employ balloons for military reconnaissance.

better known by his pseudonym Nadar, managed to take the first successful aerial photographs. Two years later, American balloonists Samuel A. King and James W. Black took the first aerial photographs in the USA from a tethered balloon flying 1,200ft (365m) over Boston. But, though the North used balloons for reconnaissance during the American Civil War and the French employed them extensively when Paris was besieged by the Prussians during the Franco-Prussian War, neither side appears to have taken photographs from them.

An important breakthrough came in 1871 when Richard L. Maddox, an English doctor, invented gelatine dry plates to replace collodion ones. Aerial photography really became practical as a result. Maddox's plates were more sensitive than their collodion predecessors; they could also be developed after returning to the ground rather than in flight. In 1896, a Manual of Military Ballooning declared confidently that "no modern army would be considered complete without balloon equipment."

POWERED FLIGHT

Aerial reconnaissance by balloon had a significant drawback. By definition, tethered balloons lacked maneuverability. The Germans believed that powered airships could be the answer; in 1900, Count Ferdinand von Zeppelin's first rigid dirigible took to the skies. Then, in 1903 at Kitty Hawk on the North Carolina coast, Orville and Wilbur Wright succeeded in getting their heavier-than-air biplane airborne. The revolutionary age of powered flight had arrived.

From the start, airplanes were recognized as potentially valuable observational tools—that was why armies bought them in the first place. Technological progress was swift. In 1912, General Sir James Grierson, one of the commanders in the British Army's summer war games, decisively outmaneuvered General Sir Douglas Haig, his opponent, largely thanks to his use of aerial reconnaissance. It was a foretaste of what was to follow when, two years later, the world went to war.

An early Zeppelin makes a safe landing, with Count Ferdinand von Zeppelin, the airship's inventor, and the Crown Prince of Germany among the onlookers. In 1915, military Zeppelins became the world's first strategic bombers, when they began an 18-month terror campaign against British targets, aiming to break civilian morale and bomb the nation into submission. Peter Strasser, their commander, put it starkly: "There is no such thing as a noncombatant any more. Modern war is total war."

AIRPLANES AND CAMERAS

Grierson undoubtedly possessed foresight. At the conclusion of the 1912 war games, he concluded: "Personally, I think there is no doubt that, before land fighting takes place, we shall have to fight and destroy the enemy's aircraft… warfare will be impossible until we have mastery of the air." Other military pundits, however, disagreed. The most notorious of them was France's General Ferdinand Foch, who is said to have opined that "aviation is a good sport, but for the army it is useless." The Russian General Alexander Samsonov was another. When war came in 1914, he ignored the information provided by his reconnaissance pilots. General Paul von Hindenburg, his opponent, did not. After his crushing victory, the German commander acknowledged that "without the airmen there would have been no Tannenberg." The defeated Samsonov killed himself on the battlefield.

Technologically, the airplanes at the start of the war were unsophisticated. Four squadrons of Britain's recently formed Royal Flying Corps (RFC) accompanied the British Expeditionary Force (BEF) to France. The airplanes with which they were equipped were underpowered, flimsy, and somewhat unstable. They could be thrown around by a heavy gust of wind, tossed about in thermals, and found it hard to make progress when faced by a strong wind. Nor were they armed. Pilots and observers fell back on rifles, sporting guns, and revolvers in an attempt to deter marauding German scouts. New airplanes were an obvious priority.

As fighting on the Western Front degenerated into the stalemate of trench warfare, it quickly became clear to the British that better cameras with longer lenses

Founded in May 1912 as part of the British Army, the Royal Flying Corps dispatched 63 aircraft to France on the outbreak of war. It expanded quickly; by the time of the Battle of the Somme in 1916, 27 squadrons with 421 aircraft between them were serving on the Western Front. By the end of the war, the RAF, as the RFC became when it was merged with the Royal Naval Air Service in April 1918, had a total strength of around 22,000 aircraft. It was the biggest air force in the world.

were required. The A-type met some of these requirements. Its main drawback was its use of 5 x 4in (12.5 x 10cm) glass-plate negatives, which had to be individually loaded and unloaded manually. Though photographic quality was excellent, actually taking the photographs was a cumbersome process that required patience and considerable skill. B-type and WA-type cameras were modified and bigger versions of the A-type; the C-type was fitted with two semiautomatic magazines to make changing plates easier.

The E-type, which was introduced toward the end of 1916, differed from its predecessors by being made of metal rather than wood. It was generally mounted externally alongside the observer or behind his seat, the lens focusing downward through a hole in the fuselage. The L-type, which superseded it, could be fitted either inside or outside the cockpit and operated either by hand or automatically. The LB- and BM-types were further important modifications.

ZEPPELINS, GOTHAS, AND GIANTS

The Germans and the Allies more or less matched each other move for move in the air war that raged over the trenches. In one respect, the Germans took the lead. They were the first of the belligerents to embark on the deliberate strategic bombing of civilian populations, so unleashing a totally new era in warfare. Peter Strasser, the fanatical commander of Germany's Zeppelin air fleet, grimly told his aircrews: "We who strike the enemy where his heart beats have been slandered as 'baby killers.' Nowadays, there is no such animal as a noncombatant. Modern warfare is total warfare."

Count Ferdinand von Zeppelin's great airships were the first bombing weapon the German High Command deployed against Britain. Two of them bombed the North Sea port of Great Yarmouth and the town of King's Lynn on the night of January 19, 1915. On May 31, London was bombed for the first time.

Flying at heights of 20,000ft (6,096m) or more,

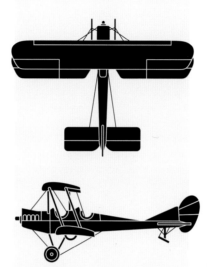

BE2-C

Type	Reconnaissance/Light Bomber
Crew	2
Length	27ft 3in (3.4m)
Wingspan	37ft (11.28m)
Speed	72mph (116km/h)
Range	3.25 hours endurance

The BE2-C was the Royal Flying Corps' mainstay during the first years of World War I. It was, said one of its pilots, "a sort of maid of all work, a general-purpose hack, which could be used for reconnaissance, artillery observation, photography, spy-dropping, or any other job that turned up."

Germany's airships seemed invincible. It was not until September 2, 1916 that Lieutenant Leefe-Robinson finally managed to shoot one down. His success was not only due to his flying skills; his airplane's machine guns were loaded with two new types of bullet, fired in sequence. The first, containing highly explosive nitroglycerine, blew large holes in the airship's hull and gas-bags; the second, an incendiary bullet, caused the resulting hydrogen and oxygen mixture to catch fire and explode.

The Germans were not beaten. They turned to heavier-than-air bombers to bring about the results they so desired. On May 25, 1917, 22 twin-engine Gotha bombers carried out a major daylight raid on targets in southeastern England. On June 12, they struck at London, again flying by day. It was not until September that they switched to night-raiding. That fall, they were joined by the aptly named Giant four-engine heavy bomber. Produced by the Zeppelin Company, it was the largest airplane to be fielded by either side during the whole of World War I.

PHOTOGRAPHING THE TRENCHES

Aerial photographs were taken vertically downward or at an oblique angle, which allowed cameras to "see" farther behind the enemy lines. They had varied and equally important uses. First and foremost, both sides used them as the basis for constructing detailed maps of enemy lines. Photographs could also pinpoint artillery positions, while pilots and observers could detect and record reinforcements of men and materials being brought up to the front.

The British were the first to make use of coordinated aerial photography. In advance of the Battle of Neuve Chapelle, which began on March 10, 1915, two RFC reconnaissance squadrons successfully photographed the entire German defensive system at the point where a salient jutted out into the BEF's positions close to their junction with the French Army. The enemy trenches shown on the photographs were traced onto a skeleton map on which details of the British plan of attack were superimposed. It was the start of a process that was to lead to the development of a whole new science of photographic interpretation, which was to play a major part in the future military direction of the war.

PHOTOGRAPHIC INTERPRETATION

Aerial success at Neuve Chapelle triggered a decision to speed up the expansion of the RFC and its photographic capabilities. In August 1915, Lieutenant Colonel Hugh Trenchard was appointed its new commander. A dominant personality with a foghorn of a voice, which earned him the nickname "Boom," Trenchard was air power's most fervent apostle. Immediately, he started to plan for a massive expansion in the size of the RFC, pushing for the introduction of faster airplanes with more powerful engines and equipped with better weapons. He also advocated the development of bombers.

Effective aerial reconnaissance was an integral part of Trenchard's master plan. He immediately put the

32-year-old John Moore-Brabazon, who in 1909 had become the first Englishman to fly in an airplane in Britain, in charge of RFC aerial photography. Sergeant Major Victor Laws, the RFC's only experienced photographic specialist, was assigned to work alongside him. In September, Laws returned to Britain to set up the new RFC School of Photography at Farnborough. Two months later, he became its head.

At Farnborough, candidates were trained in all aspects of aerial photography. They learned how to develop and print glass plates, make enlargements, maintain aerial cameras, and use photographs to make maps. They were also taught how to use shadows to measure the scale of objects on the ground, spot enemy machine gun and artillery positions, locate unit headquarters, and to analyze troop movements. Having

▼ This C-type camera is fitted to the rear cockpit of a BE 2c reconnaissance aircraft. The observer operated the shutter of the camera by pulling a cord attached to its trigger. The C-type utilized the body of the earlier A-type camera with the addition of a plate-changing top and a second magazine. The first magazine held 18 photographic plates, stacked face down over the camera's focal plane. Once exposed, each plate slid over to a frame in the second magazine, into which it fell.

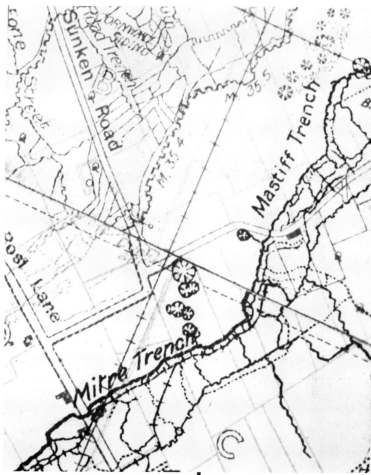

completed their training, they were posted back to France to staff the photographic units that were soon being attached to each frontline squadron.

Results became more and more impressive. Before the Battle of the Somme began in July 1916, all the German positions had been photographed by the RFC and detailed maps of them plotted. The French, with their "Plans Directeur," excelled even the RFC in the amount of detailed information their maps contained. Gleaned over time and intended primarily to assist the French artillery, they clearly identified the most vital points in the enemy defenses.

Each sector of the French-held front had its own "Chef de Cartographie," selected for his specialist knowledge of the particular area. According to one American observer, this involved "going out not only into the foremost observation posts but even into 'No-Man's Land,' as well as analyzing all the aerial photographs and other intelligence available to him." In addition, in the person of Captain Eugene Marie Edmond Pepin, the French possessed one of the greatest pioneers of aerial photographic interpretation to emerge on either side during the course of the entire war.

Before the Battle of Neuve Chapelle began on March 10, 1915, reconnaissance aircraft from 2 and 3 Squadrons of the RFC photographed the entire German defensive position successfully at the point where an enemy salient jutted out into the British front lines (*above left*). The German trenches detected on the photographs were then traced carefully onto a skeleton map (*above right*), on which details of the British plan of attack were eventually superimposed. Copies of this map were distributed to the attacking infantry and supporting artillery as part of the preparations for the British assault.

Reconnaissance photographs of the German and British positions at Neuve Chapelle were built up to create this impressive photomontage. By 1918, the British had created a vast photographic map of the whole of their sector of the Front in France. The map was kept up to date constantly with new photographs being added on an almost daily basis. Between January 1918 and the Armistice the following November, Allied photo-reconnaissance aircraft took more than 10 million photographs of the Western Front. The Imperial German Air Service was not far behind; by 1917, its reconnaissance planes were aiming to cover the entire Front twice a month.

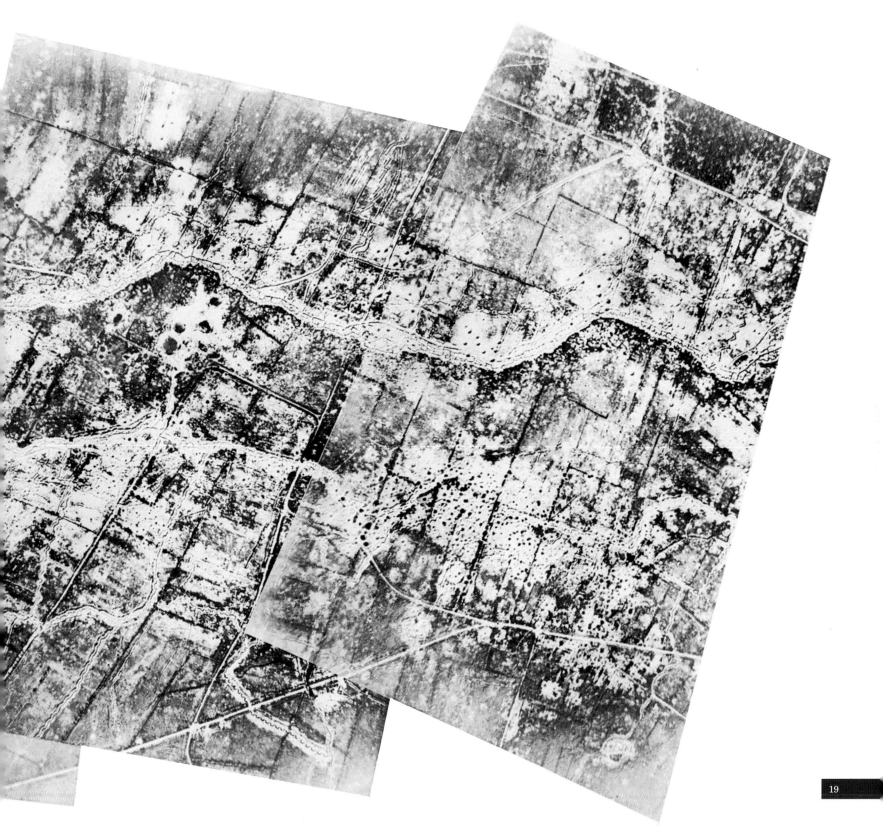

▲ A Short Type 184 seaplane taxies prior to takeoff. A two-seater fitted with folding wings, the Short served as a reconnaissance, bombing, and torpedo-carrying aircraft in the Royal Naval Air Service from the time it came into service in 1915 until the end of the war. On August 12, 1915, a Short was the first aircraft in the world to attack an enemy vessel with a torpedo; three days later, it became the first to actually sink one when Flight Commander Charles Edmonds successfully torpedoed a Turkish transport ship a few miles north of the Dardanelles.

PHOTOGRAPHS BY THE MILLION

By December 1917, a vast photographic map of the whole of the Western Front had been painstakingly built up; the map was amended constantly as new photographs were obtained. The ever-increasing number of photographs being taken enabled the Allied commanders finally to check the great German offensive of March 1918 and then to launch their war-winning counteroffensives that summer. The Germans could not match the massive Allied photographic effort, although, by mid-1917, their Imperial Air Service was taking around 4,000 aerial photographs a day, covering the entire Western Front roughly twice a month.

Between January 1918 and the Armistice that November, Allied airplanes took more than 10 million aerial photographs over France and Belgium, by which time the Americans had arrived to complement British and French efforts. Following its entry into the war, the USA was quick to learn from previous precepts. Aerial observers were taught the skills of aerial photography at Langley Field, Virginia; Cornell University in Ithaca, New York; Fort Sill, Oklahoma; Madison Barracks in New York City; and the Eastman-Kodak plant in Rochester, New York. An aerial photographic center was also established in Tours, France, where newly arrived US air observers could draw directly on British and French experience.

American realization of the importance of thorough photographic interpretation was swift. An official US Army handbook published in 1918 stated clearly how aerial photography had become "one of the most important sources of information" at a commander's disposal. The handbook continued: "In fact, it alone makes possible the exact location of the enemy's defensive works and their detailed study. The enemy, realizing its importance, tries to render this study difficult. Skillful camouflage, a large number of defenses, and imitation works are some of the means

employed. As a result, the study of aerial photographs must be entrusted to specialists, who should be provided with all possible means of verification." American photographic interpreters accordingly were tasked with studying the details of German fortifications, unit structure, and the way in which the Germans went about organizing attack and defense.

Photographic reconnaissance played its part in war zones far from the Western Front as well. Royal Naval Air Service (RNAS) airplanes scouted for the British and Australian and New Zealand Army Corps (ANZAC) when they landed in Gallipoli in 1915, while RFC and RNAS machines supported British, South African, and Belgian forces from the Congo in the campaign in German East Africa (now Tanzania). One of their successes came when an RNAS seaplane spotted and photographed the German cruiser *Königsberg* as she lay skulking in the delta of the Rufiji River in April that year. The *Königsberg* was damaged by British river monitors on July 5; she was finally sunk a week later with accurate gunnery spotting by an RNAS airplane providing the key to the ship's destruction.

Palestine and the Sinai Desert were among other areas that witnessed substantial air reconnaissance activity. It started in early 1915 when Turkish forces advancing across the Sinai on the Suez Canal were spotted by British and French airplanes. Subsequently, the Turks were repulsed. Two years later, the boot was on the other foot when a largely British and Australian army, commanded by General Edmund Allenby, advanced across the Sinai in its turn to defeat the Turks in the battle of Gaza. Allenby then pressed northward, capturing Jerusalem, occupying Palestine, and, by the time the war came to an end, securing Allied control of much of Syria.

Much of the territory over which Allenby's troops were to advance had never been surveyed or mapped thoroughly. RFC photographic reconnaissance was to change all that. In late 1916, photographic officer Hugh

Hamshaw-Thomas was put in command of aerial reconnaissance. A one-time Cambridge paleontologist now based in Egypt, Hamshaw-Thomas approached his photographic tasks in the same studious way in which he had previously unearthed Jurassic fossils. His unit constructed huge photo mosaics—sets of photographs that were literally stuck together—to create an aerial view of a large area. Hamshaw-Thomas used these to produce detailed maps of more than 500 sq. miles (1,295km²) of Egypt, Palestine, and Syria. His painstaking labors demonstrated yet again how important aerial photography was as an adjunct to military intelligence.

This aerial view of Gaza and the surrounding countryside was shot by an Australian pilot in early 1918. The RFC had started photographing the whole of the area in which the British were confronting the Turks the previous year. Air reconnaissance played an important part in paving the way for the British and Commonwealth breakthrough.

BETWEEN THE WARS

A US B4-A reconnaissance aircraft flies over the Philippines in the late 1920s. B4-As and similar aircraft were employed here and in the USA for aerial surveying and photographic mapping. The Americans developed a series of cameras specifically for topographic use. These were fitted with multiple lenses to enable them to cover more ground and shoot parallel strips of terrain simultaneously, taking both oblique and vertical shots.

In the four years of the world war, aviation had progressed by leaps and bounds. The airplanes of 1918 were far faster, more powerful, and more reliable than their predecessors. Unarmed reconnaissance machines had become armed fighting scouts; light, medium, and finally heavy bombers had been developed.

Aerial reconnaissance, too, had developed almost beyond recognition. Sophisticated cameras, fitted with better lenses, could capture detail over a large area from heights of more than 20,000ft (6,100m). Fragile glass plates were being replaced by flexible roll film. Behind the scenes on the ground, photographic interpretation had been perfected as had the art of producing detailed maps based on the photographs the aviators had collected. In sum, flying had come of age.

"AIR CONTROL"

Almost as soon as the war ended, the piecemeal dismantling of the RAF began. It was run down rapidly from around 200 squadrons to only 33. Indeed, it might well have ceased to exist altogether as an independent branch of the armed forces had not Trenchard, now

SURVEYING AND MAPPING

During the 1920s, the RAF deservedly won a high reputation for the detailed aerial surveys it carried out from which new maps and charts were compiled. In 1924, RAF DH 9As, based at Shaibah in Iraq, surveyed the area around the Abadan oil fields in Iran at the request of the Anglo-Persian Oil Company; a photograph from a later aerial survey of Bandar Shahpur is shown (*left*). Earlier RAF aircraft had surveyed a 618-mile (994.5km) stretch of the River Nile for the Egyptian government. Subsequent surveys covered vast areas of the Baluchistan and Afghan border regions in India and a stretch of the River Indus. Another survey took the RAF to the borders of British Somaliland, where it was so hot in daytime that it was possible to process photographic film only during the night.

Chief of Air Staff, fought for its survival. He persuaded key figures in the government—most notably Winston Churchill, then Secretary of State for War and Air—that what was termed "air control" would be a more economic way of dealing with attempted risings and insurrections in the British Empire.

Trenchard and his acolytes argued that bombing and strafing rebel tribespeople into submission would prove cheaper, quicker, and more effective than relying on expensive standing garrisons or punitive land expeditions to do the job. The British put "air control" into practice in oil-rich Iraq, which they now controlled under the terms of a League of Nations mandate; in British Somaliland; and on India's frequently turbulent northwest frontier. Its apparent success confirmed Trenchard in his belief that the bomber would be the war-winning weapon of the future, even if government parsimony ensured that his vision remained a dream.

The USA had its own advocate of air power in the person of General William "Billy" Mitchell, but, unlike Trenchard, Mitchell's career came to a sudden and inglorious end. By 1925, he had alienated not only his superiors in the War and Navy Departments, but also President Coolidge himself. When he publicly attacked both departments for their "disgraceful administration of aviation," Coolidge ordered his court-martial. He was found guilty of gross insubordination; in protest, he resigned his commission.

Germany, prohibited from possessing an air force by the terms of the Treaty of Versailles, had no such public advocates. Italy did. Marshal Italo Balbo, promoted to lead the Italian air force by Mussolini himself, saw it as his mission to raise the public profile of Italy in the skies. For their part, the Germans did their best to circumvent the Treaty of Versailles's provisions. From 1926 to 1933, for instance, groups of young German officers were sent undercover to Lipetsk in the USSR for secret flight training with the Soviet air force.

TOP-SECRET MISSIONS

With the war clouds beginning to gather as Hitler, having assumed supreme power in Germany, announced that he was determined to rearm, Britain and France, albeit reluctantly, slowly began to realize they, too, had to modernize and expand their armed forces. The British rescinded the so-called 10-year rule. Promulgated in the early 1920s, this laid down that Britain was not likely to be involved in a major war for at least 10 years. The French speeded up the building of the Maginot Line, a massive fortification system designed to secure the Franco-German frontier. Construction was scheduled to be completed by 1935.

Completing the Maginot Line cost the French a fortune. They had little, if any, money left over for anything else, particularly at a time of economic recession with most politicians, particularly on the left, begrudging spending anything on armaments at all. Their air force was largely left to fend for itself. The British were just as reluctant to face up to unpleasant facts. Nevertheless, facing, as they believed, the threat of overwhelming aerial bombardment, they decided to increase the size of the RAF as quickly as they could.

As the political skies across Europe darkened, Scheme A, which the British government announced in July 1934, was rapidly overtaken by Schemes C, F, H, and J. Eventually, after a dispute between the Air Marshals and Sir Thomas Inskip, the Minister for Coordination for Defence, as to whether bombers or fighters should be given priority, Scheme L was promulgated in April 1938. It called for the RAF to

SIEGFRIED LINE

The Siegfried Line or West Wall was Hitler's answer to the French Maginot Line, built to protect France from invasion by Germany in the early 1930s. It stretched for more than 390 miles (630km) from Kleve on the Dutch border as far as Weilau am Rhein on the border with Switzerland. The Nazi propaganda machine claimed that the Siegfried Line was impregnable; in fact, as General Alfred Jodl later admitted, it was "little better than a building site" when war broke out. When Field Marshal Gerd von Rundstedt inspected it, he is said to have laughed. Maverick secret agent Sidney Cotton started photographing sections of it secretly—first for the French Deuxième Bureau and then Britain's MI6—in the spring of 1939.

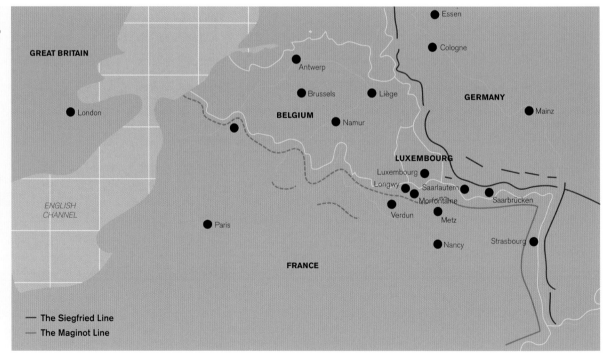

— The Siegfried Line
— The Maginot Line

TOP The Dornier Do 19 strategic bomber prototype is captured in flight. It first flew in late 1936, years ahead of its four-engine equivalents in Britain and the USA, but, after the death of General Walther Weaver, the Luftwaffe's first chief of staff, in an air crash, Goering ordered the heavy bomber program to be abandoned. The Luftwaffe, he said, was to be a tactical air force, working in close cooperation with the army and he could build many more medium bombers than heavy ones. The amount of bombs the Dornier could carry also told against it. At most, this amounted to only 3,527lb (1,600kg).

BOTTOM Nicknamed the "Ural bomber" by its supporters in the Luftwaffe, the Junkers Ju 89 first took to the air in early 1937, a few months after its rival, the Dornier Do 19. It was faster, better armed, and could carry a greater weight of bombs than the Dornier, but, just under three weeks after the prototype's maiden flight, the strategic bomber development contract was cancelled by the Luftwaffe. Goering claimed that building aircraft like the Junkers would cost the aircraft industry amounts of aluminum it could ill-afford to spare.

reach a strength of 1,352 bombers and 608 first-line fighters by April 1940. Scheme M, which followed in the fall of 1938, was even more ambitious. In the event, none of its targets was reached. When war broke out in September 1939, Britain possessed 608 first-line fighters, but only 536 bombers. The comparative Luftwaffe figures were 1,215 fighters and 2,130 bombers.

AIRCRAFT DEVELOPMENTS

Even more critical than mere numbers were the types of airplane coming off the drawing board and onto the production line. The French, for instance, were horrified to discover that the Luftwaffe's new Dornier Do 17 bomber was actually faster than their most modern fighter. Britain's Hurricanes and Spitfires suffered delay after delay in getting into production. The specification both airplanes were designed to meet was issued by the Air Ministry in December 1934. The prototype of the Hurricane flew in November 1935; the Spitfire in March 1936. By the end of January 1938, however, there were only 20 Hurricanes in service with the RAF. As for the Spitfire, in December 1937, the air ministry ceased to give any delivery dates for the airplane at all in its progress charts because "the firm state they are unable to forecast deliveries at present." It was not until the late summer of 1938 that the first few of them finally arrived.

Where the British scored was with their development of four-engine heavy bombers. In 1936, the Air Ministry issued the specifications that eventually brought the Short Stirling, the Handley-Page Halifax, and the Avro Lancaster into existence. The Germans, by contrast, scrapped their four-engine heavy bomber prototypes. In 1936, Dornier was already test flying three Do 19s and Junkers two Ju 89s. Then Goering took a hand. Two of his intimates—Albert Kesselring, the Luftwaffe's new chief of staff, and Hans Jeschonnek, commander of its Operational Development Wing— suggested to him that, given the scarcity of raw materials, the heavy bomber project should be dropped. Goering immediately asked "How many twin-engine airplanes can we make for every four-engine one?" The reply was "about two-and-a-half." Goering promptly ordered the heavy-bomber program to be cancelled. "The Fuehrer," he said, "does not ask me how big my bombers are, but how many there are."

The Heinkel aircraft factory at Rostock, photographed from the air after an RAF bombing raid. It and the Heinkel plant at Oranienburg were considered to be among the most modern in Germany. When General Joseph Vuillemin, the commander-in-chief of the French Air Force, visited the Oranienburg facility in August 1938 and saw Heinkel He 111 bombers being mass-produced, all he could find to say was *Je suis écrasé* ('I am shattered').

◄ A captured Heinkel He 177 heavy bomber is seen flying in RAF markings. Ernst Heinkel designed the aircraft to fulfill a Luftwaffe requirement for a 335mph (539km/h) bomber carrying a 4,400lb (1,995kg) bomb load and with a range of at least 1,000 miles (1,609km). Technical problems with the aircraft's coupled engines, which were prone to catch fire, and the Luftwaffe's initial demand that it should be capable of dive-bombing, delayed the aircraft's development and it never fulfilled expectations.

It was not until 1938 that Goering was persuaded to change his mind. Then together with the Reichsmarschall Ernst Udet, a veteran of the celebrated World War I Richthofen fighter squadron and now in charge of the Luftwaffe's Office of Air Armament, decided to press ahead with the development of the Heinkel He 117. It was intended that this would be the long-range strategic heavy bomber the Luftwaffe lacked. Udet, however, added a fatal extra requirement to the specification: the He 177 had to be capable of dive-bombing.

The consequences were catastrophic. Meeting Udet's demand meant that the airplane's four engines had to be coupled together in pairs to avoid weakening the wing structure. Consequently, the Heinkel and Daimler-Benz designers and engineers involved in the He 117's development were hit by major technical problems. The water-cooled Daimler-Benz engines proved anything but reliable; they were all too prone to catch fire in mid-flight. There were design flaws in the airframe as well. By August 1942, by which time the Luftwaffe had counted on having 800 He 177s in service, only 101 had been manufactured. Of these only 33 had been accepted as ready for squadron service and only two were actually operational.

AIR INTELLIGENCE

The British were obsessed with the RAF's apparent numerical inferiority to the Luftwaffe, even though this was less than people like Winston Churchill claimed. Their pioneer development of radar also gave them a priceless early warning advantage. What they failed to do was to build a comprehensive intelligence picture of the strengths and weaknesses of the German economy. Without this, there was no way of formulating any effective strategic bombing plan.

As late as 1938, the annual British Secret Intelligence Service (SIS) budget was only equal to the annual cost of running a single destroyer. A tiny branch of air intelligence had been created to study possible targeting; it was led by a retired squadron leader. Economics were barely comprehended outside the ranks of a few academics. Major Desmond Morton, controlling the Industrial Intelligence Centre, devoted the bulk of his limited resources to studying arms-related industries. He made no attempt to assess the broad industrial potential of the German economy as a whole.

The RAF, too, had lost the aerial reconnaissance capabilities it had once possessed. Attempts to photograph Italian defense installations on various islands in the Mediterranean, along the North African coast and around the Red Sea, in 1936 and 1937 were almost total failures as the photographs that were taken came out too blurred to be of any use. Nor were any of its officers being trained in the skills of photographic interpretation. Army officers were undertaking such tasks instead.

SECRET SURVEILLANCE

In any event, it was unlikely in the extreme that Neville Chamberlain's government, hell-bent on appeasing

SIDCOT FLYING SUIT

A group of pilots pose in their Sidcot flying suits, developed by Sidney Cotton in 1917 when he was serving with the RNAS. Cotton designed the fur-lined one-piece suit to overcome the cold pilots faced when flying at high altitude. The Sidcot flying suit became standard issue in both the RNAS and the RFC and was also adopted by the French Air Force and the US Army Air Corps. Even some German pilots took up the suit—Baron von Richthofen, the celebrated air ace, was wearing one when he was shot down.

the Nazis, would ever have countenanced any covert photographic surveillance of war preparations within the borders of the Third Reich. Even after war broke out, Sir Samuel Hoare, the Secretary of State for War, dismissed pugnacious backbench MP Leo Amery's suggestion that the RAF should attempt to set fire to the Black Forest with the words: "Are you not aware that this is private property? Why, you will be asking me to bomb Essen next!" The RAF was restricted to dropping millions of propaganda leaflets over the German heartlands. Joseph Goebbels sneered in his diary that they made "excellent toilet paper" for the Reich.

Fortunately as it turned out, there were others who were less pusillanimous. One of them was Frederick Winterbotham, ostensibly a squadron leader attached to the air ministry but in reality a leading light in MI6, the espionage wing of British military intelligence. Extremely well-connected and prepared to use all his contacts to further his plans, Winterbotham was on the lookout for a businessman with an airplane who was used to flying over Europe and ready to engage in covert aerial photography for him. In Australian-born Sidney Cotton, he found his man.

MAVERICK AUSTRALIAN

Cotton was a maverick entrepreneur. The son of a wealthy Australian landowner, he had been educated in Britain at Cheltenham; it was there that he developed a passion for aviation. In 1916, he joined the RNAS and soon was posted to France to serve as a bomber pilot on the Western Front. He demonstrated his natural ingenuity by inventing a new single-piece flying suit. The Sidcot, as it was named, became standard issue throughout the RFC and the RNAS. The Germans copied it, too; Baron von Richthofen was wearing one when he was finally shot down and killed.

Cotton was certainly ingenious; he also could be stubbornly obstinate. Brimming with self-confidence, he believed that he was always in the right and anyone

disagreeing with him was in the wrong. After just 18 months of service, he quarrelled with his commanding officer—he was accused of disobeying a direct order. Resigning his commission in protest, he returned home to Australia, where he sat out the rest of the war.

When peace came, Cotton returned to Europe, where he pursued an adventurous career in civil aviation, at the same time making a fortune through Stock Exchange speculations and the buying and selling of land. He also became deeply interested in photography, investing heavily in Dufaycolor, the pioneer of a new type of color film. It was through this involvement that he struck up a friendship with Alfred J. Miranda Jr., an American who was closely connected with the company. It was Miranda who introduced Cotton to Winterbotham in September 1938.

▲ Sidney Cotton photographed in the cockpit of his Lockheed Electra 12A preparing to take off from Heston, the airfield where his activities were based. He had ordered the Electra to be modified to enable two cameras to be concealed in its wings and one in its fuselage. Posing as an international businessman, Cotton flew in and out of Nazi Germany on a regular basis during the late 1930s, secretly photographing military installations, armaments plants, and other industrial targets for the British Secret Intelligence Service, also known as MI6.

SPYING FROM THE SKY

Cotton and Winterbotham reached an agreement and preparations for the first clandestine reconnaissance flights began. Miranda arranged for a Lockheed 12A six-seat twin-engine airplane to be transported from the USA to Britain; it reached Southampton in January 1939. In the meantime, Winterbotham was on the lookout for a suitable copilot who was also a trained engineer. He identified Robert Niven, a Canadian who was nearly at the end of a short-service commission in the RAF, as the ideal man for the job.

Cotton and Niven set about adapting the Lockheed for its future tasks. It was fitted with extra fuel tanks, which added 900 miles (1,448.4km) to its 700-mile (1,126.5km) range. Winterbotham had got the French Deuxième Bureau to supply a large aerial camera, which was nearly six feet long. To accommodate it, an opening had to be cut in the floor of the Lockheed's passenger cabin. The hole served a second purpose. In the event of an emergency, everything incriminating could be jettisoned through it well before the Lockheed reached the ground.

By the end of February 1939, the Lockheed was ready. Cotton and Niven flew it from Heston, a small airfield west of London, to Toussus-le-Noble, just southwest of Paris. They made their first flight over Germany on March 25 with a French secret service agent on board to operate the camera. Krefeld, Hamm, Münster, and the Dutch frontier region were photographed. The Black Forest was covered on April 1; Württemberg followed six days later. The final flight took place on April 9, when the Lockheed had to dodge a German fighter that had been sent up to intercept it. Nevertheless, Cotton managed to photograph Karlsruhe, Bruchsal, Heidelberg, Mannheim, Ludwigshafen, and Ebersbach before making an aerial dash for France and safety.

Cotton now fell out with the French. He complained about the erratic course they had insisted he flew over

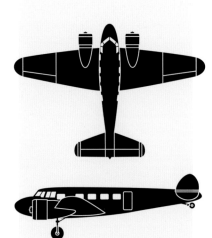

LOCKHEED 12A ELEKTRA

Type Light transport	
Crew 2 plus 6 passengers	
Length 35.0ft (10.97m)	
Wingspan 49.5ft (15.09m)	
Speed 224mph (361km/h)	
Range 800 miles (1,287km)	

Designed to be a smaller version of an existing aircraft, most Lockheed 12As ended up being used for executive travel. The aircraft came into service in 1936; by 1941, when production came to an end when the USA entered the war, 126 had been built. Why Cotton chose it for his photo-reconnaissance missions is uncertain, but its relatively high speed and maneuverability in the air may have been contributing factors.

the target areas and the quality of the photographs they had taken. To secure better photographic coverage, he also wanted to substitute three smaller RAF cameras—one of them pointing straight down, the others angled slightly to the left and right—for the single French giant camera. The French turned the request down and Cotton immediately walked out on them. He told Winterbotham bluntly: "If worthwhile results are to be obtained, I must have my own aircraft and operate in my own way." He was now convinced that the aircraft he needed for aerial reconnaissance had to be fast enough to elude intercepting enemy fighters and also be able to fly high enough to escape enemy antiaircraft fire.

MEDITERRANEAN RECONNAISSANCE

Cotton might have quarreled with the French, but he and Winterbotham were still determined to continue their aerial espionage. A new Lockheed was ordered, with extra fuel tanks behind the cockpit. Three RAF F24 cameras were fitted in the fuselage just as Cotton had specified, their identifying serial numbers being hastily scratched off so that, in the event of a forced landing or crash, there would be no obvious link between the RAF and Cotton's flights. The holes for them were cut to be slightly larger than the camera lens. This meant that at 21,000ft (6,400m)—the optimum height at which Cotton intended to fly—warm air from inside the airplane would be sucked over the cameras to stop them from freezing up. With the Lockheed painted a natty light duck-egg green—Cotton said that the color was the best possible high-altitude camouflage—he and Niven flew to Malta, from where they were to start extensive photographic reconnaissance in the Middle East. The cover story was that they were surveying a possible new route for Imperial Airways.

Cotton and Niven reached Malta on June 14, 1939. The next day, they were joined by Flying Officer

When war broke out, Cotton and his team soon proved their worth; their photo-reconnaissance efforts outdid those of the RAF, much to the annoyance of some senior officers. By the fall of 1940, things had begun to change. Cotton had been sacked and photo-reconnaissance moved to RAF Benson. Here, a Benson ground crew is testing various cameras—two F24 verticals, one F24 oblique and two F52 verticals—prior to installing them in a photo-reconnaissance de Havilland Mosquito.

Maurice V. "Shorty" Longbottom, one of the few officers serving in the RAF with practical experience of aerial photography, in photographing Comiso, Augusta, Catania, and Syracuse from the air. Cotton was now posing as a wealthy Englishman with a passion for photographing ancient ruins. On June 16, Cotton and Niven photographed two Italian-controlled islands in the Dodecanese before heading for Cairo, from where they photographed Massawa in Italian Eritrea and a possible submarine base under construction in Italian Somaliland. On their return flight to Malta, they photographed Italian military installations and airfields at El Adem, Tobruk, Derna, Bernice, and Benghazi. From Malta, they flew back to Heston, arriving there on June 25.

WAR LOOMS

Cotton managed to make more flights over Germany before war finally broke out that September. During the last few weeks of peace, he flew there on five occasions. This time, the Lockheed was fitted with two Leica cameras concealed in the wings behind panels whose opening was triggered from the cockpit. On this occasion, Cotton's cover story was that he was trying to sell Dufaycolor film to the Germans.

On July 28, Cotton flew the Lockheed to Frankfurt to attend an international air show there. His hosts were full of admiration for his American aircraft, so the next day he invited the Commandant of the Tempelhof airfield, Berlin, for a pleasure flight to see for himself how well the Lockheed flew. He suggested flying down the Rhine to Mannheim and back again. As his German guest sat back and admired the airplane, the cameras concealed in the wings clicked away, photographing the Rhine and the Siegfried Line.

This was not the end of the story. On August 17, Cotton and Niven flew to Berlin, managing to take photographs of areas north of the city. The two men were still in Berlin at the end of the month when the Nazi-Soviet Non-Aggression Pact was announced. As the skies filled with Luftwaffe fighters and bombers heading east toward the Polish border, all civilian flights were officially grounded. Waiting on board their Lockheed, Cotton and Niven were finally given permission to take off. As they headed toward the Netherlands, they spotted the port of Wilhelmshaven in the distance and what looked like the German fleet preparing to put out to sea. It was too good an opportunity to miss. Cotton hastily photographed the warships from his cockpit with a handheld Leica camera.

Cotton was luckier than he knew. His Lockheed was the last civilian airplane to get away from the city. Though he made one further flight over Germany to photograph the Frisian Islands, Heligoland, and Sylt—this time a female photographer went with him to help with the cameras—he flew nonstop back to Heston without landing to refuel. The last flight of all took place on September 1—the day the Germans marched into Poland and World War II began—at the British Admiralty's urgent request. This time, Niven flew alone in a single-engine Beechcraft long-range monoplane. He returned home with more pictures of Wilhelmshaven.

LUFTWAFFE AIR INTELLIGENCE

Though there was no doubting Cotton's professionalism, his achievements were insignificant when compared to those of the pre-war Luftwaffe. When General Werner von Fritsch, then the commander-in-chief of the German army, predicted in 1938 that "the military organization that has the best reconnaissance unit will win the next war," few doubted that in aerial reconnaissance and photography the Luftwaffe reigned supreme

After the Luftwaffe officially came into existence in 1935, its development proceeded apace. The new Heinkel He III bomber, fitted with up-to-the-minute Zeiss cameras, was its airplane of first choice for high-level photographic reconnaissance. Dornier Do 17s also carried out reconnaissance missions. By 1939, the Germans had formed 23 long-range reconnaissance squadrons, each with its own photographic laboratory where films were developed and the resulting prints analyzed and then distributed. Master prints were sent to the Luftwaffe intelligence library at Zossen, southeast of Berlin, where the 5th Abteilung of the Luftwaffe's general staff was located. Established in January 1938 and commanded by Major Josef "Beppo" Schmid, the new unit was tasked with monitoring developments in foreign air forces and preparing

▼ Sidney Cotton added a Beechcraft 18 (*below*) to his fledgling air force shortly before the outbreak of war. The Heston Flight, as it was termed initially, soon grew. Two Bristol Blenheim IVs joined the Beechcraft and Lockheed 12A toward the end of September 1939, but the prize catch was two Spitfires, which arrived at Heston on October 30. Even Wing Commander Victor Laws, one of Cotton's fiercest critics, admitted that the "one good thing Cotton did was to introduce Spitfires into photo-reconnaissance."

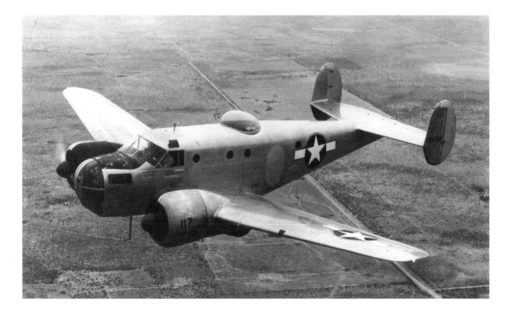

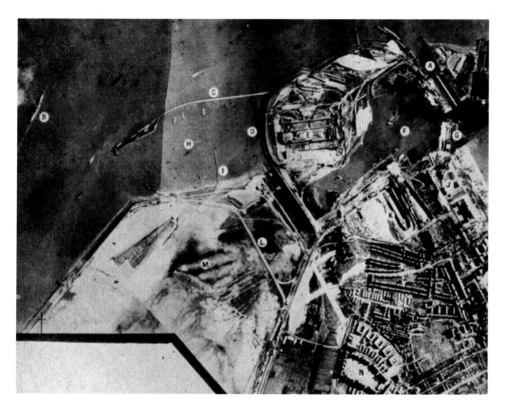

▲ This RAF photograph of the Wilhelmshaven naval base was taken in September 1939. The air force experienced great difficulty in obtaining such photographs; it believed its F24 cameras were freezing up even at moderate altitudes. Cotton demonstrated that the problem was caused by condensation and showed the RAF how to cure it. It was one of his pilots who established for the Admiralty that Germany's new battleship *Tirpitz* was not preparing to sail but still safely in dry dock.

As events were to show, Schmid certainly knew which side his bread was buttered. Thus, Luftwaffe intelligence never made the best use of the vast corpus of photography its pilots laboriously garnered.

Luckily for the Luftwaffe, it had its own Cotton. Theodore Rowehl, an experienced World War I reconnaissance pilot, began flying clandestine photographic reconnaissance missions out of Berlin in the late 1930s. The Heinkels he and his men flew were painted in Deutsche Luft Hansa colors to add credence to the cover story that they were investigating possible new routes for the airline to develop. The story gave them free access to the skies over most of Europe. During 1938 and 1939, they photographed much of eastern and southern Britain, the entire continental coast of the English Channel and the North Sea, and even penetrated as far up the Baltic coast as Leningrad.

The cameras Rowehl and his men used were huge 19.8-in (50.3cm) mapping cameras, mounted in pairs as split verticals and producing 12-in square (77.4cm^2) exposures. The results were surprisingly detailed. Yet the cameras had a major drawback. They were hard to fit into high-performance airplanes with small fuselages, such as the Messerschmitt Me 109. Though some of these fighters were eventually fitted with cameras, they did not have the range or retain the agility to make a satisfactory photographic reconnaissance platform. The Luftwaffe stuck with its Heinkels and Dorniers. Camera development stagnated as well. In the long run, these mistakes would cost Germany dear.

detailed military and economic target information for use by the Luftwaffe in time of war.

As time was to show, Schmid was an incompetent. Shrewd, sly, and notoriously cunning, he transferred to the Luftwaffe from the army in 1935, but he had no apparent interest in airplanes and air warfare. Indeed, he never even bothered to learn to fly. Adolf Galland, one of the Luftwaffe's rising stars, thought he was useless. "Beppo Schmid," he said later, "was a complete washout as an intelligence officer, the most important job of all." Erhard Milch, Goering's deputy, also recognized that Schmid was someone who "trimmed his sails to the wind" for fear of upsetting his bosses.

BLITZKRIEG

When World War II broke out, the Luftwaffe played a key role in blitzing the Poles into submission. In the months of so-called "phony war" that followed, the air forces of both sides remained relatively inactive. Contrary to pre-war expectations, no all-out bombing campaign was launched; RAF Bomber Command in the main confined itself to dropping propaganda leaflets over Germany, while the Luftwaffe had used up around half of its bombs in Poland and fresh supplies had to be hastily manufactured. In any event, the limited range of its bombers made the launching of any bombing assault against Britain from German soil impractical. It was content to sit and wait until Hitler decided to attack in the West. In Norway, the Low Countries, France, and later against Yugoslavia, Greece, and the USSR, the Luftwaffe demonstrated that aerial supremacy over the battlefield more often than not resulted in victory. The one time it failed was in the Battle of Britain and the subsequent bombing blitz, when it undertook tasks which it was not trained or equipped to fulfill.

RESTRICTED FLYING

Air reconnaissance played little part in the Polish and Norwegian campaigns. They were both over quickly as the Wehrmacht speedily proved invincible once the Luftwaffe had established total air superiority. Much the same thing happened in the West, when Hitler attacked there in May 1940. Before that, during the months of "phony war," neither the French air force nor the British Advanced Air Striking Force (AASF), which had been despatched to France shortly after the outbreak of war, made any real attempt to take the fight to the Luftwaffe over its own territory.

As far as the RAF was concerned, this lack of aerial activity was not for want of trying. At home, the government had stated publicly that it would not be the first "to take the gloves off" in a bombing war and forbade the bombing of anything other than military targets. Bomber Command, therefore, was confined to desultory attacks on German naval targets. The raids met with little or no success. If they proved anything, they showed Bomber Command's confident belief that bomber formations were sufficiently well-armed to fight their way unescorted through enemy skies to attack targets in broad daylight to be delusional.

Air Chief Marshal Sir Arthur Barratt, commander of the AASF, found himself even more constrained. Every request he made to be allowed to carry out high-altitude reconnaissance flights over Belgium was turned down flat. Terrified that the Luftwaffe would strike at Paris and their industrial centers in reprisal, the French refused to countenance taking any kind of offensive aerial action at all. When Winston Churchill, now back in the British War Cabinet as First Lord of the Admiralty, proposed dropping floating mines in the Rhine River to impede the flow of barge traffic, the French vetoed the entire operation.

PRELUDE TO DISASTER

France's refusal to take any initiative in the air was the result of the crippling weakness of its air force. Paying an official visit to Germany in August 1938, General Joseph Vuillemin, the elderly Chief of the French Air Staff, was totally overwhelmed by the seemingly stupefying strength of the Luftwaffe. "Should war break out as you expect in late September," he despondently told André François-Poncet, the French ambassador to the Reich, "there won't be a single French plane left in two weeks."

Morale was low. Even though Barratt's planes were forbidden to violate Belgian neutrality, French reconnaissance aircraft operating from Alsace-Lorraine could have easily detected the German buildup in the Ardennes, but they failed to do so. France's Bloch MB. 131s were pulled out of all daylight operations in November 1939 and henceforward allowed to fly only at night: its Breguets and Potezs were ordered to operate only "behind battery positions." For their part, Olivier LeO 45s were allowed to "approach between one and two kilometers from the lines," but only "on condition that they operated in patrols of two."

There were other explanations for this lack of activity. Some French sources put it down to bad flying conditions—the winter of 1939–40 was the harshest for many years—and the inferiority of their aircraft. General Edmond Ruby, the Assistant Chief of Staff of the French 2nd Army, wrote that French reconnaissance airplanes "could not pass over our lines except under fear of death." Barratt was less charitable. He stated bluntly that the French reconnaissance teams simply "would not leave the floor, often they gave the excuse that the weather was too bad."

Refugees flee in the face of Luftwaffe strafing in May 1940. Millions of civilians fled in panic from the forces of the advancing Wehrmacht, harried remorselessly from the air as the Luftwaffe exploited its total air superiority. At its peak, it was estimated that nearly eight million French refugees had taken flight, along with two million Belgian and Dutch fugitives. The mass of fleeing humanity totally clogged up the roads, making rapid Allied troop redeployment virtually impossible.

▼ The French Bloch MB.131 medium bomber first flew in 1936, but did not manage to get into production until 1938, by which time it was already obsolescent. The aircraft failed to live up to expectations in its primary role as a bomber, so it was hastily switched to reconnaissance use. The Luftwaffe inflicted such heavy casualties on Blochs when they flew by day that they were restricted to night sorties, in which they were just as ineffectual.

An Amiot 351 in flight, one of the few of the Amiot 350 variants that the French air force managed to get off the ground when the Germans launched their devastating offensive in the West in May 1940. The Amiot was one of the most advanced medium bombers of its day, but the chaotic state of the French aircraft industry meant that, out of the 285 that were initially ordered, only 85 were actually delivered ready for action by the time France surrendered in June 1940.

Certainly, the Luftwaffe was not deterred by bad weather. Once Hitler finally made up his mind to strike through the Ardennes, Luftwaffe reconnaissance squadrons were constantly at work, flying at high altitude to photograph the entire area. The photographs they brought back revealed that the French fortifications guarding the crossing points over the Meuse River were very far from completion. Nor was the Luftwaffe any respecter of neutrality. According to the Belgians, it carried out at least 500 reconnaissance overflights in the eight months before Hitler's armies finally struck in the West in May 1940.

Even after the great attack started, the Allies lost valuable time. The first order Barratt and General François d'Astier de la Vigerie, his opposite number, received simply ran "Air limited to fighters and reconnaissance." It was not until mid-morning that they were authorized to bomb the advancing German columns. This belated authorization contained a rider, added by General Alphonse-Joseph Georges, the commander-in-chief of the northeastern sector of the Allied front. It read: "At all costs, avoid bombing built-up areas."

By the time Georges's rider was lifted the following afternoon, it was too late. Even more crucially, Gamelin, in establishing new air priorities, ordered the maximum effort to be made in the wrong place. The bulk of Hitler's panzers continued to worm their way toward the Meuse undetected. Meanwhile, Barratt's attempts to blitz the German columns advancing through Luxembourg into Belgium met with disaster. The Fairey Battle light bombers he dispatched were decimated. Of the 32 that went into action in the first attack, 13 were destroyed and all the others badly damaged. French efforts were limited to a few Amiots dropping bombs more or less at random on German airfields and roads west of the Rhine River. Their Breguet ground attack bombers were not ready to go into action.

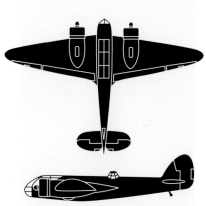

BRISTOL BLENHEIM IV

Type Light bomber/Reconnaissance	
Crew 3	
Length 42ft 7in (12.98m)	
Wingspan 56ft 4in (17.17m)	
Speed 266mph (428km/h), 198mph (329km/h) cruising	
Range 1,460 miles (2,3450km)	

The RAF intended the Blenheim IV to be its main daylight bomber, but it stood little chance when it ran up against the Luftwaffe's Messerschmitts. It was lightly built and so could take little punishment, while its defensive armament—a single machine gun in its rear turret, a fixed rear-firing gun in the port engine nacelle, and another rear-firing machine gun beneath its cockpit—was inadequate.

SIDNEY COTTON JOINS THE RAF

The Battle was by no means the only RAF airplane not fit for purpose. The Westland Lysanders and Bristol Blenheim IVs intended to undertake tactical and strategic air reconnaissance both proved inadequate. The Lysander was painfully slow. The Blenheim, too, proved to be easy prey for the Luftwaffe's marauding fighters. In the 89 reconnaissance missions they flew over the first four months of the war, 16 planes were shot down. Even more to the point, 44 of the missions failed to produce any usable photographs.

Partly this was due to the height at which the Blenheims flew to try to dodge the Luftwaffe's fighters and avoid German antiaircraft fire. They got as close to their service ceiling of around 22,000ft (6,750m) as they could, dropping down to 10,000ft (3,048m) or so to take their photographs once they had reached their targets. The problem was that the F24 cameras with which they were equipped seemed to freeze solid at high altitudes.

Sidney Cotton, still flying covert missions over Germany, was called into urgent consultation by the Air Ministry and asked what special equipment he was using. Cotton replied that he was using standard RAF cameras. The problems the Blenheims were facing, he said, were not caused by freezing, but condensation. He had solved this by directing hot air from his Lockheed's engine ducts around his cameras. The RAF experts refused to accept the explanation.

Determined to prove his point, Cotton took off again the following afternoon. He came back with clear-as-crystal photographs of Flushing and Ymuiden, which he showed triumphantly to Air Vice-Marshal Richard Peck, who had called the original Air Ministry meeting. The other senior RAF officers present erupted. One even argued that Cotton should be arrested for deliberately flaunting authority. He stormed out of the room. Much to his surprise, he was summoned back to the Air Ministry the next day to meet Air Chief Marshal Sir Cyril Newall, the RAF's Chief of Staff.

THE HESTON FLIGHT

Newall and Cotton made a deal. The former offered the latter the rank of acting wing commander and asked him to set up an experimental photography unit. Though nominally it would be part of Fighter Command, it would remain independent of RAF control. Cotton insisted on this; he also asked for carte blanche on the choice of men, machines, and equipment.

Squadron leader Alfred "Tubby" Earle, who had been an instructor at the School of Photography at Farnborough, was put in charge of photographic development. Pilot Officers Maurice "Shorty" Longbottom, whom Cotton had met in Malta before the war, Bob Niven, Hugh C. Macphail, and S. Denis Slocum were the new unit's first pilots. Flight Sergeant S. R. "Wally" Walton and Leading Aircraftsmen Whinra Rawlinson, Ron Mutton, and Jack Eggleston were its first photographers. They were joined by five fitters, three flight mechanics, two riggers, an electrician, an instrument maker, and three general aircraft hands.

The River Meuse, seen here from the air, was the key natural barrier the Germans had to cross to drive into the heart of France. On May 13, Rommel was the first across the river at Houx, closely followed by Guderian at Sedan. The panzers led the way, closely supported by the Luftwaffe's Stukas and Dorniers. The French troops trying to hold the river defenses were totally demoralized by wave after wave of Stuka dive-bombing attacks.

WESTERN BREAKTHROUGH

The Germans were swift to exploit the breakthrough their panzers made in the Ardennes, driving westwards to the English Channel and so cutting off the Allied armies in the north. This map shows the military situation on May 21, by which time the panzers had carved out an enormous bulge in the Allied line. Believing that the main German thrust was directed through Belgium, the Allied high command rushed its best troops forward to meet it. The Allies were taken totally by surprise by the Ardennes attack.

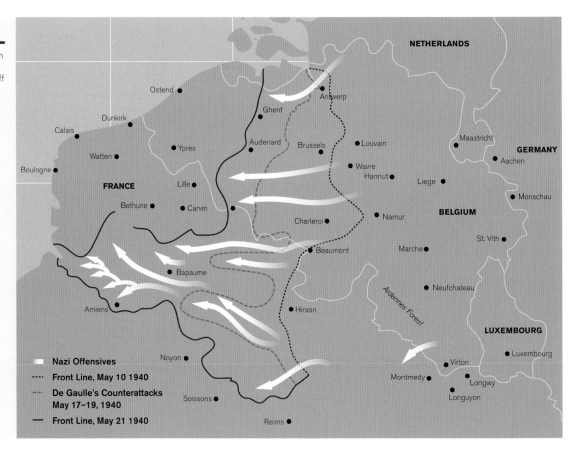

Legend:
- Nazi Offensives
- ---- Front Line, May 10 1940
- -- De Gaulle's Counterattacks May 17–19, 1940
- — Front Line, May 21 1940

Map labels: NETHERLANDS, Ostend, Antwerp, Ghent, Dunkirk, Calais, Audenard, Brussels, Louvain, Maastricht, GERMANY, Aachen, Ypres, Watten, Wavre, Hannut, Liege, Boulogne, FRANCE, Lille, Monschau, Bethune, Carvin, Charleroi, Namur, BELGIUM, St. Vith, Beaumont, Marche, Bapaume, Neufchateau, Ardennes Forest, Amiens, Hirson, LUXEMBOURG, Luxembourg, Noyon, Virton, Montmedy, Longwy, Soissons, Longuyon, Reims

What was dubbed "the Heston Flight" was in business. Cotton's Lockheed and Beechcraft were joined by two Blenheim IVs. However, these were not the airplanes Cotton wanted. He had set his heart on obtaining some Spitfires. Eventually, he got his hands on two of them, though not through a personal appeal to Air Chief Marshal Sir Hugh Dowding, the head of Fighter Command, as he later said. In fact, it was Peck who obtained the Spitfires from Maintenance Command, much to Dowding's initial displeasure.

By removing their guns and streamlining the Spitfires, Cotton's engineers raised their maximum speed from 360mph (579.3km/h) to 396mph (637.2km/h). They also fitted an additional fuel tank to boost the planes' range to 650 miles (1,0046km). By the end of 1939, the Spitfires had flown 15 high-level reconnaissance missions without loss and photographed Aachen, Cologne, Kaiserslautern, Wiesbaden, and parts of the Ruhr as well as sections of the Siegfried Line and the fortifications along the German border with Belgium. Dowding gave Cotton a dozen more Spitfires as a reward.

IMPROVING DEFINITION

Cotton's enemies in the Air Ministry were not so impressed, however. True, his Spitfires were bringing back numerous photographs, but the height at which they were flying meant that the scale was too small for intelligence use. One official report stated bluntly that "the scale of the photographs taken defies interpretation" and concluded that there was "absolutely nothing to be gained by the activities of these aircraft." Clearly, something had to be done.

Cotton quickly found the answer. He agreed with Harold "Lemnos" Hemming, an old friend now running the Aircraft Operating Company, that the 3D stereoscopes the company had been using to analyze aerial mining surveys would be used by Hemming's technicians to interpret Cotton's photographs. The

MESSERSCHMITT ME 109

Type Fighter

Crew 1

Length 28ft 6in (8.74m)

Wingspan 32ft 6in (9.925m)

Speed 398mph (640km/h), 365mph (590km/h) cruising

Range 528 miles (850km), 621 miles (1,000km) with drop tank

The Messerschmitt Me 109 was the mainstay of the Luftwaffe's fighter force. It first went into action serving in the Condor Legion of Luftwaffe volunteers during the Spanish Civil War; it remained supreme until late 1941, when the Focke-Wulf FW 190 arrived on the scene. By the end of the war in 1945, 33,000 of these angular little fighters had been built. The final variant, the Messerschmitt Me 109K, had a top speed of 450mph (724.2km/h).

devices gave the photographs increased depth. The company also owned the only Wild A5 Stereo Plotter in Britain. A huge Swiss-manufactured machine, its operator could use it to produce detailed maps even from photographs taken as high as 34,000ft (10,363m). The technical problems the Air Ministry had complained of had been resolved.

COTTON DISMISSED

Cotton's overweening self-confidence and the delight he took in circumventing official channels brought about his downfall. Many high-ranking officers in the RAF never forgave him for what they saw as a blatant attempt to play the air force off against the Admiralty. When he refused to obey orders and evacuate the 300 men he now commanded in the face of the German breakthrough in the West in May 1940, it was the last straw.

It was not until June 17 that Cotton, with the last of his men, was forced out of France. As he stepped out of his Lockheed onto the tarmac at Heston, he was handed a letter from the Air Ministry. It said that, just as the Aircraft Operating Company had been, his unit was to be officially absorbed into the RAF. What his men had dubbed "Sidney Cotton's Air Force" with its cavalier attitude to authority would cease to exist. Nor was there any place for Cotton in the new setup. Wing Commander Geoffrey Tuttle, an RAF regular who had joined Cotton a few months before as administrative officer, would take over from him.

Cotton was flabbergasted. Though he had established the principles that all subsequent aerial reconnaissance and photographic interpretation efforts were to follow, officialdom decreed that he had outlived his usefulness. The following February, he was asked to resign his commission. He played no further part in the war.

TOP LEFT Messerchmitt Me 109s pour off the Regensburg production line. The first Me 109 flew in October 1935; the plane went into squadron service with the Luftwaffe in spring 1937. Extremely fast and highly maneuverable, though tricky to get off the ground and land, it could outfly RAF Fighter Command's Hurricanes if not its Spitfires. The aircraft was the Luftwaffe's day fighter mainstay for the whole of the war, the Messerschmitt factories building 33,000 of the planes.

BOTTOM LEFT An RAF Spitfire from No. 1 Photographic Reconnaissance Unit in flight. Removing the aircraft's armament and streamlining and polishing wings and fuselage increased the aircraft's speed substantially, even though it carried extra fuel in wing tanks and an auxiliary tank behind the pilot. Experiments were carried out to find the most effective camouflage paint; light blue, light green, and even light pink were tried before the RAF settled on pure white.

OPERATION SEA LION

France had fallen. The British had been pushed into evacuating their expeditionary force from Dunkirk, leaving all its heavy equipment behind on the beaches. "In six weeks," General Maxime Weygand, the commander-in-chief of the shattered French armies prophesied, "Britain will have its neck wrung like a chicken." It had been a lightning defeat. All that now stood between the Third Reich and total victory was the English Channel and the RAF's fighter squadrons.

Even Hitler had been taken by surprise by the speed of the Wehrmacht's success. The big question for him was what to do next. General Erhard Milch, Goering's deputy in command of the Luftwaffe, was in no doubt as to the best course of action. Even before the French capitulation, he had recommended that the 2nd and 3rd Air Fleets should be moved up to the Channel coast and Britain be invaded by air immediately. Luftwaffe paratroops would capture the key airfields in southern England and fighter and dive-bomber squadrons would fly in to operate from them. Though he admitted that the proposal was risky, Milch was certain that, for the next few days, the British Army would be incapable of putting up an effective defense. He warned Goering, "If we leave the British at peace for four weeks, it will be too late."

Hitler believed that, having realized the scale of their defeat, the British would negotiate for peace, particularly as he was ready to offer them generous terms. It was not until July 16 that he ordered planning for an invasion to start. Three days later, speaking to a packed Reichstag, he made what he said was his "last appeal" to Britain. "I see no reason," he told his cheering audience, "why this war should go on." The British promptly rejected the appeal. The war would go on. Operation Sea Lion, the code name for the invasion, was set to be launched once the Luftwaffe had achieved air superiority over the RAF. On August 2, the long-awaited order went out "to overpower the English air force in the shortest possible time."

THE INVASION BARGES GATHER

Churchill and his military advisers were convinced that the invasion was coming. As RAF Fighter Command and the Luftwaffe began to battle it out in the skies above southern England, RAF photo-reconnaissance was ordered into action to scour the coastlines of the Low Countries and northern France for any telltale signs of invasion preparations. The missions went ahead regardless of flying conditions. When bad weather made high-altitude photography impractical, the pilots were sent in at low level instead.

Naturally, this made flying still more risky. Pilot Officer Peter L. Dakeyne described in a letter he wrote to his commanding officer from Dulag Luft, the Luftwaffe interrogation center for captured RAF personnel, how he had been shot down. "I rather foolishly ran into AA fire whilst preoccupied and also distracted by a third factor," he explained. "A direct hit stopped the prop, so I rolled over and fell out to land among troops! The machine made a spectacular crash full out!"

The first thing photo-reconnaissance spotted was that long-range coastal artillery was being installed in the Pas-de-Calais area. This, it was thought, might well be intended to support the amphibious landings when they were launched. There were, however, no sightings of the all-important invasion barges gathering in the Channel ports. On August 27, the Combined Intelligence Committee, which the War Cabinet had set up to assess the likelihood of a German invasion, reported that "no serious threat of invasion yet exists from the Netherlands, France, or SW Norwegian coasts."

This apparent lull did not last for long. On August 31, photo-reconnaissance revealed that 56 barges from Amsterdam and another 100 barges from Antwerp were on the move toward the Channel ports. On the same day, 18 more barges were spotted at Ostend. Over the next weeks, the number of barges assembling in the Channel ports grew constantly. The photographic interpreters counted 255 of them at Calais, 192 at Dunkirk, 230 at Boulogne, 140 at Flushing, and 227 at Ostend, while at Antwerp another 600 barges and 200 merchant ships were gathering.

It was amazing the amount of detail the photographic interpreters gleaned. Michael Spender, the operator of the Wild Stereo A5 Plotter, spotted that some of the barges moored in Rotterdam were having their bows modified to accommodate a landing ramp. Other interpreters noted that, while some of the barges were self-propelling, many of them would have to be towed across the Channel by tugs. All the information they gathered was fed through to Churchill and the War Cabinet. On September 17, the Prime Minister told the House of Commons that Hitler's invasion operations were proceeding steadily. In secret session, he reported that "upwards of 1,700 self-propelled barges and more than 200 sea-going ships, some very large ships, are already gathered at the many invasion ports."

The number of barges was still rising. On the same day Churchill was speaking in the House, Spender was busy re-counting the barges at Dunkirk. Another 130 had arrived over the previous four days. Like many others, Spender believed that the invasion was imminent.

Invasion barges for Operation Sea Lion start to gather at Dunkirk, closely monitored by RAF reconnaissance. The photographic interpreters began spotting increasing numbers of barges assembling in the major ports of Antwerp, Amsterdam, and Rotterdam toward the end of August; by the end of the first week of September, it was clear that they were moving down the Channel to the ports nearest to the British coast.

THE BOMBERS STRIKE BACK

The German build-up did not go unchallenged. At first, the Blenheims, operating mostly in daylight, bore the brunt of the burden. Then, as bombing the barge concentrations became more and more urgent, Bomber Command's medium and heavy bombers joined in night after night. Starting with Ostend and Boulogne on the night of September 7, the Channel ports came under concerted attack. More than 80 airplanes took part in the first assault, though bad weather meant that some of them missed their targets. The following night, 133 Blenheims, Hampdens, Whitleys, and Wellingtons bombed the same targets again as well as the German North Sea ports of Hamburg, Bremen, and Emden.

Just like the barge counts, the number of bomber sorties mounted. On the night of September 15, Bomber Command launched 155 of them. Most were directed at invasion shipping in the Channel ports, plus Antwerp, where the shipping in the harbor was pounded. The Kriegsmarine reported that the bombers had sunk 15 barges and three tugs, damaged six naval vessels, and put three steamers out of action.

German morale was starting to suffer as well. "The British are slowly getting on our nerves at night," Ulrich Steinhilper, a young Luftwaffe fighter pilot, wrote home to his mother. "Because of their persistent activity our AA guns are in virtually continuous action and so we can hardly close our eyes. But there is nothing else we can do about that other than curse."

SEA LION ABANDONED

Two days later, Bomber Command despatched 194 aircraft to blitz the invasion ports and targets within Germany. The ports were then attacked virtually every night until the end of the month. By this time, however, Hitler had decided that ordering Sea Lion to go ahead was too great a risk to run. On September 17, he postponed the operation; on October 12, he told his military commanders that it was cancelled until the following spring. Despite Goering's vainglorious promises, his Luftwaffe had failed to destroy the RAF and without air superiority the landings could not proceed.

The invasion fleet had already started to disperse. As early as September 20, photographs taken by a Spitfire flying over Cherbourg revealed that five destroyers and an E-boat were no longer at anchor in its harbor. At the beginning of October, more reconnaissance photographs showed that the number of barges assembled in the invasion ports was falling; by the end of the month, it had dropped to well below the number the photographic interpreters had counted less than a month before. Britain had survived to fight another day.

As September progressed, the number of barges spotted in the Channel ports grew and grew. At Boulogne (*right*), the photographic interpreters counted 230. At Calais, the total was 255, at Dunkirk 192, Flushing 140, and Ostend 227. Another 600 barges and 200 merchant ships were assembled at Antwerp. RAF Coastal and Bomber Commands bombed the concentrations day and night in what was christened the "Battle of the Barges." Eventually, after the Luftwaffe failed to beat the RAF, Hitler postponed the invasion until the following spring and the barges were dispersed.

OPERATION SEA LION

Planning Operation Sea Lion led to a clash between the German army and naval high commands. The generals planned to land on a broad front with six divisions landing between Ramsgate and Bexhill-on-Sea, four between Brighton and the Isle of Wight, and six between Weymouth and Lyme Regis. The Kriegsmarine was adamant it could cope only with landings on a much narrower front from Folkestone to Beachy Head. The one thing both sides agreed on was that, for the invasion to take place at all, it was essential for the Luftwaffe to destroy the RAF and win total air superiority.

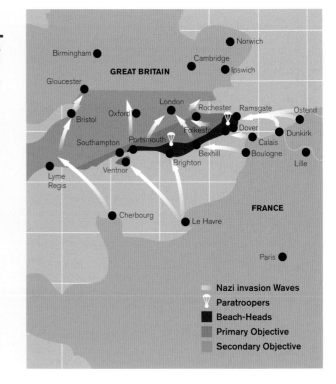

Nazi invasion Waves
Paratroopers
Beach-Heads
Primary Objective
Secondary Objective

THE BATTLE OF BRITAIN

Though Hitler's generals and admirals differed as to the best course of action when planning Operation Sea Lion—the army wanted to land on a broad front while the navy said it could protect the invasion convoys only if the landings took place on a much narrower one—both sets of service chiefs agreed on one thing. For the invasion to be attempted at all, the Luftwaffe had to win total air superiority over southern Britain and the English Channel. Hitler concurred. The RAF, he decreed, had to be "beaten down to such an extent that it can no longer muster any power of attack worth mentioning against the German crossing."

The ebullient Goering was supremely confident that his Luftwaffe could achieve what Hitler had ordained. He boasted that, given good weather, Fighter Command would be smashed in four days. On the face of it, the newly promoted Reichsmarschall had numbers on his side. The Luftwaffe had 900 fighters—Messerschmitt Me 109s and 110s—and 1,300 bombers ready for action at airfields in France, Belgium, the Netherlands, and as far away as Norway. Against them, Air Chief Marshal Sir Hugh Dowding, Fighter Command's commander-in-chief, could put 650 Hurricanes and Spitfires into the air.

HIDDEN WEAKNESSES
Numbers, however, were not everything. Though the Messerschmitt Me 109 was as fast as a Spitfire and far more maneuverable than a Hurricane, its endurance was limited. It could spend only minutes in British airspace before being forced to turn for home to refuel. The answer was to equip the Messerschmitt with auxiliary drop tanks, but when these finally arrived, it was found that they were not self-sealing and so were extremely vulnerable to enemy fire. Many pilots refused to fly Messerschmitts fitted with them.

The twin-engine Messerschmitt Me 110, which Goering thought would protect his bombers, had its problems as well. It was completely outclassed by the two RAF fighters. In any event, German fighter production

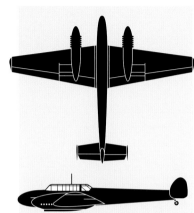

MESSERSCHMITT Me 110

Type Long-range escort fighter/
Fighter-bomber/Night fighter

Crew 3

Length 39ft 7¼in (12.07m)

Wingspan 53ft 7¾in (16.25m)

Speed 349mph (560km/h), 250mph (402km/h) cruising

Range 540 miles (869km)

The Luftwaffe had high hopes of the Me 110 as an escort fighter, but the Battle of Britain demonstrated its vulnerability. Though it could outfly a Hurricane, it was not as nimble as a Spitfire and proved unwieldy to maneuver because of its slow, wide turning circle. It also took time to accelerate from its cruising speed to its top speed and it suffered heavy casualties as a result. It scored greater success later in the war as a fighter-bomber—it could carry a bomb load of 4,410lb (2,000kg)—and as a formidable night fighter.

was now lagging well behind that of Britain. By mid-1940, British aircraft factories were churning out twice as many fighters as their counterparts in Germany.

As for the bombers, the Junkers Ju 87 dive-bomber, which had done so well in Poland and France, proved so slow and vulnerable against the modern British fighters that, after some disastrous missions, it had to be withdrawn from the battle. The Heinkel He IIIs and Dornier Do 17s were poorly armed and obsolescent if not actually obsolete. The Junkers Ju 88, which had been intended to take over from the Heinkel as the Luftwaffe's main bomber, was hopelessly late in getting into production, largely thanks to the thousands of design changes the Luftwaffe air staff had insisted Junkers made to the original prototypes. The result was far heavier and slower than had been envisaged.

Despite such deficiencies, some of which became apparent only during the course of the battle, the Luftwaffe's high command was confident of victory. Colonel "Beppo" Schmid, in charge of collating air intelligence, produced an optimistic survey, which more than confirmed this belief. "The Luftwaffe," he concluded, "is clearly superior to the RAF as regards strength, equipment, training, command, and location of bases."

Two of the glaring omissions from Schmid's report were any mention of radar and any effort to analyze the defensive system that Dowding had developed to deal with a German attack. Schmid claimed that Fighter Command's organization was rigid and inflexible, and so would buckle quickly under pressure when precisely the opposite was the case. Colonel Raymond Lee, a US observer whom Dowding took to visit the underground operations center at Fighter Command, thought differently. "I had no idea," he noted, that "the British could evolve and operate so intricate, so scientific, and rapid an organization, the tentacles of which reach out beyond the edges of the country." The Luftwaffe remained blissfully unaware of the sophisticated way in which Fighter Command was directed and controlled.

Two Junkers Ju 87 Stuka dive-bombers return from a raid on the south coast early on in the Battle of Britain. In Poland and France, the Stuka had proved itself a devastating weapon of war, deployed as "flying artillery" to demoralize enemy ground troops and clear the way for the advancing panzers. In the Battle of Britain, however, they quickly proved no match for the RAF's Spitfires and Hurricanes, taking such heavy losses that eventually they had to be withdrawn from the battle.

A FIGHT FOR SURVIVAL

One thing was clear. Hitler and Goering appeared to be in no hurry to launch an all-out aerial offensive. Though sporadic fighting began in late July with the Luftwaffe attacking convoys in the English Channel, it was not until August 2 that the order went out "to overpower the English air force in the shortest possible time." The Luftwaffe's fighters and bombers readied themselves for mass action.

Adlertag (Eagle Day) was set for August 13. It did not get off to a good start. As ordered, the first wave of bombers took to the air, but, as they approached their rendezvous point with their fighter escort, there was no sign of the fighters. The decision had been taken to postpone the attack until later because of deteriorating weather conditions, but news of the delay had arrived too late to stop the bombers from going into action. They suffered heavy casualties as a result. Even with the absent fighters present, things did not go according to plan. The two Junkers 87 groups that attacked in the afternoon were decimated, each losing around a third of its aircraft.

The battle resumed in grim earnest. Goering's strategy was simple. It was to force Fighter Command into battle by striking at targets it would be forced to defend. Chief among these were the RAF's airfields. The Luftwaffe believed that it had already destroyed several of these, though some of the airfields it blitzed belonged to Coastal Command, not Fighter Command at all. What was even stranger was that Goering ordered his bombers to stop attacking the chain of RAF radar stations along the south coast "in view of the fact that not one of those attacked has been so far put out of action." It was an extraordinary blunder that was to cost the Luftwaffe dear.

AERIAL INTELLIGENCE

As the battle hung in the balance, it became imperative for both sides to try to establish what was happening, in military parlance, is termed "the other wide of the hill." To achieve this, both the Luftwaffe and the RAF relied on air reconnaissance and photographic interpretation. Both sides took distinctly different approaches to the problem.

The German aerial reconnaissance effort concentrated on obtaining tactical information. Strategic analysis of the photographs the Luftwaffe took was lacking. The German photographic interpreters, for instance, did not succeed in pinpointing key industrial complexes, such as the Rolls-Royce plant at Derby where the Merlin

A flight of Mark XII Spitfires from 41 Squadron in the air in 1943 (*above left*) and, to the right, the original Spitfire prototype, photographed shortly before its first flight in March 1936. The aircraft was the brainchild of Reginald J. Mitchell, Supermarine's chief designer, who had previously designed the Supermarine seaplanes that won three successive Schneider Cup trophies between 1927 and 1931. Mitchell was still refining the design when he tragically died of cancer at the age of only 42 in 1937. The first Spitfire Marks were all powered by Rolls-Royce Merlin engines; for the Mark XII, a Rolls-Royce Griffon, which produced substantially more power, was substituted.

engines that powered the Spitfires and Hurricanes were produced, or the Supermarine factories in Southampton where the Spitfire itself was constructed. They also overestimated how much permanent damage the Luftwaffe was doing to Fighter Command's airfields as it battled to put them out of action.

RAF reconnaissance priorities were twofold. Day after day, reconnaissance Spitfires took to the skies, aiming to record the locations of the 400 or so airfields from which the Luftwaffe was launching its daily raids. The photographic interpreters were also trying to establish how many and what sort of aircraft the Germans had at their disposal. By monitoring construction work, such as the lengthening of a runaway or the erection of new hangars and by measuring the size of aircraft on the ground—an operation for which the Wild machine was ideally suited—they managed to get a good idea of which aircraft were flying out of which bases.

THE TURN OF THE TIDE

The Luftwaffe's onslaught intensified. On some days, its aircrews flew more than 1,000 sorties. Fighter Command shuddered under the blows, but did not break. By contrast, German bomber losses reached a point when Goering was compelled to impose a change in tactics. Instead of allowing his fighters to range freely over the aerial battlefield, he ordered them to stay close to the vulnerable bombers and protect them at all costs.

Though the Luftwaffe grotesquely exaggerated the number of RAF planes it claimed to have shot down, Fighter Command's losses started to mount. Dowding's problem was not shortage of aircraft—the factories were more than keeping pace with his needs. It was the stark fact that he was losing experienced pilots at an unsustainable rate. Then chance took a hand.

Hitler had given orders that London was not to be bombed, but on August 24 a stray Luftwaffe bomber accidentally dropped its bomb load over parts of the

capital. The next night, Bomber Command was ordered to Berlin. In response, the Luftwaffe was ordered to switch targets. On the afternoon of September 7, its bombers streamed toward London.

On September 15, fully aware that this was his last chance to win air superiority, Goering launched what he intended to be a knockout blow. More than 500 bombers escorted by 700 fighters set out to blitz the capital. After the attack ended in failure, Hitler postponed Operation Sea Lion until the following spring. Goering was soon forced to abandon mass daylight attacks altogether. Instead, the Luftwaffe turned to bombing by night. The Blitz was about to begin.

▲ Female workers at work on a Rolls-Royce Merlin engine assembly line in a factory located "somewhere in England" in 1942. Designed by Sir Henry Royce, the first Merlin ran in 1933 six months after Royce's death; the Spitfires and Hurricanes that won the Battle of Britain were powered by Merlin IIs and IIIs. Merlin engines were also employed to power other types of aircraft—most notably the Avro Lancaster, de Havilland Mosquito, and the North American P-51 Mustang, which, when its underpowered Allison engine was replaced by a Merlin, became one of the most successful long-range day fighters of the entire war.

THE BLITZ

Much to the surprise of many people, World War II did not begin with an aerial onslaught directed at the belligerents' capitals and other major cities. In Britain as early as 1920, Colonel J. F. C. Fuller, one of the foremost military thinkers of the day, predicted that in the next war "fleets of airplanes will attack the enemy's great industrial and governing centers. All these attacks will be made against the civilian population in order to compel it to accept the will of the attacker."

Basil Liddell Hart, another noted military thinker, chimed in. "A modern state is such a complex and interdependent fabric," he wrote, "that it offers a target highly sensitive to a sudden and overwhelming blow from the air.... Imagine for a moment London, Manchester, Birmingham, and half a dozen other great centers simultaneously attacked."

Sir Edward Ellington, the Chief of the Air Staff, was an equally influential prophet of doom. In 1934, he warned that, in the event of war, "we must be prepared for an attack far more severe in weight and continuity than anything experienced in this country during the last war." The likelihood was, he opined, that the war would open with a "knockout" blow delivered against London. Winston Churchill issued his own grim warning. He told the House of Commons that "one could hardly expect that less than 30,000 or 40,000 people would be killed or maimed" by a week's sustained bombing and that "at least three or four million" Londoners "would flee the capital in panic." Soon it was estimated that, if it concentrated all its aircraft against Britain, the Luftwaffe could drop up to 2,000 tons of bombs on London on the first day of an air offensive and keep up the attack for weeks.

As later events showed, such forecasts were wildly pessimistic. With the exception of the luckless Poles, whose capital was thoroughly blitzed as the Polish campaign drew to its close, the Luftwaffe did not mark the start of hostilities by launching its bombers in an

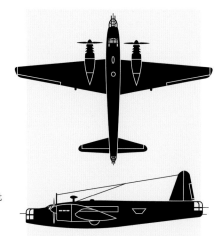

VICKERS WELLINGTON III

Type Medium bomber

Crew 6

Length 60ft 10in (18.54m)

Wingspan 86ft 2in (26.25m)

Speed 255mph (411km/h), 180mph (290km/h) cruising

Range 1,540 miles (2,484km)

Designed by Barnes Wallis, the inventor of the "bouncing bomb," the Wellington prototype first flew in 1936 and the production model a year later. When war broke out, the Wellington was used as an unescorted daylight bomber—Bomber Command thinking was that it was heavily-enough armed to deal with any fighter attack—but, after disastrous losses on two attempted attacks on the German fleet, it was switched to nighttime operations. Wellingtons were among the bombers that raided Berlin for the first time on August 25, 1940; they were also heavily involved in the first 1,000-bomber raid on Cologne in 1942.

all-out attack as had been envisaged. There were various reasons for this. Neither Hitler nor Goering had anticipated a general war. The Luftwaffe had used up more than half its bombs in Poland; it would exhaust its remaining stockpile within the first two weeks of any new campaign. Nor did its bombers have the range to strike at Britain effectively until forward air bases in Belgium, Holland, and northern France had been secured. Above all, it was a tactical, not a strategic air force. It had been built up first and foremost to provide the army with massive ground support.

WARTIME REALITY

For their part, Britain and France had decided even before the war broke out that they would not be the first to bomb civilian targets. This precluded any thought of an Allied bombing offensive even if British and French bombers had been up to the job. The French were so conscious of the weakness of their air force that they vetoed any suggestions of bombing Germany from their soil.

As for Britain, the new generation of four-engine heavy bombers the Air Ministry had ordered were still on the drawing board. Bomber Command itself was totally ill-prepared for war. Its aircrews understood little or nothing about the difficulties of night flying for long distances over blacked-out territory. In peacetime, they had been dependent on following railway lines and looking for city lights. Air Chief Marshal Sir Edgar Ludlow-Hewitt, Bomber Command's commander-in-chief, was all too aware of his force's deficiency. Before the outbreak of war, he had warned the Air Ministry that, should he be ordered to undertake a major bombing offensive against Germany, his medium bombers—the Bristol Blenheims—would be wiped out in three-and-a-half weeks. The heavy bombers—Hampdens, Whitleys, and Wellingtons—would survive a little longer. They would be totally destroyed in seven-and-a-half weeks.

A Heinkel III, photographed from another aircraft flying above it, heads for London's Docklands during the Luftwaffe's first great daylight attack on the capital on September 7, 1940. The raid might have been a success, but Goering's decision to abandon his attacks on the RAF's airfields and switch to civilian targets was to prove a major tactical and strategic blunder. Many believe that it cost the Luftwaffe its best chance of victory in the Battle of Britain.

COUNTDOWN TO THE BLITZ

Even after the Battle of Britain started, it seemed as if the Luftwaffe was still showing remarkable restraint. In fact, it had been hamstrung by orders from the top. Hitler and Goering had both vetoed the bombing of London. Then, on the night of August 24, a flight of Luftwaffe bombers, ordered to bomb an aircraft factory at Rochester, mistook the River Thames for the River Medway, flew up it and jettisoned their deadly cargoes on Millwall, Tottenham, and Islington instead.

It was an honest mistake, but one that triggered major consequences. The next night, on orders from the War Cabinet, around 50 Hampdens were dispatched to bomb Berlin in reprisal. The German capital was shrouded in cloud and only a handful of bombs fell within its boundaries. The RAF returned four nights later.

Though both raids did relatively little damage, the impact on German morale was considerable. Goering himself had assured the Berliners that their city would never be bombed. By September 4, after two more raids, an infuriated Hitler had had enough. In a speech he delivered to a 50,000-strong audience at the Sportsplatz, he vowed revenge. "If the British air force drops two, three, or four thousand kilograms of bombs," he raged, " then we will now drop 150,000, 180,000, 230,000, 300,000, or 400,000 kilograms or more in one night. If they declare that they will attack our cities on a large scale, we will erase theirs. We will put a stop to the games of these night pirates as God is our witness." He concluded with an ominous warning. "The hour is coming when one of us will break," he cried, "and it will not be National Socialist Germany."

Hitler sat down to frantic applause. His decision to attack London was welcomed throughout Germany. Lore Walb, a young student at Munich University, recorded her personal reactions in her diary. "The war of annihilation against England has now really begun," she wrote with satisfaction. "Pray God that they are soon brought to their knees!"

OPPOSITE TOP A Messerschmitt Me 110—a bold "Flying Shark" with open jaws painted on its nose—is captured in full flight over the English Channel. Though this particular aircraft looks agile enough, heavy losses quickly demonstrated that the Messerschmitts were simply not maneuverable enough when it came to battling it out against Fighter Command's Hurricanes and Spitfires. On one mission alone on August 13, only nine out of 23 aircraft taking part made it home unscathed. The Messerschmitt was much more suited to carrying out long-range, low-level ground attacks.

OPPOSITE BOTTOM An unusual action photograph, taken by a Luftwaffe bombardier, shows two strings of bombs being dropped on the port of Tilbury in October 1940. The first string is aimed at the shipping lying moored in the Thames; the second at the docks themselves. What the British christened "the Blitz" continued unabated over the following months with the scale of the attack rapidly escalating. The night raids became so frequent that it seemed as though they were practically continuous. London was bombed for 57 consecutive nights. Other target cities included Portsmouth, Southampton, Plymouth, Exeter, Bristol, Bath, Cardiff, Birmingham, Coventry, Nottingham, Norwich, Ipswich, Sheffield, Manchester, Liverpool, Hull, Middlesbrough, Sunderland, Newcastle, Glasgow, and Belfast.

SEPTEMBER 7–27, 1940

The massive daylight raid on London on September 7 marked a switch in Luftwaffe tactics, its bombers now concentrating on civilian and industrial targets rather than the RAF's vital airfields. The bombing continued throughout the rest of the month and on into the fall and winter. The problem was that it was a struggle the Luftwaffe was ill-equipped to win. It had been built up as a tactical air force and it lacked the heavy bombers it needed to successfully carry out a strategic bombing campaign. Its aircrews were tired as well. Many were being ordered to fly for more than three nights running, a burden that never would be imposed on Bomber Command's aircrews.

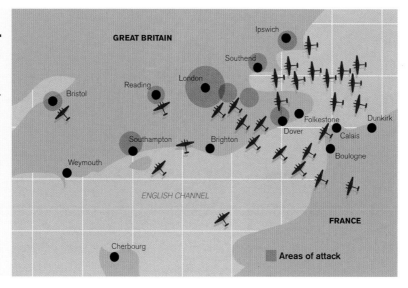

Areas of attack

The German response was not long in coming. On the afternoon of September 7, Goering, whom Hitler had dispatched to France to take personal charge of the battle, watched with his staff from the cliffs of Cape Gris Nez as wave after wave of his bombers and their fighter escorts thundered over his head. Over 900 aircraft—348 bombers and 617 fighters—took part in the attack. Relentlessly the bombers powered their way toward London's docklands in the East End, which the Reichsmarschall personally had singled out for attack. By sheer weight of numbers, they swamped the capital's defenses. Huge fires were soon raging in the docks. More and more bombers arrived to stoke them throughout the night until the raid ended around 4:30 a.m. the following morning.

What Londoners swiftly christened "Black Saturday" was over. Ernie Pyle, a leading US war correspondent stationed in the city, described it as "a night when London was ringed and stabbed by fire."

NIGHT AFTER NIGHT

The raid marked the start of the Blitz, a sustained attempt to bomb Britain into submission that lasted from September 7, 1940 to May 10, 1941. Initially, London was the Luftwaffe's prime target. Every night bar one for 10 solid weeks up to November 10, 1940, Goering's Heinkels, Dorniers, and Junkers relentlessly blitzed the capital. Thereafter, the attacks, though still heavy, became more sporadic as other cities were bombed in their turn. Southampton, Portsmouth, Plymouth, Bristol, Cardiff, Coventry, Birmingham, Nottingham, Manchester, Sheffield, Liverpool, Hull, and Newcastle all came under attack. Goering's bombers even penetrated as far north as Glasgow, where Clydeside was targeted, and Belfast across the Irish Sea.

German planning for the raids was meticulous. Each of the bomber aircrews was issued with target folders prior to the attack. The folders contained an operational plan, giving the location, a description, and topographical details of the selected target. They even included copies of relevant British Ordnance Survey maps. Oblique and vertical air reconnaissance photographs had the bombing area highlighted on them in red ink. The Germans also tried to identify individual buildings by purpose and key them into the photographs. Thus GB 10 was the shorthand for airfields and GB 73 the shorthand for aircraft engine factories.

This was by no means everything the Luftwaffe had at its disposal. Two years before the RAF eventually copied the idea, crack aircrews were grouped together as pathfinders, tasked with locating and marking the targets for the main bombing force. To help the pathfinders and bombers find their way to their target, radio-guidance beams—Knickebein, X-Gerät, and later Y-Gerät—were employed. The RAF had nothing like them.

The Germans had been developing the beams since the early 1930s. Two of them were transmitted. Just like Morse code, one of the beams was represented by a "dot" and the other by a "dash" which the pilot or navigator of a bomber could pick up in flight on their

▼ A German wireless operator is seen checking over his radio console on board a Junkers Ju 88 prior to taking off for a night raid over Britain. Originally intended to meet the Luftwaffe's requirement for a Schnellbomber (fast bomber), the Junkers first flew in 1936, but did not start to arrive in the waiting bomber squadrons until just before the outbreak of war in 1939. Partly this was due to the Luftwaffe's original insistence that the aircraft's design was adapted to give it the ability to dive-bomb. This added to the Ju 88's weight, so reducing its range and speed. Nevertheless, it was an extremely versatile aircraft, various variants serving as a torpedo bomber, fighter-bomber, reconnaissance aircraft, and night fighter.

THE GERMAN BEAMS

The map (*right*) shows how the top secret radio beams the Luftwaffe employed to aid in-flight navigation and bomb aiming intersected over their target—in this instance, the Midlands city of Coventry. Dr. R. V. Jones, a noted young physicist who had become scientific adviser to air intelligence discovered what the Germans were up to and then was tasked by the War Cabinet itself to devise effective countermeasures. His team started off by sending a "mush" of noise over the radio frequencies on which the beams were being transmitted. Then, they found out how to "bend" the beams so that the Luftwaffe aircrews relying on them for guidance dropped their bombs short of their intended targets.

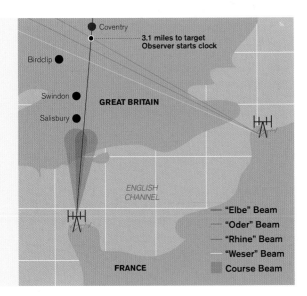

headsets. The two beams were set so that, when the aircraft was flying the correct course, the two sounds merged into a single continuous note. Off-course aircraft would hear more dots and dashes, depending on whether they had veered to the left or right. The beams intersected over the target. When the aircraft reached the point of intersection, another note was heard. It was the signal for the bomb run to start.

MOONLIGHT SONATA AND AFTER

Both the pathfinders and the beams played a crucial part in what the Luftwaffe code-named Operation Moonlight Sonata, the saturation bombing of Coventry on the night of November 14, 1940. In a 12-hour blitz, over 400 bombers dropped 500 tons of high explosive and 30,000 incendiaries on the luckless city. Three-quarters of the city center was destroyed, including the ancient cathedral; the rest of the city suffered heavy damage. Goebbels and his minions at the Propaganda Ministry coined a new verb—to "coventrate"—to describe the scale of the destruction.

Hundreds of Goering's bombers were soon to revisit the capital. On December 29—the night later labelled as the "second Great Fire of London"—the destruction stretched from Islington to St. Paul's Cathedral. The last attack of all, on May 10, 1941, was the worst. The bombers started 2,200 fires, including a giant conflagration at Elephant & Castle just south of the Thames, and killed 1,500 people. London had already suffered thousands of casualties. By the time the Blitz came to an end, 28,556 Londoners had died and 25,578 more had been hospitalized. Around 300,000 houses had been destroyed, leaving 1,500,000 people homeless.

By this time, however, the Blitz was winding down. German losses were increasing as Britain brought radar-controlled anti-aircraft guns and new night fighters into operation. On November 19,ß 1940, John Cunningham became the first night fighter pilot to shoot down a Junkers 88, using airborne radar to home

in on his target. This, though, was not the real reason for the diminution of the attacks. Luftwaffe squadrons were being transferred en masse to the East. Operation Barbarossa, Hitler's attack on the Soviet Union, was about to begin.

A German target map, showing a Scottish airfield, from a target folder of the type issued to all Luftwaffe aircrews prior to attacking Britain. Such folders contained up to six documents. The most important one was the operational plan, which gave the location, description, and other topographic details about the target. The folder also contained a rescaled copy of the relevant British Ordnance Survey map, and as up-to-date as possible oblique and vertical annotated aerial photographs of the target. The area to be bombed was normally marked in red ink on the target map with further details about the target also being added. The letters GB near the top of the map stood for Great Britain, while the numerals identified the nature of the target that it was intended to bomb.

AIR WAR IN THE MEDITERRANEAN

The air war was not confined to Europe. In the Mediterranean, following Mussolini's decision to enter the war in June 1940, the RAF faced the prospect of battling it out against the Regia Aeronautica for aerial supremacy over what the Italian Duce was pleased to call "Mare Nostrum." In North Africa, too, as Italian troops prepared to move on Egypt from Libya, close air support would be vital as both sides tried to block the long lines of communication between their bases to the front line.

Though the war started well enough for the RAF—a day after hostilities broke out, its bombers were in action against El Adem, the main Italian air base in Cyrenaica—it had only 300 first-line aircraft available to defend the 4,500,000 sq. miles (11,654,946.49km²) of territory it was committed to defend. Nine of its 14 bomber squadrons were flying Blenheims, while none of its five fighter squadrons were equipped with anything more up-to-date than obsolescent Gloster Gladiator biplanes. The Blenheims and Gladiators, plus some Sunderland flying boats and Lysander army reconnaissance machines, made up 18 of its 25 squadrons. The rest were flying a ragbag of obsolete oddments, Bombays, Valentias, Wellesleys, Harts, and Hartebeests among them. About half of these aircraft were based in Egypt, with the remainder split between Palestine, Sudan, Kenya, Aden, and Gibraltar.

To oppose the RAF, the Italians fielded 280 aircraft in Libya, 150 in Italian East Africa, and 47 in the Dodecanese. The metropolitan air force was 1,200 planes strong. The aircraft they were flying, however, were demonstrably inferior to the bombers and fighters now being produced for the Luftwaffe and the RAF. As yet, the Luftwaffe was not on the Mediterranean scene while the RAF's most modern aircraft were tied down at home and consequently not available.

The Savoia-Marchetti SM-79 trimotor was the Regia Aeronautica's workhorse bomber. It had been flown against the Abyssinians and in the Spanish Civil War,

FAIREY SWORDFISH I

Type Torpedo bomber

Crew 3

Length 35ft 8in (10.87m)

Wingspan 45ft 6in (13.87m)

Speed 136mph (224km/h)

Range 546 miles (879km)

Nicknamed the "Stringbag" by its aircrews, the Fairey Swordfish biplane went into service with the Fleet Air Arm in 1936. Despite its low speed and old-fashioned appearance, it scored notable successes. Swordfish flying from the aircraft carrier *Illustrious* crippled key warships of the Italian fleet at Taranto in 1940 and, the following May, flying from *Ark Royal* in the North Atlantic fatally crippled the crack German battleship *Bismarck* so enabling units of the British Home Fleet to engage and send her to the bottom.

but by now was obsolete. It was not equipped with blind-flying instruments or other navigational aids. In September 1940, this lack caused 75 bombers flying to Belgium at Mussolini's insistence to take part in the Battle of Britain to crash-land. With a maximum weight of only 500lbs (226.79kg), the high-explosive bombs they carried were too light to cause much damage. Italian incendiaries were equally inadequate. As the Regia Aeronautica discovered when it bombed Malta, many of them detonated in the air as soon as they were released from the bomb bays. The standard Italian bombsight was rudimentary and there was no intercom system to enable pilots and bomb-aimer to communicate directly during an attack

The open-cockpit Fiat CR 42 Falco "Hawk" biplane was the Regia Aeronautica's most numerous fighter. Ignoring developments elsewhere, the Italians had stuck with biplanes rather than switching to monoplanes, arguing that, in a dogfight, lightness and maneuverability were more important than speed, sturdiness, and firepower. It was not until the second half of 1941 that the Macchi C 202 Folgore (Thunderbolt) appeared. It was relatively fast with a top speed of 372mph (598km/h), but was underarmed. It also relied on a German Daimler-Benz engine for its motive power.

The Italian fleet still lies at anchor at Taranto, following the successful Fairey Swordfish attack on it on November 11, 1940. Note the two damaged vessels in the inner harbor. Twenty-one Swordfish attacked in two waves. The first wave torpedoed the battleships *Cavour* and *Littorio* and the second *Duilio*. *Littorio* also suffered further damage. As a result of the attacks, half of the Italian battlefleet was put out of commission. Though *Littorio* and *Duilio* were later repaired, *Cavour* never put to sea again.

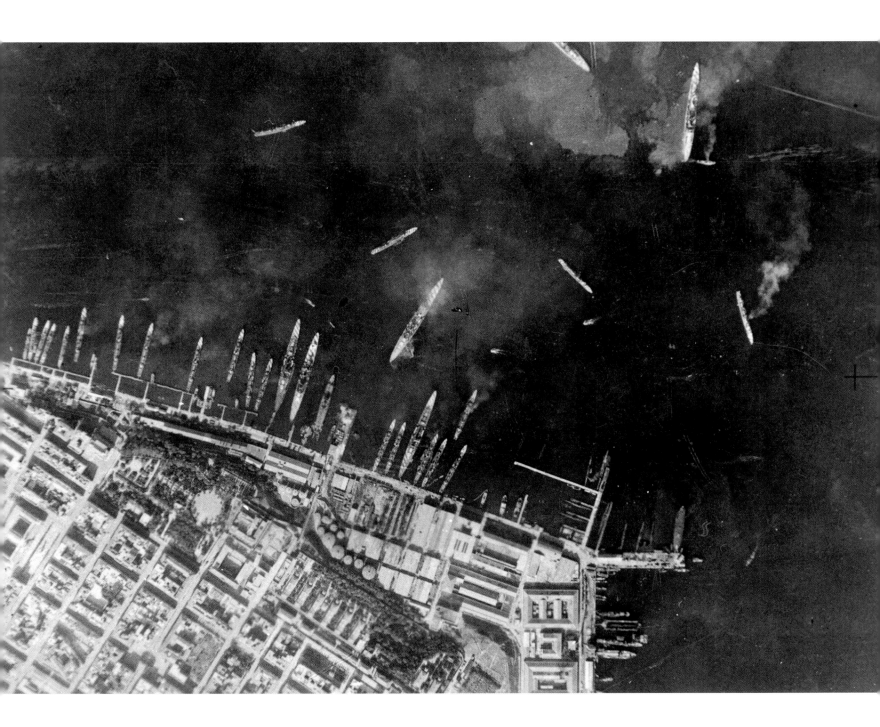

TARGET MALTA

Mussolini was totally blind to these deficiencies, just as he was to the ones in his army and navy. He spent much of his time berating Marshal Rodolfo Graziani, who had succeeded Marshal Italo Balbo as Italian commander-in-chief in Libya after Balbo had been shot down and killed by his own antiaircraft batteries, for his stubborn reluctance to take the offensive and invade Egypt. He was also plotting the surprise invasion of neutral Greece. In the meantime, he cast around for another target he could attack.

Malta seemed the natural choice. Just 60 miles (96.56km) from Sicily, it was well within reach of the Regia Aeronautica's bombers, and was undoubtedly the most vulnerable of Britain's Mediterranean bases. It was also strategically significant, situated as it was astride the main shipping routes from Gibraltar to Alexandria and from Naples to Tripoli. The Italian army's high command, however, had no stomach for any invasion attempt. Neither did the navy. Marshal Pietro Badoglio and Admiral Domenico Cavagnari, the two chiefs of staff, exaggerated the strength of the island's defenses and so managed to torpedo the idea. The Regia Aeronautica felt differently. Its airmen confidently assured the Duce that high-level bombing would "sterilize" Malta, so making an invasion attempt unnecessary.

The bombers struck first on June 11, just seven hours after Mussolini's declaration of war. Eight raids in succession struck the Grand Harbor and Hal Far, one of Malta's three airfields, The only aircraft on the island were five Fairey Swordfish torpedo bombers, four Sea Gladiators, which had arrived disassembled in packing cases and were hastily being put together, and a De Havilland DH 82B Queen Bee, a pilotless drone target plane used for antiaircraft gunnery practice. One of the Gladiators quickly crashed, to be damaged beyond repair. The remaining three—Faith, Hope, and Charity as they were soon dubbed—were all the RAF could spare to defend Malta from Italian air attack until four

Hurricanes arrived at the end of June.

Almost every day over the next two months, the Italians bombed the island. At first, the Italians flew unescorted at high altitudes, but their bomber crews soon demanded fighter protection. Eventually, they abandoned daylight raids completely in favor of attacking by night. The bombing did relatively little damage; only two of the RAF's fighters were shot down. At the beginning of August, 12 more Hurricanes were flown off the aircraft carrier *Argus* to make the loss more than good.

RECONNAISSANCE CENTER

Malta's grimmest hours were to come; in January 1941, the Luftwaffe arrived in force. Before that, however, the RAF flew in three Martin Marylands to the island for air reconnaissance duties. The Marylands—twin-engine American light bombers with a range of some 900 miles (1,448km) and capable of flying at 31,000ft (9,500km)— were ideally suited for the task. From Malta, they could overfly the whole of Sicily, the Italian mainland as far north as Genoa, much of North Africa, and track enemy

▲ The prototype of the US-built Martin Maryland I is seen on the tarmac in April 1939. Originally ordered by the French Air Force to serve as a light bomber, Britain took over the unfulfilled part of the order after France's surrender in June 1940. Initially, the RAF decided the Maryland was best suited to use as a long-range photographic reconnaissance aircraft. Marylands flying from Malta scouted Taranto harbor in preparation for the successful Swordfish torpedo attack on the Italian fleet. A later Maryland variant, the Maryland II, served for a time as a light bomber in North Africa.

Valetta, the capital of the Mediterranean island of Malta, and its Grand Harbor photographed from the air, probably by an enemy reconnaissance aircraft flying from Sicily. The island was bombed for the first time on June 10, 1940, the day after the Italians entered the war. By the time the raids came to an end in November 1942, it had been attacked 3,343 times and the Regia Aeronautica and Luftwaffe had dropped 15,000 tons of bombs on it between them. The Axis plan was to bomb and starve Malta into submission; its people's courage in the face of protracted aerial siege won their homeland the George Cross, Britain's highest gallantry award for civilians.

shipping movements throughout the eastern Mediterranean. Brindisi and Taranto were major targets as were Messina and Palermo in Sicily and Tripoli and Benghazi in Libya.

Adrian Warburton, who arrived on Malta with the Marylands, was to emerge as one of the most celebrated photographic reconnaissance pilots of the entire war. His RAF career, however, got off to a chequered start. He was nearly kicked out of flying school because of his poor takeoffs and bumpy landings. For that reason, he was not allowed to fly a Maryland to Malta, but was told to navigate one of them instead. It was only because the other Maryland pilots were all incapacitated with stomach upsets after their arrival on the island that he got the chance to fly as a pilot again. He immediately proved to be a natural in the air; as his daring exploits were to demonstrate, he also seemed impervious to fear.

ATTACKING TARANTO

Warburton's first aerial exploit was to photograph the Italian battlefleet at anchor in Taranto Harbor. In 1940, the fleet included six battleships, around 20 cruisers, 61 destroyers, 70 torpedo boats, and more than 100 submarines. After France's surrender and the consequent neutralization of the French fleet, it was notionally the most formidable navy in the Mediterranean. However, its ships were not equipped with radar or sonar, while the fleet lacked aircraft carriers to provide it with air cover of its own. Even more significantly, its admirals seemed extremely reluctant to come out of port and fight. Admiral Sir Andrew Cunningham, the commander-in-chief of the British Mediterranean Fleet, was equally determined to bring the Italians to action. As they refused to sail out to meet him, he decided that his best course of action was to launch an aerial attack.

Warburton was ordered to reconnoiter Taranto, establish which ships were anchored there, whether they were in the inner or outer harbor, and check to see if barrage balloons and torpedo nets were protecting them from air assault. He made his first flight on November 10. In appalling weather, he made two low-level sweeps over his objective and then, despite heavy antiaircraft fire, dived even lower to make a third. This enabled him to note down the actual names of the five battleships, 14 cruisers, and 27 destroyers he had spotted, along with their precise locations. He flew so low that his Maryland retuned to Malta with a ship's radio aerial dangling from its tail wheel. The next day, he flew over Taranto again. The information his photographs revealed was passed on to the waiting torpedo-bomber aircrews on board HMS *Illustrious* (HMS *Eagle*, Cunningham's other aircraft carrier, had been damaged in action and was under repair).

The plan was a bold one, especially since the Swordfish torpedo-bombers Cunningham was relying on to carry out the attack were obsolete even before the war broke out. Ungainly and slow—at most they could fly at only 138mph (222.09km/h)—these cumbersome three-man biplanes were a sitting target for modern fighters and fair game for antiaircraft guns. In all, Cunningham could muster 21 of them ready for launch.

THE SWORDFISH ATTACK

The attack went ahead on the night of November 11. The Swordfish took off in two waves spaced about an hour apart. Two planes in each wave were to fly high and drop flares to distract the Italians' searchlights and antiaircraft guns. The remainder would skim at low level over the water, dodging the barrage balloons to launch their torpedoes at the anchored ships.

The first wave's opening shot was at the battleship *Conte di Cavour*, perfectly silhouetted by the falling flares. A torpedo hit her toward the bow and the forecastle promptly erupted in flames. She sunk a little later. Two more torpedoes hit the *Littorio*, which, though badly damaged, remained afloat. All the Swordfish bar one got back to the *Illustrious* safely.

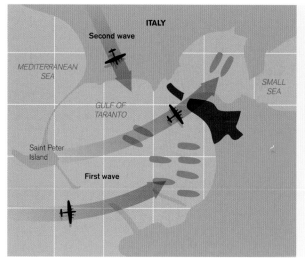

Littorio photographed steaming at speed in November 1939. She and her sister ship *Vittorio Veneto* were faster and better-armed than anything in Cunningham's fleet. Despite this apparent superiority, Italy's admirals were reluctant to take the offensive. When they were forced to do so, their sortie ended in disaster. Off Cape Matapan, *Vittorio Veneto* and the cruiser *Pola* were torpedoed from the air by Albacore torpedo bombers. Though the badly wounded battleship managed to limp back to port, *Pola* stopped dead in the water. The surface fleet sank the cruisers *Fiume* and *Zara* and two destroyers. *Pola* was torpedoed after her crew surrendered.

Map labels: ITALY, Second wave, MEDITERRANEAN SEA, SMALL SEA, GULF OF TARANTO, Saint Peter Island, First wave

ATTACK ON TARANTO

Admiral Sir Andrew Cunningham, commander of the British Mediterranean fleet, planned his attack on Taranto carefully. Two high-flying Swordfish in each wave of the attack would drop flares to light up the Italian fleet and distract its antiaircraft defenses. The remaining aircraft would skim the water, dodging the barrage balloons to launch their torpedoes at the anchored warships. The attack was a complete success. Cunningham boasted that he had done more damage in just an hour than the entire Grand Fleet had managed to inflict on the Germans at Jutland in 1916 during the course of a day.

The second wave struck at midnight. The *Caio Duilio* was hit; the *Littorio* suffered further damage. Both battleships were out of action for six months. Though the *Conte di Cavour* was raised, she never went to sea again. Another Swordfish was lost over the harbor.

More than half the Italian battle fleet had been put out of action and the naval balance of power in the Mediterranean shifted in favor of the Royal Navy. Cunningham boasted that he had inflicted more damage on the Italians in an hour than Admiral Jellicoe's Grand Fleet had done to the German Imperial High Seas Fleet at Jutland, the greatest naval clash of World War I. Even more significantly, Cunningham's triumph finally settled the 20-year argument as to whether or not capital ships were vulnerable to air attack. Unfortunately for the British and the Americans, Japan was the nation that took the lessons

of Taranto most to heart, applying them at Pearl Harbor and off Malaya, when Japanese planes swiftly sank HMS *Prince of Wales* and HMS *Repulse*.

As for Hitler, he was enraged by this latest example of his ally's military incompetence. He had been worried enough by Mussolini's decision to attack Greece, but his warnings to the Duce had been ignored. His forebodings were fully justified. Within weeks, the ill-equipped, ill-prepared, and ill-led Italians were being forced back toward Albania all along the line. The news of Taranto was the last straw. In January 1941, the Luftwaffe arrived in Sicily in force. The protracted aerial siege of Malta soon began.

END OF THE BEGINNING

By 1941, it was clear that, if Britain was not to fight the war blind, the RAF needed more and better equipment to photograph Occupied Europe and the Third Reich itself effectively. It also needed the specialists to interpret the photographs and build up a visual picture of everything that was happening in Nazi-occupied territory. Specially modified Spitfires, later joined by De Havilland Mosquitoes, and improved cameras solved the first part of the problem; the setting-up of a new Central Interpretation Unit the second. The airmen took RAF Benson, not far from London in rural Berkshire as their headquarters. The photographic interpreters, whose original home at Wembley was blitzed by the Luftwaffe, moved to Danesfield House, a mock-Tudor mansion situated above the River Thames just outside the Buckinghamshire village of Medmenham between Henley-on-Thames and Marlow. From May 1941 onward, as the most important center for the interpretation of aerial photographs for the RAF and later the US Army Air Force, RAF Medmenham, as it was christened, was the heart of Allied air intelligence for the rest of the war.

AN AIR INTELLIGENCE REVOLUTION

When General Werner von Fritsch, the then commander-in-chief of the German Army, predicted in 1938 that "the military organization which has the best reconnaissance unit will win the next war," few doubted that, in aerial reconnaissance and photography, the Luftwaffe reigned supreme. This, however, proved to be far from the case. Although the Germans began World War II with an efficient air reconnaissance and photographic interpretation system, they did not develop or improve it as the conflict widened and progressed. Though starting from far behind, the British, in contrast, were to bring about a revolution in aerial photography and air intelligence that was to play a vital part in transforming the fortunes of the war. As the RAF slowly began to gain air superiority over the increasingly hard-pressed Luftwaffe, nothing, it seemed, escaped the probing of its photographic spies in the skies.

SPITFIRES AND MOSQUITOES

Choosing the right aircraft was the key to success. Where Sidney Cotton had pioneered the way, the RAF followed. The Spitfire, in its various reconnaissance versions, became the main aircraft of choice for its photo-reconnaissance squadrons. Unarmed—except for one low-flying variant, which retained its original eight machine guns—it relied on speed and altitude to ensure its survival.

Consequently, throughout the war, there was a steady increase in performance within the Spitfire reconnaissance family. The last of the wartime variants, the Spitfire XIX, could fly over 100mph (160km/h) faster, two miles (3.22km) higher, and more than four times farther than Cotton's pioneer PR 1A. However, the Spitfire XI, of which 471 were produced, was the most numerous of these magnificent aircraft. It could fly at 422mph (679.14km/h), possessed a service ceiling of 44,000ft (13,411m), and had a maximum range of more than 2,000 miles (3,220km).

DE HAVILLAND MOSQUITO DH 98

Type Light bomber/Reconnaissance/ Night fighter/Fighter-bomber

Crew 2

Length 41ft 2in (13.57m)

Wingspan 54ft 2in (16.52m)

Speed 415mph (668km/h)

Range 1,300 miles (2,400km)

Geoffrey de Havilland's revolutionary Mosquito was one of the most versatile aircraft to be produced during the whole of World War II. It was given the official go-ahead in March 1940 and made its operational debut the following year as a photographic reconnaissance machine. Bomber, night fighter, and fighter-bomber variants followed. Its speed, range, and ability to fly at great heights made it almost impossible to shoot down, as the Luftwaffe found to its cost.

As good as the Spitfire was, the twin-engine de Havilland DH 88 Mosquito was probably the best all-round photo-reconnaissance aircraft to go into service with the RAF during the entire war. The first, the PR 1, was delivered to the RAF on June 2, 1941. Seven variations were to follow. Fast, agile in the air, and lightweight thanks to its wooden airframe, the Mosquito could fly as quickly, sometimes quicker, than a Spitfire and enjoyed double the Spitfire's range. By early 1942, UK-based Mosquitoes were regularly flying reconnaissance sorties as far away as northern Norway, East Prussia, and the north of Italy.

Despite its small size, the Spitfire's fuselage was still big enough to accommodate a variety of camera configurations, while cameras could also be mounted in the wings to provide oblique photographic coverage. The mounting-point in the fuselage was just behind the centerline fuel tank. The cameras were split verticals with the largest lenses that could be fitted into the airframe. The Mosquito's fuselage was roomier and so could accommodate any required camera configuration. The commonest involved three cameras—a single short-lens area collector and two long focal length ones, mounted as split verticals for taking more detailed shots of specific objectives. Forward obliques could be taken from the nose or from wing pods to gather stereo images.

Some of the mounting points could be accessed by the aircrew—the Mosquito accommodated a navigator as well as a pilot—which meant that film magazines could be changed in flight. Naturally, this greatly increased the number of photographs that could be obtained.

A Mark XVIII Mosquito fighter-bomber specially
adapted for low-level attacks and fitted with a
six-pounder (57mm cannon). This variant proved
particularly effective in combating German
U-boats and surface shipping; on April 9, 1945,
for instance, Mark XVIIIs sank three U-boats
caught heading for Norway in quick succession.
Other Mosquito bombing marks—most notably the
BXVI—excelled in precision attacks. One of their
most important roles was acting as pathfinders for
Bomber Command's heavy-bomber squadrons.

RECONNAISSANCE ROUTINE

When the weather was clear, reconnaissance pilots often flew several reconnaissance sorties a day—at their peak, in the run-up to D-Day in 1944, many were averaging up to eight. With up to 500 exposures on each roll of film the pilots brought back, staffing levels at RAF Medmenham increased exponentially. At the start, Medmenham had an establishment of 114 officers and 117 other ranks. By the end of the war, there were around 550 officers and 3,000 other ranks working there. They included many Americans.

The staff—mostly an eclectic mix of boffins and academics with quite a few women among them—comprised some of the best brains in the country. Geoffrey Stone, an army photographic interpreter posted to Medmenham prior to D-Day, recalled that the place was nothing like a "regimented military establishment." It was "much more like an academic institution full of civilians in uniform." Glyn Daniel, the first Cambridge archaeologist to be recruited to the Medmenham operation, described his new colleagues as "an ill-assembled collection of dons, artists, ballet designers, newspaper editors, and writers." There was no doubting, however, the dedication they brought to their new jobs.

Archaeologists like Daniel were prized because of their ability to piece together tiny scraps of information to produce a comprehensive intelligence picture. Dorothy Garrod, Disney Professor of Archaeology at Cambridge, joined Medmenham as a member of the Women's Auxiliary Air Force (WAAF), became a Section

A recruiting poster appeals for Britain's women to come forward and volunteer to serve in the ATS (Auxiliary Territorial Service) and the WAAF (Women's Auxiliary Air Force). In September 1940, the first batch of WAAFS arrived at Wembley, then the headquarters of RAF photographic interpretation. At first, they worked as plotters, marrying the routes flown by reconnaissance aircraft and the photographs they took onto large maps to build up a composite aerial picture, but it was quickly recognized that they could be trained to become fully fledged photographic interpreters.

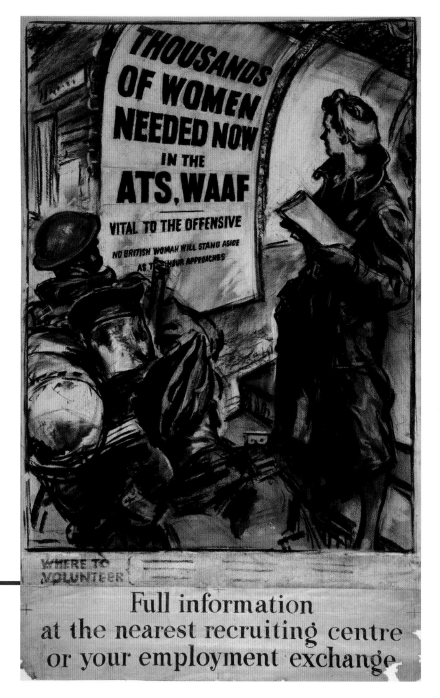

Officer and made herself Medmenham's expert on the movement of supplies and troops by train. Explorers and geologists were equally valued. Many found their peacetime experiences invaluable. Constance Babington Smith, a young WAAF officer who had been a pre-war journalist on *The Aeroplane*, won fame for being the first to identify one of the Third Reich's most-closely guarded secrets, the VI Flying Bomb.

Not everyone took to the life. Elizabeth Johnston-Smith, a 19-year-old WAAF who came to Medmenham to train as a photographic interpreter, said the place had "a fuddy-duddy, middle-aged feel to it," which she did not care for at all. The hours were long, the tasks taxing, and the pressure unrelenting. Night and day every day of the year, work went on continuously. To cope with the burden, Medmenham personnel worked a shift system. For day workers, the norm was 12 hours on and then 24 hours off. Nightshift personnel worked from 8:00 p.m. to 8:00 a.m. They got 36 hours off.

TRAINING PHOTOGRAPHIC INTERPRETERS

All prospective photographic interpreters posted to Medmenham had to undertake an introductory training course. There were no exceptions, regardless of any past experience. Douglas Kendell, who had worked with the Aircraft Operating Company before the war and then with Sidney Cotton, was put in charge of setting up the course; Pilot Officer Alfred Stevenson eventually took over from him. By the end of the war, he had trained 1,300 would-be photographic interpreters successfully.

The course lasted two weeks, during which time its participants learned the basics of the various skills a proficient photographic interpreter required. Some, like patience, attention to detail, and a good visual memory could not be taught. Successful photographic interpreters also possessed the kind of mind that enjoyed solving what often proved to be knotty problems. The starting point was learning how to

identify objects on the ground as seen from high up in the air. Railways, for instance, had to be distinguished from roads as did fighter airstrips from bomber airfields. Next, the students were introduced to stereoscopic viewing. They were taught how to handle a stereoscopic viewing frame—this was universally referred to simply as a "Stereo." The two photographic prints that fitted into it were termed a "Stereo Pair."

Viewing objects on the ground in 3D made it easier to identify them. It also made it possible to measure them. The logical first step was to work out the scale of the photographs. Once this had been established, the size of every object in them could be calculated, though many found it hard to master the intricacies of working with a slide-rule. Finally, the trainee photographic interpreters were taught how to distinguish objects of military significance and especially how to seek out any telltale signs denoting untoward enemy activity.

▼ Flight Lieutenant H. W. Williams demonstrates the workings of a giant Wild A5 photogrammetric mapping machine to press visitors at RAF Medmenham. The first Wild machine to reach Britain was imported from Switzerland by The Aircraft Operating Company shortly before the war and Sidney Cotton seized on it as the way of improving the amount of military information photographic interpreters could glean from small-scale high-altitude photographs. Two consecutive aerial photographs—a Stereo Pair—were mounted within the machine. Looking through its twin eyepieces, the operator could see a three-dimensional image and a floating dot. The latter could be mechanically controlled to trace off outlines and contours.

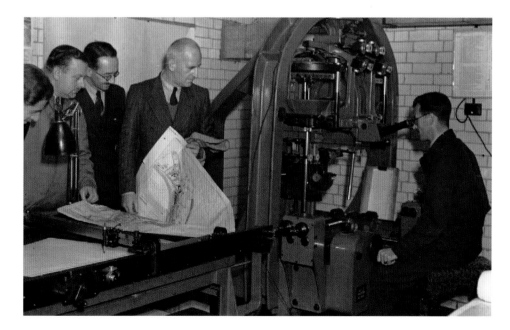

PHOTOGRAPHIC INTERPRETATION IN ACTION

Actual photographic interpretation involved several phases or stages. The First Phase, as it was termed, was carried out as soon as possible after the photographs had been developed and printed. The aim was to spot urgent military information. Second Phase analysis followed. This was a more elaborate process, undertaken by a large team examining the photographs in more detail. What the team detected formed the basis for the daily reports RAF Medmenham produced, summarizing every aspect of enemy activity.

The Third Phase was the key to building a greater understanding of specific aspects of the enemy war effort. It involved close photographic analysis by specific dedicated working sections. Section A dealt with enemy shipping. It had plenty of material to work with—from 1941 onward, every port in Occupied Europe was photographed at least once a week, provided the weather was favorable. One of the section's key figures was David Brachi, another of those who came to RAF Medmenham having worked for the Aircraft Operating Company. Among his achievements was his identification of a new class of German destroyer, but his real speciality was monitoring U-boat construction. By carefully charting each stage of the process, he was able to amass enough evidence to be able to deduce how many new U-boats were being built up to a year ahead. In early 1941, for instance, he predicted that U-boat production would double by the end of the year. The report went straight to the highest levels of naval intelligence, then to the chiefs of staff and finally to the War Cabinet, where it was seen by Churchill himself.

Section C studied enemy airfields, while Section E devoted itself to spotting all kinds of camouflage. Section F concentrated on railways, roads, and river and canal transport. Section L specialized in aircraft identification, while the aptly-named Section N concentrated on night photography. Other sections focused on industry, army sites, and bomber targeting and damage assessment. During the entire course of the war, none of the other belligerents managed to build up such a sophisticated air intelligence operation.

Section C, in particular, was faced with an arduous task. There were 400 Luftwaffe air bases in France and the Low Countries alone and hundreds more scattered through the Mediterranean. The photographic interpreters first set about establishing which aircraft flew from what bases. The Luftwaffe's fighters, for instance, more often than not flew from smaller bases with grass landing strips. German bombers and transport aircraft, on the other hand, usually needed longer concrete runways in order to be able to take off and land without damage.

This was by no means all Section C spent its time observing. Its photographic interpreters also kept a close watch-out for signs of airfield expansion, particularly the building of new hangars and taxiways or the extension of runways and the installation of flare paths. They had to be able to recognize existing aircraft types and spot new ones as and when they were introduced. Often, building activity was an anticipation of the arrival of new aircraft. In 1944, for instance, when the Luftwaffe started to prepare to receive its first jets, the interpreters spotted not only that runways were being lengthened but that new fuel dumps were also being built to accommodate the needs of the new aircraft. They went on from this to predict the approximate number of jets the Germans, in theory, would be able to deploy.

Only the most talented photographic interpreters were considered suitable for working on Phase Three analysis. Constance Babington Smith was one of them. As well as being the photographic interpreter who first spotted a V1 Flying Bomb on its way for testing, she was the first to spot the Messerschmitt Me 163 rocket fighter, the Heinkel He 28, the world's first jet fighter, and the revolutionary Messerschmitt Me 262, the

A Vought SB2U Vindicator from the US aircraft carrier *Ranger* flies an antisubmarine patrol over a convoy heading for Cape Town. The problem was that until relatively late in the war, only a few aircraft with the range to offer long-distance convoy protection were available to fly in the Battle of the Atlantic. The "bomber barons" resolutely refused to detach any of their aircraft to help with the job. Grand Admiral Doenitz's U-boat wolf packs were quick to take advantage of the opportunity they were offered. In 1942 alone, they sunk 1,661 merchant vessels.

twin-engine jet fighter that, fortunately for British and American airmen, Hitler insisted be redesigned to be deployed as a fighter-bomber. She and her team detected other top-secret German aircraft prototypes into the bargain.

Babington Smith's photographic detective work in Section L was praised by no less a person than Group Captain Frank Whittle, the inventor of the original jet engine. He visited her at RAF Medmenham where he appeared to fall for the WAAF officer. Babington Smith later discovered that he had tried to find out from her colleagues what sort of scent she was wearing. It was Guerlain's *L'Heure Bleue*—a classy French perfume that was hard to find in wartime Britain. Babington Smith wore it, she said, to try to counteract the masculine effect of her service uniform.

MAPS AND MODELS

Map-making was another important part of RAF Medmenham's activities. The route of each photographic reconnaissance sortie and outline plots of the photographs taken on it had to be traced onto small-scale maps to create a permanent record of what had been photographed—and, more often than not, photographed again—when and where. The latter was particularly important, since the photographic interpreters needed all the photographs that could be mustered for purposes of comparison.

It was precision work, which required great skill and fine attention to detail. It was reckoned that a first-class tracer could plot around 100 photographs an hour. The finished plots were cut out and mounted on a master map for future reference. The original prints were dispatched to RAF Medmenham's Photographic Library. This housed a truly mammoth photographic collection, which expanded at the rate of about a million photographs a month as the war reached its height.

The long rolls of negative film shot by the reconnaissance Spitfires and Mosquitoes were also stored in the capacious library. New prints from them could be requested whenever they were needed. A vast Williamson Multiprinter from Kodak speeded up the process. Working flat out, it could print up to 1,000 photographs an hour. The librarians—there were 275 of them—boasted that they could find or produce prints of photographs taken almost anywhere over Europe in a matter of minutes. By 1944, they were producing up to 140,000 duplicate photographs a month and, by the end of the war, they were storing approximately seven million photographic prints from all the main fighting fronts.

Section V was responsible for model-making. Initially, the section was based in the basement of Danesfield House, which was converted into a carpenter's workshop, but it soon spread to outbuildings scattered through the grounds. Geoffrey Deeley, a successful sculptor, was the chief model-maker. Others included

OPPOSITE TOP A model-maker shows off one of the model maps that were produced as part of RAF Medmenham's D-Day preparations. Three types of model map were produced. Small-scale ones showed the landscape and key communications of large areas of northern France. Larger-scale ones showed stretches of coastline in detail to a depth of around 12 miles (19.31km). Even larger-scale ones were devised to help to brief the troops taking part in parachute and glider landings.

OPPOSITE BOTTOM One of the many models Medmenham produced was this detailed model of the German Würzburg radar station at St. Bruneval on Cap d'Antifer near Le Havre in France. It was used as a briefing guide by paratroops from the 1st Airborne Division who raided the site on the night of February 27, 1942. The model was based on photographs taken by No. 1 Photographic Reconnaissance Unit, stationed at RAF Benson. Tony Hill, who flew the first mission, spotted the Würzburg's antenna, which, he said, looked like "an electric bowl fire."

Alan Sorell, a well-known artist, and Leslie Durbin, a celebrated silversmith.

The section used the aerial photographs that were passed across to them as reference for the three-dimensional models they spent their time lovingly creating. Initially, they started by making individual models of ships, aircraft, tanks and other military vehicles, military installations, other buildings, and even railway locomotives and goods wagons. New photographic interpreters used them as recognition guides. Soon, however, the model-makers grew more ambitious. They began creating models of entire landscapes that could be as much as 20 sq. ft (1.85m²). Cliffs, beaches, ports, harbors, dams, and specific groups of buildings, such as radar stations, were all produced in full detail precisely to scale. They were triumphs of the model-makers' art.

BUILDING THE MODELS

Each model was constructed as follows. First, the model-makers built up an accurate representation of the overall terrain by layer on layer of hardboard cut-outs on a baseboard. They used maps as extra reference to back up their photographs. Then they covered the layered cutouts with rubber or plastic to create a more realistic effect.

The next step was even more complicated. It involved creating a mosaic of vertical aerial photographs over the model. This was a skillful job, as it usually meant cutting out several photographs to give the model what might be termed a photographic "skin." This was painted to simulate the look of a real landscape, complete with rivers, roads, fields, woods, and trees. Finally, individual models of key installations or buildings were made separately and then placed carefully in position. During every stage of the process, Third Phase specialists checked and double-checked the model-makers' work to ensure that what was being produced was as accurate as possible.

By the time the war ended, Medmenham's model-makers had churned out more than 1,400 models. Some, like the models of the Möhne, Eder, and Sorpe dams used to brief the Dam Busters prior to their famous 1943 air attack, were extremely elaborate. Such was the reliance Bomber Command placed on them that, according to Paul Brickhill, author of *The Dam Busters*, the aircrews taking part in the attack were instructed to "look at these until your eyes stick out and you've got every detail photographed on your mind. Then go away and draw them from memory, come back and check your drawings, correct them, then go away and draw them again till you're perfect."

Sometimes, too, the models were photographed lit in a way that replicated exactly what the location must look like on a moonlit night. The biggest task Section V undertook involved building 97 separate models of the Normandy beaches as part of the preparations for the June 1944 D-Day landings. In order to produce the many copies of the models the Overlord planners required, the model-makers made plastic molds from the originals in order to produce the required number of duplicates.

SPOTTING DECOYS

As the RAF's bombing offensive slowly built up its strength, the Germans tried to divert the bombers away from their targets by setting up hundreds of decoy sites. There was nothing new in this; the British had done much the same thing when they implemented Operation Starfish to try to fool the Luftwaffe during the Blitz. The German plan worked for a time, until Geoffrey Dimbleby began studying the countryside around priority RAF targets in the Ruhr Valley and along the Rhine. He spotted hundreds of craters in fields where, by triggering decoy fires, the Germans had tricked the bombers into dropping their bomb-loads.

It was an easy enough mistake to make. Many Bomber Command aircrews were already bombing on estimated time of arrival over their targets and their accuracy was substantially inaccurate as a result. Seen from 20,000ft (6,100m) or so, the fires the Germans set could easily be mistaken for burning buildings. Dimbleby was put in charge of a new section—Q Section—at RAF Medmenham with orders to solve the problem the various decoy sites were posing. They got to work and, around Cologne alone, quickly identified 17 different decoy sites.

The Germans even attempted the Herculean task of trying to camouflage their capital. The surface of the East-West Axis, the city's most important distinguishing landmark, was sprayed with dark green paint to blend in with the surrounding Tiergarten. An overhead cover of wire matting, interwoven with green material to resemble vegetation, was also strung over it for a considerable distance. In Hamburg, the main railway station had a false roof built over it in the shape of a small hill. The photographic interpreters, though, found such efforts relatively easy to spot in photographs, as opposed to with the naked eye from the air, because the camouflaged areas looked visually different to the actual landscape surrounding them. Comparing photographic coverage shots could also be a dead giveaway. E Section, headed by WAAF officer Molly "Tommy" Thompson, briefed photographic interpreters on what to look out for and how to spot it.

Dummy airfields featured prominently in the German decoy scheme. They were often sited close to actual airfields and populated with dummy airplanes in the hopes that attacking aircraft would be fooled into bombing and strafing them. The dummies were often so realistic that even experienced photographic interpreters sometimes found it difficult to distinguish them from the real thing. Oil depots and storage tanks were shrouded with camouflage netting to look like fields. The Germans used smokescreens as well—both to try to conceal actual targets and as decoys. Despite their efforts, the majority of the bombers got through.

Both the British and Germans created elaborate deception sites — such as these decoy sites pictured showing the remains of Sliverknowes and Cramond in Scotland — designed to fool the spies in the sky and divert hostile bombers from their real targets. The British called their effort Operation Starfish. The first Starfish sites were set up in December 1940. By the end of the war, there were 237 of them, protecting 81 cities, factories, and other potential targets. The Germans went even further than the British. One of their main efforts was an attempt to divert Bomber Command away from Berlin itself.

KRIEGSMARINE

An RAF aerial reconnaissance photograph shows the battlecruiser *Scharnhorst* in dry dock in Kiel harbor. The arrow in the lower center marks her exact position. Both *Scharnhorst* and her sister-ship *Gneisenau* had been damaged in Operation Cerberus, their successful attempt to break out from Brest and steam for home through the English Channel in February 1942. *Prinz Eugen*, the heavy cruiser that had accompanied *Bismarck* on her ill-fated Atlantic sortie, went with them. Despite being forewarned by the French Resistance, the audacious move took the British completely by surprise. The Germans were already 300 miles (482km) up the Channel before they were detected.

Though, thanks to the sacrifices Hitler had demanded of it during the 1940 Norwegian campaign, the weakened Kriegsmarine was no match for the Royal Navy in fleet action, it nevertheless remained a potent threat to Britain's trans-Atlantic lifeline. Keeping the sea lanes open was of critical importance for the island's very survival. Grand Admiral Karl Dönitz's U-boats, though there were not enough of them to win the battle of the Atlantic outright, were a constant menace, sinking thousands of tons of shipping a month. If Grand Admiral Erich Raeder's powerful surface ships—the battlecruisers *Scharnhorst* and *Gneisenau* and, when they were ready for sea, the crack battleships *Bismarck* and *Tirpitz*—broke out into the Atlantic, the consequences would be catastrophic. The pocket battleship *Admiral Graf Spee* had already demonstrated what a determined commerce raider could accomplish.

SCHARNHORST AND GNEISENAU

While these mighty modern warships were anchored in their home ports, they presented a threat, rather than an immediate danger. Photographic reconnaissance was the only way of keeping tabs on them. So, when it was discovered that *Scharnhorst* and *Gneisenau* had

The *Gneisenau* was also photographed in dry dock in Kiel. She was about to sail for Norway when she was hit by a single bomb during an RAF air raid. The bomb penetrated her foredeck and exploded, its detonation triggering a further internal explosion in the ship's magazine. The damage was so severe that *Gneisenau* was ordered to the Polish port of Gydania to be rebuilt. Work had barely started when Hitler personally ordered her to be decommissioned. She was eventually sunk as a blockship outside Gydania in early 1945.

both slipped out of Kiel on November 27, 1940, it was little wonder that the alarm bells rang at the Admiralty. The naval panic that ensued was fully justified. In three months, *Scharnhorst* sunk eight merchant ships and *Gneisenau* 12. Approximately 120,000 tons of British shipping had been sent to the bottom of the Atlantic Ocean.

It was not until March 28, 1941 that the two battlecruisers—the "ugly sisters" as the navy christened them—were spotted again by a photo-reconnaissance Spitfire, flying from St. Eval in Cornwall. Pilot Officer Gordon Green, flying in atrocious weather, took advantage of a brief break in the clouds covering Brest to make two swift passes over the harbor. In the teeth of ferocious German antiaircraft fire, he and his precious photographs made it home safely.

The RAF's response was immediate. While photo-reconnaissance Spitfires conducted an almost continuous surveillance of the port, Bomber and Coastal Command blitzed Brest by night and sometimes by day. Losses were heavy and the damage inflicted minimal. Then, on April 5, luck presented the RAF with a golden opportunity. Photo-reconnaissance revealed that *Gneisenau* had been moved from the safety of the dry dock, where she had been refitting, out into the inner harbor. It was later discovered that the move had been decided on by the German port authorities because of the risk posed to the ship by an unexploded bomb. It proved to be a costly decision.

The next morning, a flight of Beaufort torpedo-bombers was dispatched from St. Eval to attack *Gneisenau* while she was still vulnerable. Thanks to bad weather and heavy German antiaircraft fire, only one of the Beauforts, piloted by Flying Officer Kenneth Campbell, managed to locate the target. Undeterred by the hail of antiaircraft fire that greeted his arrival, Campbell managed to fire his torpedo directly into the helpless ship. The 40ft (12m) hole the torpedo blew in her hull put *Gneisenau* out of action for six months.

HUNTING DOWN THE BISMARCK

The British now faced another and even more dangerous menace. On May 19, 1941, *Bismarck*, Germany's newest and most powerful battleship, sailed from Gydania in the Baltic in company with the heavy cruiser *Prinz Eugen*. Raeder had ordered her to sail through the Kattegat and then to Grimstadfjord, a little south of Bergen on the Norwegian coast, preparatory to heading through the Denmark Strait between Greenland and Iceland and out into the Atlantic. *Prinz Eugen* sailed to Kalvanes Bay, slightly farther to the south.

It was the turn of the reconnaissance Spitfires based at Wick, right at the tip of northeast Scotland, to hunt down and identify what the Admiralty had been told, via the British naval attaché in Stockholm, were simply "two large warships." On the morning of May 21, two aircraft were dispatched accordingly to make a sweep over the Norwegian fjords. One flew along the coast near Oslo, while the other, piloted by Flying Officer Michael Suckling, headed farther north toward Bergen to reconnoiter the coast there.

Suckling flew high, banking every few minutes or so to catch a glimpse of the fjords scattered along the coast. Suddenly, he caught sight of a group of ships below him and dived to take a closer look. He identified one of them as a cruiser, surrounded by destroyers and an oil tanker. Turning on his cameras, he made a pass across the fjord before heading for Bergen to check out the harbor there. Then he turned for home. As he did so, he spotted another group of ships below him. He activated his cameras again, photographed the ships, and resumed his homeward course.

The Spitfire reached Wick safely early that afternoon. It took about an hour to process Suckling's films. Then, David Linton, a geographer who had been enrolled as a photographic interpreter shortly after the outbreak of war, examined the prints. Suckling thought he had seen two cruisers, or possibly one cruiser and a battleship.

Linton identified them as a Hipper-class heavy cruiser and *Bismarck*. Moreover, he spotted that neither ship had protective torpedo nets deployed. It was more than likely, he deduced, that they were preparing to sail. The prints were rushed south to Coastal Command in London, who confirmed the identification. The following day, another reconnaissance flight—this time by a Martin Maryland from the Naval Air Training Station at Scapa Flow—confirmed that the ships indeed had left the fjords.

THE NET CLOSES

Admiral Sir John Tovey, commander-in-chief of the Home Fleet, had already taken precautionary action. He had dispatched five cruisers—two to patrol the Denmark Strait and three to scout the passage between Iceland and the Faeroe Islands. The veteran battle-cruiser *Hood* and the *Prince of Wales*, a brand-new battleship which had just joined the fleet, were sailing north, ready to intercept the Germans. The rest of the fleet would follow once the enemy had been sighted.

On May 23, the *Suffolk*, one of the two cruisers patrolling the Denmark Strait, struck lucky. A lookout spotted *Bismarck* and *Prinz Eugen* steaming together roughly seven miles (11km) away. As *Suffolk* signalled she had sighted the enemy, the Germans opened fire on *Norfolk*, her sister-ship. Both British vessels took cover in a convenient fog bank, from where *Suffolk* continued to track *Bismarck* by radar. *Hood* and *Prince of Wales*, who were around 1,590 miles (2,560km) away, altered course to intercept the enemy. They were soon steaming so fast that their escorting destroyers found it near impossible to keep up with them in the heavy seas. Then, the news came through that *Suffolk* had lost radar contact with the enemy. Fortunately, or so it seemed at the time, it was not long before she regained it.

Bismarck, the pride of the Kriegsmarine, was spotted by Pilot Officer Michael "Babe" Suckling sheltering in a Norwegian fjord near Bergen on May 21, 1941. He had caught sight of the heavy cruiser *Prinz Eugen* in a nearby fjord moments before. Suckling's sighting, when confirmed, triggered the most celebrated sea-chase of the entire war. At first, *Bismarck* struck lucky, sinking the battlecruiser *Hood* and damaging the battleship *Prince of Wales* before giving her pursuers the slip. Then, crippled by a torpedo hit on her rudders by a Fleet Air Army Fairey Swordfish strike, she was caught and sunk by the Home Fleet when it closed in for the kill.

At around dawn, *Hood* and *Prince of Wales* sighted the Germans. The British ships steamed toward the Germans head-on, maybe to close the range quickly and present as small a target as possible. Shortly before 6:00 a.m., they opened fire. There apparently was some confusion as to which German ship was which; both *Hood* and *Prince of Wales* engaged *Prinz Eugen* rather than *Bismarck*. It took a couple of salvoes before they corrected the mistake. Both German vessels concentrated their fire on *Hood* right from the start.

The battle did not last for long. A salvo from *Prinz Eugen* started a fire on *Hood* near the base of her mainmast. Minutes later, as the British ships finally started to turn to port so they could bring all their main armament into action, *Hood* was devastated by a huge explosion. A shell from *Bismarck* had pierced her outdated armor plating and exploded in her aft magazine. She sank almost instantly. The heavily-damaged *Prince of Wales* was forced to break off the action. The Germans did not pursue her.

It seems that the Germans had scored an overwhelming victory. *Bismarck*, however, was losing oil. One of the few shells that struck her had penetrated a fuel tank, which had started to leak. Admiral Günther Lütjens, the commander of the German squadron, realized that it was impossible for the *Bismarck* to continue as planned. Accordingly, he ordered *Prinz Eugen* to proceed on her own into the Atlantic, while he headed for Brest.

ATTACK FROM THE AIR
The Home Fleet started to track *Bismarck*, but, thanks to her sudden change of course, lost her. By the time Tovey realized where she was heading and re-established contact, she had established a commanding 130-mile (209km) lead. Something had to be done to slow her down before she got within range of protective Luftwaffe air cover. Fortunately for Tovey, he had two aircraft carriers to hand. *Victorious* had already

launched one strike against *Bismarck*, but her Swordfish torpedo-bombers had failed to score any hits. Now it was the turn of *Ark Royal* to show what her torpedo-bombers could do.

The first attack from *Ark Royal* was a fiasco. Her Swordfish mistook *Sheffield*, the light cruiser that was now shadowing *Bismarck*, for the German battleship and attacked her instead. Luckily for *Sheffield*, the magnetic firing mechanisms of the Swordfish's torpedoes malfunctioned. The torpedoes exploded prematurely as they hit the ocean. The chastened Swordfish pilots returned to their carrier to rearm the aircraft with old-style contact torpedoes and then tried again. This time, they were successful. Their attacks were pressed home with the utmost gallantry. According to a German account, "the aircraft came down to the attack and darted through the barrage like flashes of lightning. The courage displayed by the pilots in pressing home their attack in this fashion was beyond praise."

One torpedo struck *Bismarck* amidships, but caused no damage. The other hit her starboard side close to her stern and jammed her rudders. The great battleship began to turn in circles. Attempts to steer her with her screws failed and she started to head inexorably on a collision course toward Tovey and his avenging battlefleet. Lütjens realized that his ship was doomed. He signalled Naval Group West: "Ship unable to maneuver. We will fight to the last shell. Long live the Fuehrer!"

The final battle was fought the next day. It did not last for long. The British pounded the stricken battleship mercilessly, soon putting almost all its guns out of action, killing most of the senior officers on board—including Lütjens—and reducing her to little more than a blazing hulk. Yet despite everything Tovey and his ships could throw at her, she resolutely refused to sink. The British ceased fire in bewilderment. Tovey, in particular, was getting frustrated. His ships were

Fairey Swordfish torpedo bombers prepare for launch from the flight deck of the aircraft carrier *Victorious*. They attacked *Bismarck* around midnight on May 24 with no success. A second strike the following afternoon, however, proved decisive. The torpedoes launched by the Swordfish damaged the battleship's starboard propeller, wrecked her steering gear, and jammed her rudders. It proved impossible to repair the damage. Admiral Günther Lütjens signalled his shore command: "Ship unmaneuverable. We will fight to the last shell. Long live the Fuehrer!"

low on fuel and soon would be forced to break off the action and turn for home. He signalled to the cruiser *Dorsetshire*: "Get closer and sink her with torpedoes."

Dorsetshire obeyed. The three torpedoes she fired all struck home. *Bismarck*, already listing heavily to port, capsized and sank with the loss of all but 110 men of her 2,300-strong crew. Whether or not it was the torpedoes alone that sent her to the bottom is still a matter of historical controversy and debate. Some say that her crew scuttled her to prevent her from being captured. What is indisputable, however, is that, without *Ark Royal* and her Swordfish, the British probably would have found it impossible to snatch victory from the jaws of defeat.

THE BATTLE FOR CRETE

In the history of World War II, the battle for Crete stands out for two distinct reasons. To begin with, it was the first time Ultra intelligence, by cracking the Luftwaffe's Enigma code, alerted Britain to a German attack plan in advance. Secondly, it was the first time that airborne troops were deployed to capture an important strategic objective on their own.

Crete had been garrisoned by the British since November 1940, though General Sir Archibald Wavell, the commander-in-chief in the Middle East, lacked the troops to do the job thoroughly. Suda Bay, the island's main harbor, was held by a weak brigade group, while the RAF built three airstrips, the most important one being situated at Maleme practically next door to Suda. That was the full extent of the British involvement, though with the Greeks successfully fighting off the Italians on the mainland, the chances of an Axis attack on Crete were considered to be slight.

In fact, Hitler had had half an eye on Crete since July, though, at the time, he left the decision on whether or not to strike at the island to his Italian allies. When the Italians faced disaster after their ill-timed and ill-judged attempt to invade and conquer Greece, he changed his mind. He told Count Ciano, Mussolini's son-in-law and foreign minister, that Italian military incompetence was threatening the entire Axis position in the Balkans. It was something the Fuehrer could not tolerate. In particular, he feared that the British, who were on the brink of dispatching an expeditionary force to assist the Greeks, would turn Crete into a springboard from which RAF bombers could strike at Ploesti and the Romanian oil-fields. These were Germany's sole source of high-grade crude oil.

Hitler told Ciano that in April he would be ready to strike. In the event, the Wehrmacht moved simultaneously against Yugoslavia as well as Greece. Both countries were forced to capitulate within a couple of weeks. The British were forced to evacuate as much of their expeditionary force as they could. The Axis triumph was swift and complete.

OPERATION MERCURY

Driven out of Greece and mindful of Crete's strategic potential, Churchill was determined to hold onto it at all costs. Alerted by Ultra to the fact that the Germans were preparing an imminent attack, he brushed aside the objections raised by Wavell and his other military advisers, who warned that the island was fundamentally indefensible. Ships sailing there had to pass through the Kaso Strait to the east or the Kithira Channel to the west, where they would be sitting ducks for aircraft attack. Crete itself possessed only one inadequate main road, running its 180-mile (290km) length roughly parallel to the shore. Moreover, Major-General Bernard Freyberg, the commander of the New Zealand division whom Churchill insisted was the best man to take charge of the island's defense, was, despite a brilliant fighting record in World War I, relatively inexperienced in dealing with the demands of modern warfare.

The British premier believed that British naval superiority in the eastern Mediterranean would put paid to any seaborne invasion attempt. Equally, Goering and his Luftwaffe commanders were confident that an airborne assault would succeed. The Reichsmarschall persuaded an initially reluctant Fuehrer to give Operation Mercury the go-ahead. Lieutenant-General Kurt Student, commander of Fliegerkorps XI, was put in charge of planning the invasion.

A fighter ace in World War I, Student had been Germany's leading advocate for the development of airborne forces ever since he had witnessed a mass parachute drop as a guest military observer at the 1937 Soviet Army maneuvers. He had already proved his point by masterminding the capture of Fort Eben-Emael in May 1940. Now, he was to be given the chance to put his theories into practice on an even larger scale.

At dawn on May 20, 1941, Luftwaffe bombers launched their pre-invasion air strike against Crete, blitzing Maleme and Canea in an attempt to demoralize the defenders and silence their supporting ground and antiaircraft artillery. Student's gliders were next to arrive on the scene, closely followed by the Junkers 52 transport planes carrying his first wave of paratroops. The initial attack did not go according to plan. By the end of the day, half of the attackers had been killed and none of the vital Cretan airfields had been captured.

He had at his immediate disposal a paratroop shock regiment, a parachute division, an airfield-landing division, and 500 Junkers Ju 52 transport planes.

Student's plan for the attack on Crete was daringly simple. Paratroops were to be dropped on the airstrips at Maleme, Heraklion, and Rethimnon along the island's northern coast. Once these had been secured, the paratroops would be reinforced by airborne infantry from the 5th Mountain Division with swarms of dive-bombers and fighters flying into the airstrips to provide aerial support. The British, Student argued, would become disorganized and confused by the sheer speed of the attack. Lacking adequate communications and without a hope of attaining air superiority, they would be unable to resist a subsequent amphibious landing.

The plan was fraught with risks. General Wolfram von Richthofen, commander of Fliegerkorps VIII, which would be providing the bulk of Student's air support, did not like it at all. "Student plans his operations upon pure suppositions and preconceived motives," he noted in his diary. Despite such opposition, Student pressed ahead. The biggest danger was one he naturally could not have foreseen—thanks to Ultra, the British were aware of every detail of the plan.

THE INVASION BEGINS

Freyberg reached Crete on May 1. Sure that the German invasion was imminent, Freyberg concentrated his New Zealand division, supported by 3,500 Greek troops, around Maleme to defend the airstrip there. Around 5,000 Australians and Greeks were ordered to defend Rethimnon and 8,000 British and Greeks Heraklion. Royal Navy warships stationed themselves to the south and west of the island—out of German air

Junkers 52s unload their cargo on the airfield at Maleme, following its capture by German paratroops. Capable of carrying 16 to 18 fully equipped paratroopers 800 miles (1,287.5km) at a cruising speed of 132mph (214.43km/h), General Kurt Student relied on these somewhat ungainly transports to get the majority of his paratroopers and their supporting equipment into Crete. The Junkers were supported by DFS 230 gliders, each glider capable of carrying a pilot and nine fully equipped airborne soldiers. Student was confident of quick success, but, thanks to top-secret Ultra intercepts, the British were aware of exactly what he had planned.

range, but ready to intervene in the event of any amphibious assault.

The attack began at dawn on May 20, with Ju 87 dive-bombers blitzing the New Zealand positions around Maleme and Canea. The first and second waves of airborne troops swiftly followed. The paratroops dropped first, followed by glider-borne assault troops from Student's shock regiment. Freyberg's men were ready for them. By the evening, more than half the attackers had been killed and none of the vital airstrips had been captured.

It was then that things started to go wrong. For some unknown reasons, the New Zealanders withdrew from the knoll defending Maleme to the south. Student's battered paratroops rallied and captured it and part of the airstrip itself the following morning. Reacting quickly, Student ordered reinforcements to be dropped west of Maleme, while his Ju 52s started to land on the airstrip even though it was still not occupied completely. The cost was high—more than 80 Ju 52s were written off—but the results were worth it. By the end of the day, Maleme was firmly in German hands.

EVACUATION

This was the turning point of the battle. Freyberg failed to appreciate that Maleme was the key to holding onto Crete. Instead, many of his troops were still facing seawards at Canea and Suda, ready to parry the amphibious assault when it came. He also believed that Heraklion, rather than Maleme, was the ultimate German objective. Nevertheless, the New Zealanders did mount a counterattack. Though initially it looked like succeeding, it eventually failed. The Germans drove the New Zealanders almost back to Canea. On May 27, the town was overrun. Suda Bay fell the next day.

The battle for Crete was lost. Freyberg ordered as many of his soldiers as possible to trek over the mountains to Sphakia on the south coast from where they could be evacuated. Some 15,000 got away, plus another 5,000 from Heraklion. However, almost 12,000 were abandoned on the beaches when the heavy losses inflicted on the navy by the Luftwaffe brought the evacuation to an end. Its bombers sunk two cruisers and six destroyers. Two battleships, an aircraft carrier, and 16 other warships were badly damaged.

Student and his paratroops had won their battle, but it proved to be a pyrrhic victory. Shocked by the German casualty figures, Hitler vowed not to mount such an operation again. For the rest of the war, the paratroops were never employed in a strategic role.

The airfield at Maleme seen from above is littered with the remains of crashed Junkers 52s. In an attempt to capture the airfield at all costs, Student ordered his planes to belly-flop onto the runway, which the New Zealand defenders had left unblocked. By nightfall on May 21, Maleme was firmly in German hands, though the attack had cost Student more than 80 of his transports. As the paratroopers started to push east, the tide of the battle began to turn in their favor. The British mistake was to keep many of their troops at Canea and Suda, waiting to parry an amphibious assault that never came.

BARBAROSSA AND AFTER

To launch Operation Barbarossa, his surprise attack on the Soviet Union in June 1941, Hitler amassed the largest invasion force the world had ever seen. More than 3,000,000 German soldiers, together with a further 500,000 troops from the Reich's allies, were ready to pour across the Soviet border on a 1,000-mile (1,600km) front, stretching from the Finnish frontier in the north to the Black Sea hinterland in the south. On the ground, they were backed by 3,600 tanks and 700,000 pieces of artillery.

The Fuehrer was supremely confident that Barbarossa would succeed. He anticipated that the new campaign would be over in no more than two months. "We only have to kick in the door," he assured his generals, "and the whole rotten structure will come tumbling down." He continued: "When the attack on Russia commences, the world will hold its breath." Speed and surprise were to be the twin keys to throwing the opposing Soviet forces into complete disarray.

THE LUFTWAFFE PREPARES

Hitler's audacious plan relied on one further factor—the ability of the Luftwaffe to establish total air superiority over the fighting front. It was well-placed to achieve this. Even though the Russians theoretically had more aircraft at their disposal—German air intelligence estimated that there were 7,300 Soviet planes stationed in western Russia with more in reserve—most of these were obsolescent or downright obsolete. Their pilots had little or no experience of actual air combat and the majority of them were ill-trained. Even the best of the Soviet fighters, the new Yak-I, was demonstrably inferior to the Messerschmitt Me 109. Soviet bombers, in the main, were slow, ill-equipped, and lacked the necessary range to take the fight to the enemy.

By contrast, the Luftwaffe was at the peak of its powers. Over the preceding months, more than half of its entire strength had been shifted eastward to take up position behind what soon would become the Eastern Front. Hitler himself had set out its task. It was "to release such powerful forces for the eastern campaign that a rapid conclusion of the ground operations may be anticipated."

Systematic air reconnaissance of the Soviet Union had been authorized as far back as the end of September 1940. During the months that followed, Luftwaffe reconnaissance aircraft mounted some 500 sorties. Flying at heights of up to 36,000ft (10,973m), they began by probing the Russian frontier areas, continuing by flying as far to the east as Murmansk, Moscow, and Rostov. The number of sorties increased as the date Hitler had set for the launch of Barbarossa neared. The Soviet air force was well aware of what the Luftwaffe was up to, but Stalin, determined to appease Hitler at all costs, personally forbade any attempt at interception or retaliation. Eventually, he decided to purge the air force's leadership. Lieutenant-General Pavel Rychagov, commander of Russian tactical aviation, was dismissed and replaced by Lieutenant-General Pavel Zhigarev. As a result, the bewildered air force was left rudderless. It was totally unready for the Luftwaffe's actual attack.

Junkers 88 bombers power into action. The Luftwaffe attacked at dawn on June 22, smashing much of the Soviet Air Force on the ground before its pilots could get their planes into the air. A first wave of 637 bombers and dive-bombers swooped on 31 Soviet airfields, destroying an estimated 1,800 aircraft. In a second attack, the Germans destroyed a further 700 planes. Total Luftwaffe losses were two aircraft in the first wave and 33 in the second. It was clear that the Germans were well on the way to achieving air superiority.

OPERATION BARBAROSSA

On June 22, 1941, Nazi Germany, Finland, and Romania launched Operation Barbarossa, Hitler's gigantic surprise invasion of the Soviet Union. It took just a week for the German forces to advance 200 miles (320km) into Soviet territory; destroy nearly 4,000 Soviet aircraft; and kill, wound, or capture some 600,000 Red Army soldiers. This map shows the main thrusts of the initial German attacks, carried out along a front stretching from the Baltic to the Black Sea.

SWEDEN · FINLAND · ESTONIA · Leningrad · LATVIA · Moscow · BELORUSSIA · Warsaw · POLAND · RUSSIA · UKRAINE · Kiev · Kharkov · HUNGARY · ROMANIA · Odessa

- ■ Nazi Offensives
- --- Front Line, June 1941
- — Front Line, September 1941
- — Stalin Line
- ■ Main Russian Pockets

DAWN ATTACK

At dawn on June 22, the Luftwaffe took to the air. Some 500 bombers, 270 dive-bombers, and 480 fighters headed east in two waves, thundering over the heads of the advancing ground troops. The targets were the key airfields on which the Russians had concentrated the majority of their planes and the aim was to take the Soviet air force by surprise and catch it on the ground. The attack was completely successful. The first wave destroyed an estimated 1,800 Soviet aircraft, almost all of them before they were able to take to the air. The second wave claimed to have destroyed a further 700 Russian planes. Total Luftwaffe losses were 35 aircraft.

The carnage continued over the following days. By the beginning of July, Luftwaffe high command calculated that the Russians had lost 4,990 aircraft at a cost to the Germans of 491 planes destroyed and 316 damaged. The air superiority Hitler had demanded had been achieved. Such was the scale of the Luftwaffe's success that many of its pilots confidently expected to be transferred back to the west to take up the fight against the RAF no later than the beginning of September.

THE ADVANCE CONTINUES

With its command of the air assured, the Luftwaffe focused on supporting the Wehrmacht's ground forces in their headlong advance as they smashed through the Soviet defenses and inflicted huge losses on Stalin's ill-prepared armies. All three of Hitler's army groups were making amazing progress. By July 14, Army Group Center had already taken 600,000 prisoners. It had fought its way into Smolensk and its panzer spearheads were pushing on toward Moscow. The Luftwaffe began blitzing the Soviet capital on July 21, forcing Stalin and his entourage to take refuge in the tunnels of the city's metro system. Army Group North had overrun Latvia, Lithuania, and much of Estonia and was advancing on Leningrad (present-day St. Petersburg). Army Group South was driving fast toward Kiev, gaining control of much of Ukraine in the process. The Finns had cut off Murmansk and were making toward Leningrad from the north, while German and Romanian troops were entering Bessarabia in the far south.

German progress was such that, within weeks of the opening attack, many of the Luftwaffe's squadrons were operating from improvised new bases 372 miles (599km) east of their home airfields. The constant moves forward and the consequent supply difficulties both had an impact on the number of sorties the Luftwaffe could mount, while the number of serviceable aircraft also started to decline significantly. By September 6, the day the attack on Kiev began, its three Air Fleets could field only 1,005 aircraft serviceable between them.

What was becoming clear was that the German aircraft industry was failing to keep pace with the Luftwaffe's losses, let alone increasing its fighting strength. Its average losses were now running at 741 aircraft a month. The prototypes of the new fighters and bombers the Air Ministry had been counting on all had serious teething troubles and were far from ready to go into full-scale production. The Russians, on the other hand, were starting to make good their losses, re-equipping their stricken air force with up-to-date fighters and bombers, In common with other armaments and munitions plants, aircraft manufacturers were being shifted east from the endangered industrial regions of Ukraine to beyond the Urals, well out of range of the Luftwaffe's bombers. The operation started in July and concluded in November. By the time it was over, 1,360 armaments factories had been successfully transferred eastward. It took 1,500,000 railway wagons to do the job. What could not be taken was sabotaged or destroyed.

Leningrad, the Soviet Union's second city, is seen from the air in this covert Luftwaffe air reconnaissance photograph taken before the German onslaught. The German reconnaissance effort was masterminded by Colonel Theodor Rowehl, who had been photographing the USSR clandestinely since 1934. Systematic air reconnaissance was authorized by Luftwaffe high command on September 21, 1940. Over the ensuing months, Rowehl's airmen flew some 500 sorties, not only probing the frontier areas but also as far east as Moscow, Rostov, and Murmansk.

THE FREEZING WINTER

As the German advance slowed and the Fuehrer and his generals disputed on the best course of action to take, many senior commanders on the Eastern Front were coming to the conclusion that Soviet strength and resilience had been gravely underestimated. General Franz Halder, Chief of the Army General Staff, noted in his diary: "At the onset of the war, we reckoned with about 200 enemy divisions. Now we are already counting 360. These divisions are certainly not armed and equipped in our sense of the words and tactically they are often poorly led. But they are there. And when a dozen of them have been destroyed, then the Russians put up another dozen."

The Luftwaffe was facing its own problems. Though Field Marshal Albert Kesselring, commander of Air Fleet 2, was able to muster 1,320 aircraft—half the Luftwaffe's remaining strength on the Eastern Front—to support the attack on Moscow, the Russians managed to field 708 planes against him, 344 of which were the capital's air defense shield. The wear and tear of almost continuous flying was beginning to tell. Despite the air raids it was launching against Russia's major cities—as well as Moscow, Leningrad, Kiev, and others were heavily bombed—its Dorniers, Heinkels, and Junkers were unable to inflict significant damage on the centers of Soviet war production. The fall rains had arrived as well, turning many of its improvised airstrips into mud and sludge.

As the panzer spearheads neared the outskirts of Moscow, the Soviets prepared to counterattack. Made aware by his spies that Japan had no intention of entering the war against him, Stalin was able to shift reinforcements to the front defending his threatened capital. On December 5, the Russians attacked, driving the Germans back in confusion before them.

In addition to these reinforcements, the Soviet supreme command had a natural ally. The temperature was plummeting to well below freezing and heavy snow was starting to fall. The Russian winter had arrived. Though, thanks to Field Marshal Erhard Milch and unlike the rest of the Wehrmacht, the Luftwaffe had been equipped with thick winter clothing, the number of sorties it could fly dwindled. The snow stopped many of its aircraft getting off the ground.

Keeping the Luftwaffe's remaining aircraft airworthy in the Arctic winter conditions was tricky. Many of them had to be dug out of the drifting snow. Metal tools became brittle in the freezing cold, engine oil froze, hydraulic fluid turned into glue, and the rubber aircraft tires crumbled. Engines had to be turned over regularly to stop them from freezing up completely. The complicated cold-start equipment proved too delicate for the conditions and it emerged that many ground crews were ignoring the simpler procedure—thinning the oil with a little petrol while the engine itself was still warm—that the Luftwaffe itself had pioneered.

▼ A flight of three Ilyushin Il-2 ground attack aircraft power-dive into action. Known to Red Army soldiers on the ground as the "flying tank," the Ilyushin was one of the most successful Russian aircraft of the war. Stalin regarded its continued mass-production as vital, angrily telegraphing the manager of a factory that had fallen behind in its deliveries that Ilyushins "are as essential to the Red Army as air and bread." He concluded ominously: "I demand more machines. This is my final warning!"

The Tupolev Tu-2 high-speed daylight bomber was the Soviet equivalent of the Junkers Ju 88. It went into action for the first time in March 1942 and rapidly became the USSR's second most important twin-engine bomber. Able to carry a heavy bomb load, it could still maneuver almost as well as a fighter. It was also constructed toughly enough to withstand substantial enemy battering.

AIR RELIEF

With the Wehrmacht falling back in confusion outside Moscow, Hitler acted swiftly to stop the rot. He sacked Field Marshal Walther von Brauchitsch, the commander-in-chief of the army, and took over command himself. He had already fired Field Marshal Gerd von Rundstedt, commander of Army Group South, for allowing General Ewald von Kleist-Schmenzin to pull back his panzers from the outskirts of Rostov, where they ran the risk of encirclement. General Heinz Guderian, probably Hitler's best panzer leader, and General Erich Hoepner also paid the price for disobeying the Fuehrer. Hitler had one simple mantra: the armies in the east had to stand fast and hold their ground along the entire line.

Even though the front was eventually stabilized, the military situation remained uncertain as the Russians strove to eliminate the pockets of German resistance that had been left jutting into their new front line. On February 9, 1942, Soviet forces cut off Lieutenant-General Walter von Brockdorff-Ahlefeldt's 2nd Army Corps on Army Group North's vulnerable right. Some 95,000 men were encircled at Demyansk and 5,000 more at Kholm to the southwest. The only way they could hold out until they were relieved was for the Luftwaffe to supply them by air. Hitler personally promised to transfer 337 extra transport aircraft to Air Fleet 1 within a week to add to those that General Alfred Keller, acting on his own initiative, had already committed to the operation.

The airlift succeeded. Thanks to the Luftwaffe, the pocket was able to hold out for nearly three months until it was finally relieved. The success, however, would have fatal consequences. From that time onward, Hitler was convinced that determined, though isolated, German garrisons could hold out against any number of Soviets provided they were supported by an airlift. The Wehrmacht and the Luftwaffe were to pay the price for this belief within nine months—at Stalingrad.

▲ A formation of Yakolev Yak-9 fighters is seen in flight over Sebastopol in the Crimea. A lighter version of the Yak-7, it first went into action during the Battle of Stalingrad toward the end of 1942. At lower altitudes, it was faster and more maneuverable than the Messerschmitt Me 109 and Focke-Wulf FW 190s, which were its chief opponents on the Eastern Front, though less well-armed than the German aircraft.

PEARL HARBOR AND THE PACIFIC

When the Japanese struck at the US Pacific Fleet at its base in Pearl Harbor on December 7, 1941, the attack took the Americans completely by surprise. Air reconnaissance could well have detected the Japanese aircraft carriers before they launched their devastating first strike, but the forces on Hawaii lacked the airplanes to carry it out. It also did not help that the attack was launched on a Sunday and the newly installed radar station that otherwise could have detected the Japanese planes as they approached had been shut down for the day.

At the time the Pacific war broke out, neither side had made much provision for collecting and analyzing aerial intelligence. Though the Japanese had mapped Malaya and the Philippines meticulously from the air before the war, narrow-minded military thinking and bitter interservice rivalry combined to prevent them from exploiting air reconnaissance to its full potential.

Some 20 photographs, taken by handheld cameras during the attack on Pearl Harbor, were used to assess the damage the Japanese dive-bombers and torpedo planes had caused; the Mitsubishi C5M2 "Babs" aircraft that, flying from Japanese-occupied French Indochina, also took photographs when they located the British battleship and battle-cruiser *Prince of Wales* and *Repulse* off the Malayan coast. The Japanese also photographed the beaches at Lingayen Gulf prior to their invasion of Luzon, the largest island in the Philippines, while photographs taken of Dutch Harbor in the Aleutians during the first bombing raid on the harbor were used effectively to help plan subsequent bombing attacks there.

Other than these instances—though the Japanese did fly some aerial photo-reconnaissance sorties in China—Japan hardly employed aerial photography at all in the Pacific theater of war. As a post-war US assessment put it: "The few Japanese officers who realized the broader possibilities of photo-reconnaissance met with only small success in their

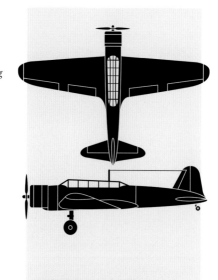

NAKAJIMA B5N KATE

Type Torpedo bomber

Crew 3

Length 33.79ft (10.3m)

Wingspan 50ft 11in (15.52m)

Speed 235mph (378km/h)

Range 1,237 miles (1,990km)

Although nearing obsolescence, the B5N was still generally regarded as the best torpedo bomber in the world after its 1941 exploits; B5Ns scored substantial successes during the Japanese air assault on Pearl Harbor that December. At least 144 B5Ns took part in the attack, one of them sinking the battleship *Arizona*. They were also responsible for the sinking of the US aircraft carriers *Hornet* and *Lexington* and the disablement of *Yorktown* (the abandoned vessel was eventually sunk by a Japanese submarine while under tow) later in 1942.

efforts to convince doubting superiors." When the Japanese navy finally rushed 100 men into training as photographic interpreters at Yokosuka naval base, it was too few and too late. The unit they were intended to form never became operational. The army fared little better when, in June 1945, it attempted to employ aerial photo-reconnaissance against the US forces invading Okinawa.

This neglect proved to be a costly oversight—the more so because in the twin-engine Mitsubishi Ki-46 "Dinah" the Japanese possessed what was potentially the most outstanding aerial reconnaissance aircraft produced by either side during the course of the war. With a top speed of just under 400mph (643km/h), a service ceiling of 36,000ft (10,973m), and an effective range of over 2,400 miles (3,862km), it impressed the Germans so much that, after it made its debut in July 1941, they started negotiating to be allowed to manufacture it for themselves under the terms of the Japanese-German Technical Exchange Agreement. The plan came to nothing. For their part, the Japanese took advantage of the plane's impressive performance to press it into service as a high-altitude fighter to take on the American Boeing B-29 "Superfortress" long-range strategic bombers that became such a thorn in the Japanese side later in the war.

This aerial view of Battleship Row, Forde Island was one of many taken by Japanese aircrew during their strikes on Pearl Harbor in December 1941. It shows torpedo bombers flying into the attack. Three defenseless US battleships have already been torpedoed; *West Virginia* and *Oklahoma* are spewing fuel oil and listing to port. The white smoke in the distance is rising from Hickam Field, where many US aircraft had been caught napping and destroyed on the ground.

THE PROBLEM OF DISTANCE

Japan and the Allies had to cope with the same geographical problem: distance. As far as the Allies were concerned, after the US airfields on Wake Island and Luzon were lost to the Japanese in the early months of the war, most important strategic points in the Pacific theater were out of range of all but carrier-borne aircraft. The Americans decided that their Pacific Fleet's three precious carriers could not be risked for anything less than a major fleet action or for combating a full-scale Japanese seaborne attack.

The Japanese were confronted by the same problem before the war started. The only way that they could photograph Pearl Harbor, the US Pacific Fleet's most important naval base, from the air was by sailing their aircraft carriers to within range of Hawaii. If their reconnaissance flights were detected, the Americans would be alerted to the likelihood of imminent attack. This was probably why Admiral Isoruko Yamamoto, commander-in-chief of Japan's Combined Fleet, discounted any advance aerial reconnaissance when he laid his plans.

"TORA, TORA, TORA!"

In the late fall of 1941, the Pearl Harbor task force secretly assembled in Tankan Bay in northern Japan. It consisted of the cream of the Combined Fleet. The aircraft carriers *Akagi, Hiryu, Soryu, Kaga, Zuikaku* and *Shokaku* were its core, supported by battleships, heavy cruisers, destroyers, and screening submarines. Vice-Admiral Chuichi Nagumo was in command.

On November 26, the task force weighed anchor and sailed, taking the northern route to Hawaii. Even though the weather was bad and seas rough, the Japanese believed that the winter storms would serve to mask their approach. For the same reason, the task force observed strict radio silence. On December 2, however, Nagumo received a message from Tokyo. It read simply, "Climb Mount Niitaka." It was the signal

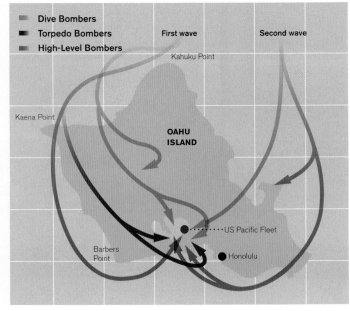

PEARL HARBOR

The Japanese struck at Pearl Harbor in two waves. The map here shows the overall plan of attack. The first wave, consisting of 49 high-level bombers, 51 dive-bombers, 40 torpedo planes, and 40 fighters, reached Pearl Harbor at around 7:50 a.m. They had been launched from the six Imperial Japanese Navy fleet aircraft carriers 250 miles (400km) north of Oahu. The aircraft did not all arrive together— the fighters flew ahead of the bombers to establish air superiority over the target. The second wave, some 170 aircraft strong, took off at 7:15 a.m. and reached Pearl Harbor at 8:50 a.m.

for the attack to go ahead. Four days later, the Japanese were 230 miles (370km) north of Oahu, well within striking distance of Pearl Harbor. At 6:00 a.m. precisely the following morning, the great carriers turned into the wind and launched the first wave of attack planes. It was led by Lieutenant-Commander Mitsuo Fuchida, the Japanese Navy's top air ace. He and Lieutenant-Commander Minoru Genda, Japan's leading aerial tactician, had drawn up the detailed plan for the aerial attack. The second wave followed an hour later, by which time Fuchida was well on the way to his target.

Fuchida struck at 7:50 a.m. Within a quarter of an hour, his torpedo bombers had sunk five US battleships and badly damaged three more, while swarms of strafing fighters and dive-bombers had attacked the airfield at Kaneohe, Hickham, Ewa, Bellow, and Wheeler, catching practically all the American planes on the ground. The second wave, which arrived above Pearl Harbor at around 8:50 a.m., continued the attack still virtually unopposed. At 9:45 a.m., the Japanese brought their assault to an end. They had lost only 29 aircraft out of the 360 that Nagumo had launched.

All eight battleships of the Pacific Fleet had been sunk or put out of action, yet the attack was not the total success for which Yamamoto had hoped. He had counted on sinking or disabling the fleet's three aircraft carriers as well, but they were at sea and so escaped unscathed. Even more to the point, because Nagumo did not know where the missing carriers were, he cautiously decided to turn for home rather than dispatching reconnaissance aircraft to hunt them down or launching the third air-strike against Pearl Harbor that Yamamoto had called for in his original master-plan. Though more than 3,500 Americans had been killed or wounded, 18 ships sunk or badly damaged, and more than 350 US aircraft destroyed, Pearl Harbor's vast oil storage bunkers survived untouched. Had the Japanese attacked again and destroyed them, as Yamamoto had intended, the Pacific Fleet would have been put completely out of action for many months.

MALAYA AND SINGAPORE

Like the Americans at Pearl Harbor, the British were taken by surprise when Japanese invasion convoys were reported heading into the Gulf of Siam bound for the coastline of Thailand and northern Malaya. They were first spotted on December 8; two days later, having flown up the Malayan Peninsula the previous day, an RAF Beaufort photo-reconnaissance aircraft took off at first light from Kota Bharu to reconnoiter. While taking its photographs at 20,000ft (6,096m), the Beaufort was bounced by a patrol of Japanese Zeroes. Its pilot, Flight Lieutenant P. D. F. Mitchell, recorded what happened next.

"Believing what we had been told about the slow performance of Japanese aircraft," he wrote, "I thought it would be some time before they got up to our height and we went on taking our photographs. The next thing I knew they were all around us like hornets... After the first pass, I went into a steep spin. Then the port engine was hit and the Beaufort rolled on her back and started to spin. We went down to about 10,000ft (3,048m) before I got her out of it and headed for the nearest cloud."

Mitchell and his battered Beaufort made it back to Kota Bharu, only to find it under intensive and practically continuous air attack. He flew low over the jungle for a while, waiting for a pause in the bombing and strafing, then made a hurried landing. In fact, the

▼ A Douglas TBD-1 torpedo bomber from the US aircraft carrier *Enterprise* patrols over Wake Island on February 24, 1942. Note the fires burning probably as a result of prior American bombing attacks in the lower center. The Japanese made capturing this tiny atoll in the Central Pacific a military priority because of its strategic significance. They began bombing US positions on the atoll just hours after the attack on Pearl Harbor and on December 11, 1941 attempted an initial landing. Though the US garrison rebuffed this, a second attempt on December 23 was successful. The garrison managed to hold out for three hours before being forced to surrender.

This photograph, taken from a Japanese high-level bomber, bears witness to what happened to Britain's ill-fated Force Z off the coast of Malaya on December 10, 1941. The battlecruiser *Repulse*, near the bottom of the picture, had just been hit by a single bomb; the splashes surrounding the ship denote near misses. The battleship *Prince of Wales* near the top is generating considerable amounts of smoke. Force Z had gone to sea without air cover and thus lay open to the relentless Japanese aerial attack. After being torpedoed multiple times, *Repulse* was the first to sink at 12:33 p.m. *Prince of Wales* capsized at 1:18 p.m., striking the destroyer *Express*, which was trying to evacuate her crew, a glancing blow as she turned turtle and sank.

Japanese invasion had been in full swing since the previous day, with securing control of the airfields at Kota Bharu, Gong Kedah, Sungei, Patani, Butterworth, and Alor Star among its initial objectives.

FORCE Z

Singapore took the news of the Japanese landings calmly. Duff Cooper, the Chancellor of the Duchy of Lancaster who had been sent by Churchill to the Far East three months before to assess the situation there, recorded how at 3:00 a.m. on December 8, he and his wife were woken by his secretary, "who put his head into our room and said 'The Japs have landed on the northeast coast of Malaya'. There was nothing we could do about it," Duff Cooper continued, "so we composed ourselves to sleep again, only to be roused by the familiar sound of falling bombs, followed by explosions, followed by guns, and finally by air-raid warnings. So the Japanese war had begun."

The landings should not have come as a surprise. In May 1937, the Chiefs of Staff in London had warned that the Japanese might well aim "to land army forces in the Malayan Peninsula to advance on Singapore. The Japanese," they continued, "may hope by the combined effect of attrition, air, and land attack to force our garrison to surrender before our fleet can arrive to relieve it." British defenses in Malaya were weak. "If no reinforcements have reached Singapore," the Chiefs of Staff concluded, "the forces at our disposal may be unable to prevent a landing in Malaya... These limited forces... are unlikely to prevent the Japanese from establishing themselves in Southern Johor within two months of the outbreak of war."

Everything therefore turned on British ability to reinforce its ground and air forces and send its battlefleet to Singapore in good time. On the ground the 9th Division of the Indian Army was stationed in the west of Malaya around Kuala Lumpur and the 11th in the north. The 8th Australian Division was defending Johor, the southernmost Malay state just north of Singapore Island. The British were notably weak in the air. Though the Chiefs of Staff had stated that 336 aircraft were the minimum needed to mount a successful air defense with another 327 in reserve, the continual demand for air reinforcements in the Middle East meant that area was given priority. Churchill, too, had insisted on sending 300 Hurricanes to Russia against the advice of his advisers, who argued that they would be far better deployed in Malaya than on the Eastern Front. When Robert Menzies, the Australian premier, pressed for the Hurricanes to be dispatched to the Far East as well, he was soft-soaped with the assurance that the Brewster Buffaloes, 170 of which arrived instead, "appeared to be eminently satisfactory."

As for the battlefleet the naval base at Singapore had been built to house, it never arrived. Instead, the Admiralty dispatched *Prince of Wales*, a new battleship, and *Repulse*, an ageing World War I battlecruiser, to the Far East. There was nothing else to send. Duff Cooper described their arrival on December 2. "It was a great moment when they came round the bend into the narrow waters of the straits that divide Singapore from the mainland," he wrote. "We were all at the Naval Base to welcome them and they arrived punctual to the minute with their escort of four destroyers. They conferred a sense of complete security."

Why Duff Cooper should have been so complacent remains a mystery, though Admiral Tom Phillips, in command of the newly arrived squadron, shared his confidence. He even made light of the fact that he had no independent air cover of his own—the British ships should have been accompanied by the new aircraft carrier *Indomitable* but she had run aground during her proving trials in the West Indies and could not be repaired in time to send.

FORCE Z SAILS NORTH

After Japanese aerial reconnaissance confirmed the presence of the two capital ships at Singapore, more torpedo-bombers were dispatched to reinforce the ones already stationed in Indochina. The RAF made it clear to Phillips that it was unlikely that it would be able to provide him with any meaningful air support. Nevertheless, on receiving news of reported Japanese landings, Phillips decided to sail as fast as he could to the invasion area.

Force Z sailed in the late afternoon of December 8. Phillips intended to steam northward to Kota Bharu, where a major Japanese landing was reported as being in progress, destroy the invasion barges, and withdraw. The plan depended on Force Z remaining undetected by the Japanese. On December 9, Phillips' squadron was spotted by Japanese aircraft. That evening, he canceled the operation. Force Z headed back toward Singapore.

Phillips then received a report of another Japanese landing—this time at Kuanton far farther south. He changed course to investigate, but when he arrived there was nothing to be seen. The destroyer *Express* he sent close to shore to reconnoiter reported, "All is quiet as a wet Sunday afternoon." Phillips resumed his course southward.

THE JAPANESE STRIKE

The delay was probably the nail in Force Z's coffin. Around 10:15 a.m. on December 10, it was spotted again by Japanese aircraft. An hour later, the Japanese bombers and torpedo planes closed in for the kill. There were 85 of them—34 Mitsubishi G3M "Nell" high-level bombers and 57 Mitsubishi GM4 "Betty"; torpedo aircraft. As they converged on Force Z for the assault, the first wave flying in high to distract the two ships' antiaircraft gunners while the second flew in at low level to launch its torpedoes, Phillips still did not break radio silence to ask for air cover of his own even after the attack began. Instead, he signalled Singapore

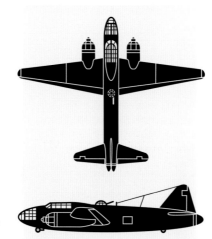

MITSUBISHI GM4 MODEL 11 "BETTY"

Type	Medium bomber/Torpedo bomber
Crew	7
Length	65ft 6¼in (19.97m)
Wingspan	81ft 7¾in (24.89m)
Speed	256mph (428km/h), 196mph (315km/h) cruising
Range	1,771 miles (2,862km)

The "Betty," as the Allies codenamed it, was the main land-based bomber used by the Imperial Japanese Navy during World War II. Its structural lightness allowed for impressive range, which meant a lack of armored protection for its crew. The failure to provide the aircraft with self-sealing fuel tanks make it easy to shoot the aircraft down in flames. Admiral Isoruko Yamamoto, mastermind of the Pearl Harbor attack and commander-in-chief of the Japanese fleet, was killed when he was shot down flying as a passenger in one in April 1943.

tersely, "Emergency. Have been struck by a torpedo on port side. *Repulse* struck by 1 torpedo. Send destroyers."

Quite what Phillips thought more destroyers could accomplish remains unknown. His next signal was to ask Singapore to dispatch "all available tugs." It was the last transmission he made. The next signal came from the destroyer *Electra*. It read simply "HMS *Prince of Wales* sunk." *Repulse*, whose captain had managed to dodge 19 torpedoes, had already fallen victim to the Japanese attack. The Japanese lost a grand total of three aircraft, downed by antiaircraft fire, in the two-hour encounter.

SINGAPORE FALLS

Things were going equally badly on the mainland. The Indian troops holding the forward positions had never seen armor before and as soon as Japanese tanks appeared they fell back in confusion. It was the start of what swiftly became a rout. By February 8, 1942, the Japanese had reached the southern tip of Malaya and were poised to cross the Johor Strait. Even though Singapore's garrison far outnumbered the invading force, the western part of the island had fallen to them by the evening of December 10. Soon, the Japanese had captured all but one of Singapore's airfields and gained control of the island's freshwater reservoirs.

With fresh water running out and with no prospect of relief, Lieutenant-General Arthur Percival, the British commander, decided he had no option but to surrender. On February 15, he ordered his troops to lay down their arms. It was, said Churchill, "the most disastrous and largest capitulation in British history." It also signalled that even well-handled capital ships could not survive aerial attack. The age of the battleship was over—that of the aircraft carrier had begun.

ABOVE Mitsubishi GM3 "Nells" photographed in flight. Like the "Betty," the "Nell"—Japan's main heavy bomber at the start of the war—had an impressive range. Though by 1941 "Nells" were rapidly nearing obsolescence, they were nevertheless employed to bomb Singapore, flying from bases in Japanese-occupied French Indochina (Vietnam). They also joined in the bombing of Darwin, in Australia, when 188 Japanese aircraft struck at the city on February 19, 1942. For this operation, they were based in the Dutch East Indies (present-day Indonesia).

LEFT Mitsubishi Ki-67s fly in a classic stepped formation. The Japanese called the aircraft "Hiryu," meaning "Flying Dragon"; the Allies dubbed it "Peggy." Designed initially for use by the Japanese Army Air Service, the "Peggy" was armored and fitted with self-sealing fuel tanks—its designers had obviously learned from past mistakes. By the time the aircraft was ready to come into service in October 1944, however, Allied bombing raids were impeding its production with the result that it was possible to manufacture only 698 Ki-67s before the end of the war. Novice aircrew and fuel shortages also contributed to the aircraft's lack of success.

TURNING THE TIDE

After the USA's entry into the war in December 1941, Roosevelt and Churchill set about devising a grand strategy that would win them and the Soviet Union total victory over the Axis powers. Both men agreed that Germany must be defeated before Japan; the underlying and unspoken reason for the decision may have been the fear that otherwise the bloody and battered Soviets might decide to come to terms with Hitler, leaving the Western powers to face the Wehrmacht on their own. The question was what they could do, other than supply arms under the terms of Lend-Lease, to satisfy their Soviet allies and at the same time take a major step along the road to winning the war. A strategic bombing offensive, launched on an unprecedented scale, seemed the obvious answer. RAF Bomber Command would strike at the Third Reich by night and the United States Army Air Force would precision-bomb it by day. Though the offensive would not get into full swing until 1943, the stage was set for the launch of the greatest and most prolonged aerial conflict of the entire war.

THE AMERICANS ARRIVE

Even before the USA entered the war, the US Army sent Captain Harvey C. Brown Jr. to be trained in photographic interpretation at RAF Medmenham. Upon his return to the USA, Brown put his newly gained knowledge to good use. He helped to set up a photographic interpretation school at Harrisburg, Pennsylvania, to complement the existing one at Lowry Field, Denver. It was from these relatively small beginnings that US aerial reconnaissance grew.

ENTER ELLIOTT ROOSEVELT

In April 1942, Major Elliott Roosevelt, the second son of the US President, arrived at Freetown, the capital of Sierra Leone, then a British colony in West Africa, flying in a Boeing B-17 Flying Fortress bomber. Roosevelt initially was less than enthusiastic about being posted far away from any fighting, but no less a personage than his father explained to him exactly how important his mission was. He and his team were to map North Africa from the air in preparation for Operation Torch, the Allied invasion of Algeria and Tunisia that was to take place later in the year.

Roosevelt did the job well. Following the successful Torch landings, he was promoted to the rank of Lieutenant-Colonel and put in charge of the 3rd Photographic Operation Group, flying specially modified Lockheed P-38 Lightnings and based in Algiers. There, he got to know some of Britain's leading reconnaissance fliers in the Mediterranean theater of war. Though he admired them, there were also clashes between the American photographic interpreters and their more experienced British counterparts. Roosevelt stubbornly tried to keep American photo-reconnaissance separate from that of the British. It was a foretaste of the policy he was to adopt when he was posted to the UK in early 1944 to take charge of US photographic intelligence in Britain in the run-up to D-Day and the launch of Operation Overlord.

A DAMAGING DISPUTE

The first US photographic interpreters arrived at RAF Medmenham in September 1942, just a month after the US 8th Army Air Force had launched its first daylight bombing raids against targets in Occupied France. Some of the Americans got on with the British, but others did not. Fortunately, whatever issues there were between the two nationalities did not fester. More Americans arrived to be integrated into the Medmenham machine. The original 30 soon doubled to 60. By the beginning of 1944, the number had reached 163.

It was then that Roosevelt arrived on the scene. His aim was still to ensure that American photographic reconnaissance and intelligence operations were conducted entirely separately from those of the British. Together with General James Doolittle, the commander of the 8th Army Air Force, he urged that all US photographic interpreters currently stationed at RAF Medmenham should move to Pinetree, where the headquarters of the 8th Army Air Force were based and set up a new independent operation there. The British high-ups and the majority of senior Americans were horrified by the scheme. Not only would implementing it be a wasteful, expensive, and time-consuming duplication of effort, it also went completely against the spirit of total Anglo-American cooperation that General Dwight D. Eisenhower, now designated supreme Allied commander in Europe, was doing everything he could to foster. Eisenhower warned that any US officer finding it impossible to establish cordial relations with the British or caught running them down would find himself on the next boat home, however high his rank.

Roosevelt refused to be deterred. He threatened to take the dispute to his father to settle even after James Winant, the US Ambassador in London, warned him bluntly that his stubbornness "might jeopardize the whole future of Anglo-American relations." Eventually, thanks to Winant and General Carl Spaatz,

One out of the hundred B-17s that raided the Focke-Wulf aircraft plant at Marienburg on October 9, 1943 flies away from the burning factories. General Carl Spaatz, the US 8th Army Air Force's commander, argued from the moment he and his aircrew arrived in Britain that daylight precision bombing of key industrial targets would be the quickest way of bringing the German war economy to its knees.

commander-in-chief of all US strategic air forces in Europe, a compromise was brokered between the disputants. It involved the setting-up of a new body—the Joint Photographic Reconnaissance Committee—on which the Americans and British were equally represented. The committee laid down the priorities for aerial reconnaissance. RAF Medmenham, renamed the Allied Central Interpretation Unit, retained control of photographic interpretation with the exception of damage assessment, which moved to Pinetree. Actual RAF and USAAF reconnaissance flights would still be flown separately—the RAF operating from Benson and the US 8th Reconnaissance Wing from Mount Farm. Roosevelt had lost his battle. In November 1944, he was recalled to Washington and reassigned to the Pentagon.

THE "BOMBER BARONS"

Of course, this was by no means the only disagreement between the two Western Allies. The issue was when and where the invasion of Occupied Europe should take place. The Americans were all for an invasion of France as soon as possible, for which the Soviets were pressing constantly as well. The British response was that this would be impossible before 1943 at the earliest and more likely impractical until 1944. Instead, Churchill and his military advisers argued that, once Axis forces had been driven out of North Africa, the best option would be to keep up the pressure on them in the Mediterranean, invading mainland Italy to knock the Italians out of the war and moving on to liberate the

Balkans. The Americans reluctantly agreed to go along with the first part of the plan.

The one thing Washington and London both agreed on completely was that a massive strategic bombing offensive should be launched to carry the war into the heartland of the Third Reich. Air force commanders on both sides—the so-called "bomber barons," as they were nicknamed—enthusiastically endorsed the decision, but differed as to how best to carry it out.

Sir Arthur Harris, who took over as commander-in-chief of Bomber Command in February 1942, was in no doubt that area bombing by night, carried out on an unprecedented scale, would overwhelm the German air defenses, break civilian morale by the sheer scale of the destruction it would cause, and so win the Allies the war. "Having watched the bombing of London," he wrote, "I was convinced that a bomber offensive of adequate weight and the right kind of bombs would, if continued for long enough, be something that no country in the world could endure." The four-engine Stirling, Halifax, and Lancaster heavy bombers that the British aircraft industry was churning out in ever-increasing numbers were the tools he needed to do the job. Revolutionary new radar aids and a new Pathfinder force would help his aircrews to find their targets and bomb them accurately on even the blackest of nights.

The Air Ministry obligingly issued Bomber Command with a list of priority targets. Essen, Duisberg, Düsseldorf, and Cologne were termed Primary Industrial Areas. Lübeck, Rostock, Bremen, Kiel, Hamburg, Hanover, Frankfurt, Mannheim, Stuttgart, and Schweinfurt were among the Alternative Industrial Areas Harris was enjoined to attack as well. The assault by Harris's aerial armadas would continue until, as he put it, "the heart of Nazi Germany ceases to beat." He was utterly confident of success.

US Army Air Force chiefs were just as convinced as Harris that strategic bombing would succeed. Where they differed from him was the way in which they thought it should be best implemented. After its disastrous experiences in 1939 and 1940, the RAF had concluded that mounting daylight raids with unescorted bombers was tantamount to suicide and that, for whatever reason, British aircrews were incapable of achieving the level of accuracy precision bombing demanded. The Americans begged to differ on both counts.

THE BOMBER AND THE BOMB-SIGHT

In the Boeing B-17 Flying Fortress, the Americans were convinced that they possessed a strategic bomber capable of carrying out unescorted daylight missions over Germany regardless of anything the Luftwaffe might throw at it. Flying in tight formation, each bomber "box" supporting its partners, Flying Fortresses would blow any attacking fighters out of the sky.

The Boeing certainly was a magnificent piece of aviation engineering. Flying at a cruising speed of

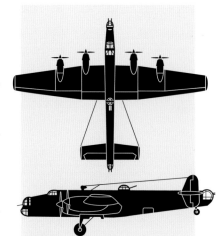

HANDLEY PAGE HALIFAX HP57 III

Type	Heavy bomber
Crew	7
Length	71ft 7in (21.81m)
Wingspan	104ft 2in (31.74m)
Speed	282mph (454km/h)
Range	1,860 miles (3,000km)

Though overshadowed by its counterpart, the Avro Lancaster, despite having entered service more than a year before it, the Halifax nevertheless was one of the most versatile aircraft produced for the RAF during World War II. As well as serving as a strategic bomber, it flew as a pathfinder, air ambulance, glider-tug, transport, and maritime reconnaissance aircraft. The first Halifaxes, however, were too slow. They also suffered from rudder problems that could throw the aircraft into an uncontrollable spin. It was not until the Type III was produced that these problems were fully rectified.

260mph (418km/h), with a range of 3,750 miles (6,035km) and a 35,600ft (10,668m) service ceiling, it was heavily armored and heavily armed with no fewer than between 11 and 13 machine guns. Its drawback was its lack of bomb-carrying capacity. A Flying Fortress could carry only a 4,800lb (2,177kg) bomb load as opposed to the 14,000lb (6,350kg) of an average Lancaster.

The Americans, however, believed that they had another trump card up their sleeves. It was the Norden bomb-sight, one of the air force's most closely guarded secrets and one of the most advanced pieces of bombing technology to see service during the course of the entire war. It was a mechanical analog computer, which a bombardier could use to determine the precise moment at which he had to drop his bombs to hit their target accurately. The sight was claimed to be accurate enough for a bombardier to hit a 100ft (30.4m) circle from a height of 21,000ft (6,400m), though, in actual combat conditions, accuracy was understandably somewhat less. It was also affected by the generally overcast flying conditions in European skies.

THE FIRST ATTACKS

The 8th Army Air Force finally got into action on August 17, 1942, when it flew its first mission. This was to bomb the marshalling yards at Rouen in northern France. Only 18 bombers took to the air—12 attacking the marshalling yards while the others flew a diversionary sweep along the Channel coast. All of

This vertical reconnaissance photograph shows some of the damage inflicted on Düsseldorf in the Ruhr after it was heavily bombed by 479 Bomber Command aircraft on September 10, 1942. The Deutsche Rohrenwerke factory, an important steel tubing works in the Lievenfeld district of the city, was almost totally destroyed. This was not the first or last time Düsseldorf was raided. Bomber Command launched its first Main Force Attack on August 31, 1942 and its last one on November 2, 1944. In total, it raided Düsseldorf ten times and destroyed an estimated 64 percent of the city.

them returned home safely, having bombed on or close to their target. General Ira Eaker, commander of the 8th Army Air Force who had flown as a passenger in one of the bombers, was quick to claim it had been a complete success. He omitted to point out, however, that his Flying Fortresses had been escorted throughout by RAF Spitfires—four squadrons on the outward leg of the mission and another five on the way back—so it was hardly a fair test of the American claim that Flying Fortresses were capable of dealing with the Luftwaffe on their own.

Between then and the end of December, the 8th Army Air Force flew a further 26 operations over Europe, though none of them were targeted against Germany

▶ Second lieutenant Everett Glen Hanes crouches over his Norden bomb-sight in the nose of a Martin B-26 Marauder serving in the 344th Bomb Group of the 9th US Army Air Force. The sight was a complicated 50lb (23kg) mechanical analog computer, made up of gyros, motors, gears, and a telescope containing some 2,000 precision parts. The bombardier's job was to feed the sight the information it needed to compute an accurate course to the target and then to release the bombs. Prior to the Manhattan Project, it was the USA's most secret weapon.

itself. It lost only 32 aircraft in 1,547 sorties, a casualty rate of less than two percent. Flying Fortress gunners claimed to have shot down scores of Luftwaffe fighters. On the surface, at least, it seemed that American hopes were being more than justified. Eaker was certainly of that view. He stated that, provided he had 20 Bomber Groups operational by June 1943, these would be adequate "coupled with the British night-bombing effort, completely to dislocate German industry and commerce and to remove from the enemy the means for waging successful warfare."

General Carl Spaatz, in overall command of US air forces in Europe, shared Eaker's optimism. So, too, did Harris. He did not mind what the Americans did, provided that he was not expected to abandon his cherished area bombing offensive. As for the Americans, they were also indifferent to what Bomber Command might or might not do, as long as they were given the chance to fight the bombing war in their own way.

The Casablanca Conference, held in January 1943, confirmed that what was now officially labeled the Combined Bombing Offensive would become official Allied policy. Its goal was simple—"to weaken Germany's war-making capacity to the point to which invasion would become possible." The directive to the Allied bomber commanders continued: "Your primary aim will be the progressive destruction and dislocation of the German military, industrial, and economic system, and the undermining of the morale of the German people to a point where their capacity for armed resistance is fatally weakened.

The policy was clear-cut. It was now time for the RAF and the USAAF both to put their respective plans into action. It remained to be seen whether either of them would succeed.

US 8th Army Air Force B-17s release their bomb loads through layers of thick cloud over Bremen on November 13, 1943. The signal to bomb was given by aerial markers dropped from Pathfinder aircraft fitted with H2X airborne radar, a substantially improved version of the RAF's H2S. Until H2X came on the scene, the cloud cover the B-17s frequently encountered over Western Europe made visual precision bombing impossible. Even the Norden bomb-sight could not cope with overcast conditions. Radar-led bombing was to overcome the problem for good, though it did not provide the complete accuracy US bombing chiefs ideally required.

THE DOOLITTLE RAID

As the seemingly invincible Japanese swept all before them in the aftermath of their devastating attack on Pearl Harbor, President Franklin D. Roosevelt spoke for the American nation when he urged his military chiefs to devise a plan that would enable the USA to strike back urgently at Japan. Roosevelt's motives were twofold. First, he sought to show the Japanese people that, despite what their government had told them, they were not invulnerable to US assault. Second, an American success would give a timely shot in the arm to US morale on both the domestic and fighting fronts.

There were substantial difficulties to overcome. The US Pacific Fleet was in no fit state to mount an immediate attack. Even if it had been, its own aircraft lacked the range and could not carry the bomb-loads required to deal the Japanese a significant blow. The Doolittle Raid—a strike by carrier-borne land bombers against targets on the Japanese home islands—was the answer. The idea came from an unlikely source. Captain Francis Low, the US Navy's Assistant Chief of Staff for Anti-Submarine Warfare was the man who had the original notion, but it was Lieutenant-Colonel James Doolittle of the USAAF who volunteered to plan and lead the attack.

Doolittle was an all-American hero, who first achieved public prominence in 1922, when he flew a De Havilland DH 4 solo across the USA from Florida to California. His other flying achievements included winning the Schneider and Mackay Trophies in 1925, the Harman Trophy in 1930, the Bendix Trophy in 1931, and the Thompson Trophy in 1932. In 1928, he had smashed the world speed record for land aircraft. However, he was more than simply a daredevil pilot. He helped to pioneer blind flying—that is, flying solely with the aid of instruments. No US aviator could have been better suited to taking on such a hazardous job. For successfully leading the raid, in which he flew himself, Doolittle was to be awarded the Congressional Medal of Honor.

PLANNING THE RAID

Admiral Ernest King, Chief of Staff of Naval Operations, and General "Hap" Arnold, commander of the USAAF, both were enthusiastic supporters of the idea. King had Captain Donald Duncan, his Air Operations Officer, conduct a feasibility study. This indicated that a force of twin-engine Mitchell B-25 medium bombers could be launched successfully from an aircraft carrier and be able to fly the 2,000 miles (3,218km) or so the proposed mission would require. However, there was one immediate drawback. Though the Mitchells might take off from a carrier safely, there was no way they could be retrieved once they had completed their task.

Doolittle took over the practical planning. He calculated that the Mitchells could be launched from a carrier 500 nautical miles (926.5km) away from the Japanese home islands and reach Tokyo with a 2,000lb (907kg) bomb load. Once having bombed key industrial and military targets there and elsewhere on Honshu, the Mitchells would fly in to Nationalist-held territory in China and land at airfields there.

The next step was to try out the idea for real. On February 2, 1942, two lightly loaded Mitchells were flown off the flight deck of the new aircraft carrier *Hornet*, which was undergoing her sea-trials in the Atlantic off Norfolk, Virginia. Following this success, Doolittle set about having the Mitchells he would lead on the flight fitted with extra fuel tanks and selecting, briefing, and training his aircrews for the mission. Like him, they were all volunteers. The training was intense, but short. The time allowed for it was just three weeks.

GETTING UNDERWAY

In the meantime, *Hornet* was sailing from the Atlantic to California via the Panama Canal. Her first port of call was the naval base at San Diego, where she picked up her own fighters and dive-bombers. She then sailed again—but for an unexpected destination. On March 28, Captain Marc Mitscher, her commander, was

Lieutenant-Colonel James Doolittle and his all-volunteer aircrews pose on the flight deck of the US aircraft carrier *Hornet* before their daring attack on the Japanese home islands. The B-25s took off earlier than planned at around 8:00 a.m. on April 18, 1942; *Hornet* had been spotted by Japanese picket boats while still some 600 miles (965km) out from the raid's target. Mitchell led 16 B-25s into the air. Most of them reached and bombed the Tokyo area, though a few hit Nagoya instead.

Though only a small amount of damage was inflicted, Mitchell's successful attack was a deep embarrassment for the Japanese High Command. The plan was for the B-25s to fly on to safety in Nationalist-held China, but things went awry. Fifteen of the B-25s either crash-landed—the picture here shows the wreckage of Doolittle's own plane—or their crews were forced to bail out. One plane landed in the USSR, where its crew was interned. Eight fliers were captured by the Japanese and put on trial for war crimes. Three were shot and one died in prison. The other four survived their captivity.

handed secret orders. Instead of heading for Pearl Harbor to join the three aircraft carriers of the Pacific Fleet, he was told to steam to Alameda Naval Air Station, San Francisco. There, he was to pick up Doolittle's Mitchells and load them on board.

Hornet arrived at Alameda on March 25, the same day the Mitchells flew into the base from Sacramento. Within 24 hours, all 16 of them had been loaded onto the flight deck—they were too large to fit onto the hangar deck below. Once they had been tied down in expected launch sequence, the air- and ground crews came on board. Hornet cast off and moored in San Francisco Bay. It was a foggy night and Mitscher did not want to risk maneuvering the carrier out of the bay in the dark. She finally sailed the next morning, with two escorting cruisers, four destroyers, and a fleet oiler.

On April 13, northwest of Midway, Hornet and its escorts made their rendezvous with Vice-Admiral William "Bull" Halsey's task force, which had sailed from Pearl Harbor two days before. It consisted of the aircraft carrier Enterprise, two more cruisers, another fleet oiler, and four more destroyers. Enterprise was to provide air cover during the initial stage of the attack.

THE RAID IS LAUNCHED

By April 17, the Mitchells were ready for their mission. Each had been armed with four 500lb (226kg) bombs—three were filled with high explosives, while the other was an incendiary. Then chance took a hand. The following day, the Americans were still 150 nautical miles (278km) from their planned launching point when the task force was spotted by a Japanese picket boat. One of the escorting cruisers quickly sank her, but not before she had radioed a warning.

Halsey decided to launch the strike at once, 12 hours earlier and farther away from Japan than had been planned. The weather was worsening into the bargain. Winds were gusting at speeds of up to 20 knots and huge waves were breaking over the ships' bows. To

NORTH AMERICAN MITCHELL B-25

Type Medium bomber

Crew 6

Length 52ft 11in (16.3m)

Wingspan 67ft 7in (20.60m)

Speed 272mph (438km/h), 230mph (370km/h) cruising

Range 1,350 miles (2,174km)

Named after US aviation pioneer Major-General Billy Mitchell, the B-25 started off life as a conventional medium bomber. Doolittle chose it for his celebrated raid because it was light enough to take off from an aircraft carrier, though it was too heavy to land on one. This meant that his B-25s had to fly on to land in Nationalist China after their attack on Japan. Later, the aircraft revealed its substantial potential as a ground attack aircraft in the Pacific theater of war. It also served with the RAF and other Allied air forces.

make the launch even more problematic, none of the B-25 pilots—including Doolittle himself—had ever taken off from an actual aircraft carrier before.

Starting at 8:20 a.m., it took around an hour to launch the planes, but all 16 of them managed to get into the air. They then set course for Japan in groups of two to four, dropping almost to wave level as they approached the coast to lessen the chances of detection. Arriving over Japan at around noon, they spread out to attack their allocated targets—10 in Tokyo; two in Yokohama; and one each in Kobe, Osaka, Nagoya, and Yokosuka. The air defenses were taken by surprise. Antiarcraft fire was light, while no fighters managed to get into the air in time to intercept the raiders. The low-flying bombers were actually cheered by civilians, who thought that they were Japanese.

AFTERMATH

After the raid 15 bombers headed southwest for China as planned; one, already low on fuel, made for nearby Soviet territory. It landed successfully, but its crew were interned (Russia did not enter the war against Japan until 1945). None of the China-bound aircraft reached their destination. Running out of fuel, their crews were forced to abandon their aircraft and parachute to safety, or try to crash land. Three crewmen died while bailing out and eight were captured by the Japanese. Three were executed and a fourth died in captivity. The others made it to safety.

Doolittle was one of the men who evaded capture. He was convinced that the raid had been a dismal failure, thanks to the loss of all his aircraft and the minimal damage inflicted on the Japanese. He was mistaken. The Japanese were shocked by the attack. Fighter squadrons were speedily recalled to defend the Home Islands. Even more importantly, the raid provoked Admiral Yamamoto into hastily organizing a strike against Midway in revenge. The consequences of that decision were to prove catastrophic for Japan.

THE BATTLE OF MIDWAY

After their success at Pearl Harbor, the Japanese Navy's six crack fleet carriers—and the 400 or so aircraft they carried between them—became the dominant naval force in the Pacific. They ranged as far as the Indian Ocean, where they sank British warships seemingly at will, to within striking range of Northern Australia, where their planes hammered Darwin from the air. Having overrun much of the southern and western Pacific, the Japanese looked unstoppable.

It was not until early May 1942 that the Japanese rampage was checked in the inconclusive Battle of the Coral Sea. Though the Americans lost more ships than the Japanese, two out of Japan's six fleet carriers were damaged. Logic dictated that all the carriers should return to their home ports to refit.

This, in fact, had been Admiral Yamamoto's original intention, but then an unexpected event changed his mind. On April 18, Lieutenant-Colonel James Doolittle led 16 US Army Air Force Mitchell B-25 bombers in a daring air raid on Tokyo and other cities on the Japanese home islands. Though the damage the bombers inflicted was slight, the psychological impact on Japanese civilian morale was immense. The mortified Yamamoto ordered a fresh attack.

PREPARING FOR BATTLE

Yamamoto chose Midway, a barren but strategically important island outpost some 1,200 miles (1,931km) west of Hawaii, as his target. The plan the Japanese commander-in-chief evolved was a complicated one. To confuse the Americans, he decided to launch a diversionary attack against the Aleutian Islands first to draw his enemies north. The following day, however, his main force—Vice-Admiral Chuichi Nagumo's carriers in the lead with Yamamoto's battlefleet following behind—would strike at Midway itself. The Americans, hurrying south to defend the island, would fall neatly into the Japanese trap. To make double certain of success, Yamamoto ordered a submarine screen to be deployed between Midway and Pearl Harbor to intercept any US naval reinforcements putting to sea.

Admiral Chester Nimitz, the US naval supreme commander, knew that, in terms of numbers, he was outmatched. He had to outwit his enemy. Here, he had a priceless advantage. His cryptologists had broken the Japanese naval code and were listening in to the signal traffic between Yamamoto and his widely dispersed fleet. Forearmed with this intelligence, Nimitz acted. He secretly sent more planes to reinforce the ones already stationed on Midway, while dispatching only a token task force to the Aleutians. He split his main strength into two strong carrier groups, commanded by Rear-Admiral Raymond Spruance and Rear-Admiral Frank Fletcher respectively. The first group consisted of the carriers *Hornet* and *Enterprise*, escorted by six cruisers and nine destroyers. The carrier *Yorktown*, which the Japanese believed they had sunk, but in fact had been hastily repaired, was the flagship of the second. It was escorted by two cruisers and five destroyers.

Six dive bombers from *Hiryu*, the last surviving Japanese carrier, managed to stop *Yorktown* dead in the water. She finally got underway, only to be hit again. The carrier stopped again and took on a severe list. Fearing that his command was about to capsize, her captain ordered his crew to abandon ship. *Yorktown*, however, refused to sink. The coup de grace was administered by a Japanese submarine, which managed to penetrate the carrier's destroyer screen, and torpedo her again.

▼ This Japanese aerial reconnaissance photograph of Darwin was taken before the bombing of the city on February 18, 1942. There were two consecutive attacks, involving 54 land-based bombers and around 188 other aircraft flying from Japanese aircraft carriers. The first strike began just before 10:00 a.m.; the second followed an hour later. The Japanese plan was to cripple Darwin's military potential, so leaving them free to invade Timor. They were the first air raids to be launched on a target in mainland Australia.

BATTLE BEGINS

By June 2, the two US carrier groups were at battle stations some 250 miles (402km) northeast of Midway, poised to turn the tables on the Japanese. The problem was that they had no idea of where the enemy was. It was not until the next day that a long-range reconnaissance flight spotted the troop transports of the invasion force and it was not until the morning after that a Catalina flying boat caught sight of Nagumo's carriers. The Americans steamed at full speed toward the last reported position of the Japanese carriers.

Nagumo launched his initial strike at Midway at 4:30 am. He believed that a single attack would be enough to knock out the island's defenses, but he was soon disillusioned. As his bombers powered toward their target, US fighters scrambled to intercept them while Midway's torpedo and Marauder bombers counterattacked his carriers.

Though the latter were driven off without inflicting any significant damage, it was clear that Midway was still operational and a second strike would be needed. The cautious admiral hesitated. He had ordered his remaining aircraft to be armed with torpedoes and armor-piercing bombs in case of an American naval attack. Now they would have to be rearmed with incendiary and high-explosive bombs. He gave the necessary orders.

THE US COUNTERSTRIKE

It seemed safe enough as Nagumo was still completely unaware that the US carriers were present, let alone approaching his position. Then, as his ground crews started to work feverishly to swap around the bombers' armament, he received two alarming air reconnaissance reports in succession. The first was vague. A scouting seaplane reported sighting some US warships 200 miles (321km) or so away. It was not until 8:30 a.m. that more precise intelligence arrived. The message

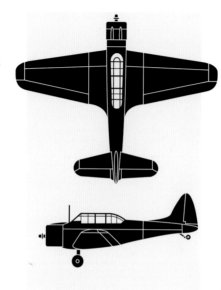

DOUGLAS SPD-5 DAUNTLESS

Type Scout plane/Dive-bomber

Crew 2

Length 33ft 1.25in (10.09m)

Wingspan 41ft 6.75in (12.66m)

Speed 255mph (410km/h)

Range 1,115 miles (1,759km)

The US Navy's principal carrier-borne bomber from mid-1940 to mid-1944, the Dauntless was arguably the war's best dive-bomber. It played a decisive part in winning the Battle of Midway for the US Pacific Fleet; on land, flying from Henderson Field on Guadalcanal, it inflicted lethal losses on Japanese shipping. Its crews loved the plane—it was rugged and dependable. A total of 5,936 were produced.

read tersely; "Enemy force is accompanied by what appears to be a carrier."

Nagumo hesitated again. The second wave's rearming was nearly completed. Now it would have to be reamed again. Also, his fighter screen was running low on fuel while he had to recover his first wave into the bargain. Accordingly, he hastily ordered all the aircraft crowding his flight decks to be taken below and as many of them as possible to be rearmed with torpedoes, while the fighters and the planes that had flown as his first wave landed.

The result was near chaos. As Nagumo altered course eastward to deal with the American threat, the flight decks of his carriers were crowded with airplanes—some unarmed, others being rearmed, some refuelling and others waiting their chance to launch. Then the American fliers from *Hornet* and *Enterprise* started to arrive on the scene. Douglas Devastator torpedo-bombers, plus their escorting Grumman F4F Wildcat fighters, made their way at low level toward Nagumo's fleet, while above them Douglas Dauntless dive-bombers from *Enterprise* and *Yorktown* were also prowling, waiting for their chance to strike once they had located their target.

The first attack met without any success. Fifteen Devastators from *Hornet* were all shot down, some by antiaircraft fire and others by Nagumo's fighter screen. Eleven out of the 14 Devastators from *Enterprise* met the same fate. When *Yorktown's* 12 Devastators eventually arrived, they, too, were decimated. Only two survived the attack. Not a single torpedo hit was scored on the Japanese carriers.

Nagumo believed he had regained the initiative. As his rearmed aircraft prepared to take off, however, the dive-bombers from *Enterprise* and *Yorktown* launched their attack. Nagumo's fighters were in no position to tackle them. Fifty-five powered down from the skies, catching the Japanese antiaircraft batteries off-guard. *Akagi*, Nagumo's flagship, was the first carrier to be hit,

followed by *Kaga* and *Soryu*. Soon, all three were ablaze. All the carriers eventually sank—*Akagi* was torpedoed by the Japanese themselves after being abandoned by her crew.

This left Nagumo with *Hiryu* as his sole carrier. Believing that he was only up against *Yorktown*, Nagumo ordered his surviving aircraft to sink his tormentor. Having lost a third of her aircraft over Midway, the carrier launched every remaining plane she possessed. Eight dive-bombers out of 18 got through to attack *Yorktown*. They scored three hits. Two hours later, she was attacked by four torpedo planes. Two torpedo hits left her dead in the water. The following day, as she was being towed toward Pearl Harbor, a Japanese submarine torpedoed her again. Her crew abandoned ship. She capsized and sank a couple of hours later.

AFTERMATH

Midway was the first battle in naval history to be fought entirely by aircraft without the involvement of surface ships. Once he learned of the disaster that had befallen his carriers, Yamamoto, still hundreds of miles to the west, reversed course for Japan. The Americans, fearing another trap, declined to pursue what was left of Nagumo's task force. In one day, the Japanese had lost their entire fleet carrier force and with it their naval command of the Pacific. They were now thrown onto the defensive as the strategic balance shifted inexorably against them.

US torpedo bombers on the flight deck of *Enterprise* prepare for launch. Their attacks on the Japanese aircraft carriers at Midway were unsuccessful, but the dive-bombers *Enterprise* also dispatched had more luck. They sank *Akagi* and *Kaga* and contributed to the sinking of *Hiryu* later in the battle. Planes from *Yorktown* sank *Soryu*. Right from the start, the Japanese were wrong-footed and taken by surprise. The subsequent indecision of Admiral Chuichi Nagumo, the task force's commander, was decisive in tipping the scales of battle firmly in the USA's favor.

THE 1,000-BOMBER RAID

Bathed in pale moonlight filtering through a curtain of fleecy cloud, Cologne, Germany's third-largest city, was awoken just after midnight on May 30, 1942 by the wailing of its air-raid sirens. Grumbling, its sleepy citizens made their way slowly down to the safety of their air-raid shelters and cellars. The city had been bombed before, so they were accustomed to the drill. This time, however, it was to be different. An aerial armada of 1,046 RAF bombers was on its way. Once they reached the Rhineland city, they flew over it in three giant waves at a rate of roughly one aircraft every six seconds, Wellingtons, Whitleys, and Hampdens striking first, followed by Stirlings and Halifaxes with Manchesters and Lancasters bringing up the rear. Halifax aircrews on their return spoke of aircraft milling over Cologne "like the traffic at Piccadilly Circus."

On the ground, chaos reigned. Many of the city's antiaircraft batteries were forced to cease fire because their transport could no longer get through the city with fresh supplies of ammunition for the guns. Searchlights meandered drunkenly across the sky. The bombers dropped a total of 1,650 tons of high-explosive and incendiary bombs during what seemed to be an eternity to Cologne's terrified inhabitants. In fact the whole thing was over in an hour-and-a-half.

ASSESSING THE DAMAGE

When the all-clear sounded, about 600 acres (242ha) of Cologne had been reduced to rubble. Much of the destruction was concentrated in the city center, around 90 percent of which had been destroyed. More than 12,000 fires were raging—the intensity of the blaze was such that the bomber crews could see it from the Dutch coast 150 miles (241km) away. As they flew over the stricken city, it looked to the awed aircrews as though Cologne was ablaze from end to end. 3,330 homes were utterly destroyed, more than 2,000 badly damaged and over 7,000 partially damaged. Forty-five thousand

people were left homeless. Industry suffered equally badly. Thirty-six factories were totally destroyed, 70 heavily damaged and more than 200 partially damaged. The water mains were breached, power and gas supplies severed and the telephone system wrecked. The railway system was severely dislocated, while the city's tramways were totally put out of action for a week. Some 4,500 of Cologne's citizens were killed and 5,000 wounded.

It was disaster on an epic scale, even though Goering refused to accept it. Albert Speer, Hitler's recently appointed Minister of Armaments, accompanied by Field Marshal Erhard Milch, called on the Reichsmarschall the morning after the attack. As the two men arrived, Goering was on the telephone to Josef Grohe, Cologne's Gauleiter, who had already advised Hitler himself of the scale of the attack and the consequent devastation. "The report from your Police Commissioner is a stinking lie," Goering roared. "I tell you as the Reichsmarschall that the figures cited are simply too high. How dare you serve up such fantasies to the Fuehrer?" Unfortunately for Goering, the reports were no exaggeration. RAF reconnaissance aircraft, taking off at dawn, returned to report that an enormous pall of smoke still hung over the city.

While Hitler was driven into paroxysms of fury by the attack, Winston Churchill was delighted at its success. "I congratulate you and the whole of Bomber Command," he wrote to Air Marshal Sir Arthur Harris, its recently appointed commander-in-chief, "upon the remarkable organization which enabled you to dispatch over 1,000 bombers to the Cologne area in a single night, and, without confusion, to concentrate their

Two aerial photographs, taken by RAF air reconnaissance the day after the first-ever 1,000-bomber raid on May 30, 1942, show some of the devastation inflicted on Cologne. The attack was the brainchild of Air Chief Marshal Sir Arthur Harris, the recently appointed head of Bomber Command. He more than succeeded in his objective.

actions over the target in so short a time as one hour and a half."

Churchill ended his message with a promise—and a warning. "This proof of the growing power of the British bomber force," he concluded, "is also the herald of what Germany will receive city by city from now on."

AREA BOMBING

The Germans should have been forewarned. Even before he became commander-in-chief, Harris had been convinced of the need to totally rethink the RAF's current bombing strategy. Trying to precision-bomb specific industrial targets required a degree of navigational accuracy and bomb-aiming skills that Bomber Command, so far, had found impossible to achieve. For this reason, Harris favored blanket or carpet bombing. There was to be no more time wasted on what he contemptuously dismissed as "panacea targets," such as individual oil plants and aircraft factories. Instead, he intended to concentrate on the progressive, systematic destruction of the Third Reich's great urban conurbations until the German people turned into a nation of troglodytes, scratching around for survival in the ruins and ready to sue for peace.

Harris had powerful backers. Lord Cherwell, a personal friend of Churchill who had appointed him his Chief Scientific Advisor, supported the commander-in-chief to the hilt. So, too, did Sir Charles Portal, the Chief of Air Staff, and Sir Archibald Sinclair, the Secretary of State for Air. Harris would be given the opportunity to level entire industrial areas to the ground. He was supremely confident that Bomber Command would prove more than capable of fulfilling the task. "There are a lot of people who say that bombing cannot win the war," he declared in a newsreel interview he gave shortly after his appointment. "My reply to that is that it has never been tried yet." Given time, enough aircraft, and sufficient aircrew, Harris was sure that he would succeed.

Time, though, was something that Harris did not necessarily have on his side. Some other military chiefs were united in their criticisms of what Bomber Command had achieved in the past and what they saw as its over-inflated claims for the future. The Royal Navy was especially critical. Infuriated admirals attacked Bomber Command for its refusal to release aircraft to help them win the Battle of the Atlantic or put up more formidable opposition to the Japanese. "If only some of the hundreds of bombers who fly over Germany (and often fail to do anything because of the weather) had been torpedo aircraft and dive-bombers," one of them wrote, "the old Empire would be in a better condition than it is now."

Professor Pat Blackett, a scientific adviser to the Admiralty, concurred. "I say emphatically," he wrote in February 1942, "that the present policy of bombing Germany is wrong; that we must put our maximum efforts first into destroying the enemy's sea communications and preserving our own; that we can only do so by operating aircraft over the sea on a very much larger scale than we have done hitherto, and that we shall be forced to use much longer range aircraft... The heavy scale of bombing will only be justified in the concluding stages of the war when (or if) we are fortunate enough to have defeated the enemy at sea and have command of it." Lord Beaverbrook, a prominent member of the Cabinet, chimed in. "The policy of bombing Germany, which in any event can yield no decisive results within any measurable period of time, should no longer be regarded as of primary importance," he wrote. "Bomber squadrons should be flown forthwith to the Middle and Far East."

THE BUILDUP

Harris needed a success—and he needed it quickly. He began on March 9 by ordering 235 of his bombers to attack the Renault truck works at Boulogne-

Aerial photographs of the Renault plants at Boulogne-Billancourt in the suburbs of Paris show the destruction the RAF caused when 235 Bomber Command aircraft bombed the complex on March 9, 1942. Renault had been producing 14,000 trucks a year for the Wehrmacht before the attack. The aircraft employed new tactics. After a first wave of bombers had dropped flares on the target, a second wave followed up with thousands of incendiaries to set fire to the target's center. The main force bombed last with high-explosive bombs. In all, 470 tons of bombs were dropped. The raid was hailed as a great success. However, Renault was put out of action for less than two months, while, as German propaganda was quick to point out, French civilian casualties were high.

Billancourt, a suburb of Paris. Then, on March 28 his aircraft bombed the medieval city of Lübeck on the north German coast. The target had been chosen not because of its military significance, but because it was something that Harris's bombers could find, strike, and utterly destroy. As Bomber Command's town-planning advisers were at pains to point out, its close-packed medieval buildings would be far easier to set fire to than those of a modern metropolis.

Ten Wellingtons led the attack, laying flares over the city. They were followed by a wave of 40 fire-raising aircraft loaded with incendiaries. Then the main force arrived, their bomb-bays stuffed with more incendiaries and 4,000lb (1814kg) high explosive "cookies" that were to become Bomber Command's standard weapon for its heavy bombers in the future. Striking at low level in clear skies, they scored a complete success. The medieval area of the city was completely destroyed. Out of the 191 bombers that claimed to have attacked, only 12 were lost.

Harris had not finished yet. He ordered Rostock, another medieval north German coastal town, to be bombed—this time over four consecutive nights. His attacking bombers were given two targets to aim at—the center of the city and the suburban area to the south containing the Heinkel aircraft factory. The first raids, which took place on April 23 and 24, produced disappointing results. The third and fourth, carried out by 128 and 107 aircraft respectively, were a complete success. Central Rostock was left ablaze. Thousands fled in panic from the blazing ruins. Goebbels wrote in his diary almost hysterically: "Community life in Rostock is almost at an end." Hitler ordered the Luftwaffe to launch its so-called "Baedeker Raids" on historic provincial town and cities in Britain in attempted retaliation.

COLOGNE AND AFTER

The following month, Harris prepared to launch his greatest attack yet. Hamburg was the original target, but weather conditions forced a last-minute change of plan. On the night of May 30, 1,046 Bomber Command aircraft took off for Cologne.

To muster such an enormous force—Bomber Command's frontline strength at the time was no more than 400 aircraft—Harris was forced to adopt various expedients, especially after the Admiralty refused to allow Coastal Command to take part in the operation. Harris was forced to fall back on pupils, instructors, and aircraft from his Operational Training Units to make up his numbers. Despite having to field these

▼ A post-raid reconnaissance photograph highlights the damage the RAF inflicted on the Heinkel aircraft plant in the suburbs of Rostock as part of a four-night attack on this north German city in late April 1942. Bombers from 3 and 5 Groups blitzed the plant at low level, while the rest of the attacking force bombed the center of the city with a lethal mixture of incendiaries and high-explosive bombs. The damage was immense, with thousands of people fleeing in panic from the blazing ruins.

tyros, he lost only 40 aircraft during the course of the operation, an acceptable 3.8 percent of the number that had been dispatched. One of them was a Manchester from 50 Squadron, piloted by Leslie Manser. Badly damaged by antiarcraft fire, his aircraft struggled back toward the Dutch coast until it became clear that it could not be kept in the air much longer. Fighting to keep the Manchester as steady as he could and waving away the parachute his flight engineer was offering him, Manser told his crew to bale out. Posthumously, he was awarded the Victoria Cross for valor.

Harris only conducted two more 1,000-bomber raids after Cologne, targeting Essen and Bremen respectively. Nor did he manage to get 1,000 bombers into the air again—Essen was attacked by 956 aircraft and Bremen by 904. The Essen attack on June 1 was not a success. Bad weather frustrated the bombers—so much so that the Germans did not realize that Essen had been singled out for mass attack, instead reporting there had been "widespread raids over Western Germany." Thirty-one aircraft were lost. On June 25, in a last throw before dismantling his 1,000-bomber force and returning the aircraft and crews he had co-opted to their original units, Harris bombed Bremen on June 24. This time, he lost 44 aircraft—4.9 percent of the attacking force. Another 65 were seriously damaged.

For now, Harris had shot his bolt. For the rest of the summer, Bomber Command confined itself to attacking Germany on a much wider front and far less intensively. Nevertheless, he had made his point. His success had also come at a time when his country, facing repeated disasters in the Middle and Far East, most needed it.

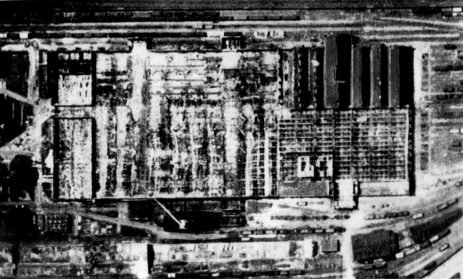

Like Lübeck, Rostock was an old medieval city and so relatively easy to set on fire. Yet, despite the confident assertion from the Ministry of Economic Warfare that "Rostock has for the time being ceased to exist as a going concern," industrial production there returned to normal with astonishing speed. Even the severely damaged Heinkel plant was back in business churning out Heinkel III bombers within a matter of weeks.

THE DAM BUSTERS

Though Harris was still totally opposed to any attempt to divert Bomber Command's efforts away from area bombing, others were not so certain that the policy was correct. When Barnes Wallis, the much-respected Assistant Chief Designer at Vickers Aviation, came up with the idea of a revolutionary new "bouncing bomb" which he argued could be used to destroy the great dams of the Ruhr—the Möhne, the Eder, and the Sorpe—in a single precision attack, he managed to win substantial high-level support. Destroying the dams, he assured them, would have "a paralyzing effect upon the industrial activity in the Ruhr."

Wallis had been working on the idea since 1940. Eventually, he designed two bombs, not just one. The smaller version, codenamed "Highball," could be carried by a Mosquito and was best suited to be used as an antishipping weapon or for bombing the hydroelectric plants dotted along the Norwegian fjords. The larger one, codenamed "Upkeep," was, he maintained, the ideal weapon for attacking and destroying the Ruhr dams.

The way Upkeep was intended to work looked simple, at least on paper. Spinning at around 500rpm, the bomb would be dropped onto a dam's reservoir at a very low altitude—Wallis thought that 150ft (45.7m) would be the optimum height—from a Lancaster flying level at no more than 240mph (386km/h) some 1,200–1,500ft (365–457m) away from the dam face. Skipping over any protective antitorpedo netting, it would bounce across the surface of the water until it made contact with the dam. Sinking to a predetermined depth, the bomb would detonate hard up against the dam's inner wall. The shock waves produced by the explosion would crack open the entire structure and the pressure of millions of gallons of water would do the rest as it poured out into the valley below.

It all sounded fine on paper, but, by January 1943, Wallis still had not been given official authorization to even build a prototype of the bomb, let alone start its mass production. Nor had work begun on modifying the

AVRO LANCASTER

Type	Heavy bomber
Crew	7
Length	69ft 4in (21.11m)
Wingspan	102ft (31.09m)
Speed	282mph (455.6km/h), 200mph (322km/h) cruising
Range	2,530 miles (4,073 km)

The RAF's main heavy bomber after its introduction in February 1942, the Lancaster became one of the iconic aircraft of the war. For Operation Chastise, the codename for the attack on the Ruhr dams in May 1943, specially modified versions of the aircraft were produced. The bomb-bay doors and much of the internal protective armor plating were removed in order to reduce weight and allow the plane to carry Barnes Wallis's massive dam-busting bomb.

30 or so Lancasters Wallis believed would be needed to carry his bombs. Above all, Harris was not convinced that "Upkeep" would function as intended at all. "This is tripe of the wildest description," he wrote at the foot of a memorandum describing the new wonder-weapon. "There are so many ifs and buts that there is not the smallest chance of it working." He was also convinced that his Lancasters would find it impossible to fly with the precision Wallis required.

Wallis appealed to Harris personally and then to Sir Charles Portal, Chief of the Air Staff, himself. "I cannot too strongly depreciate any diversion of Lancasters at this critical time in our affairs," he wrote, "on the assumption that some new weapon, entirely untried, will be a success." Portal assessed "Upkeep" carefully. Then he decided to back Wallis and gave what was soon called Operation Chastise the green light to go ahead. The decision, which was taken toward the end of February, was only just in time. The dams, Wallis had always insisted, had to be attacked while they were still full. This meant striking before the end of May at the latest. Otherwise Chastise would have to be postponed until the following year. "Finally," he concluded, "we have made attempt after attempt to pull successful low-level attacks with heavy bombers. They have been, almost without exception, costly failures."

617 SQUADRON

Once the decision had been taken, however, Harris gave it his full support. He ordered Air Vice-Marshal Cochrane, commander of 5 Group, to form a new crack squadron to undertake the job. He had already chosen Wing Commander Guy Gibson to be its commanding officer. Cochrane briefed Gibson on March 10; a few days later, 617 Squadron began to form as its first aircrews arrived at RAF Scampton, the base in Lincolnshire that Harris and Cochrane had chosen for it.

Gibson had no idea of what or where his target was. All he was told was that he and his aircrews must be able to fly level at a constant and predetermined speed at a set height over a stretch of still water. He told his aircrews that they had to "practice low flying all day and all night until you know how to do it with your eyes shut." He and his aircrews set to work. By April 6, they had undertaken 26 low-level cross-country flights; four days later, the number had risen to 62. The navigators were practicing flying by dead reckoning, honing their map-reading skills and perfecting their visual navigation. The bomb aimers were provided with a simple wooden device to act as a primitive range-finder; conventional bomb-sights would not be effective at such low altitudes. Finally, the Lancasters were fitted with two spotlights—one in the bomb bay and the other in the bomb aimer's camera position—to enable them to maintain their height accurately as they attacked. The lights were angled so that, at 150ft (45.7m), they converged to form a figure of eight.

Meanwhile Wallis was working flat out to get "Upkeep" ready for test-dropping. The first trials were failures—the bomb's outer casing shattered when it was dropped. Wallis decided the only solution was to do without it. He also told Gibson that, for "Upkeep" to work, 617 Squadron would have to fly even lower—at 60 (18.2m) rather than 150ft (45.7m)—at a speed of 232mph (373km/h). Gibson thought deeply and then

said it could be done. It still took Wallis more time to get "Upkeep" to work. He finally succeeded just a week before the raid was scheduled.

BOMBING THE DAMS

Everything was ready to go at last. RAF photographic reconnaissance pilots, who had been monitoring the dams since February, reported that they were full. The model-makers at RAF Medmenham used the photographs the pilots took to construct amazingly accurate replicas of the dams to help to brief Gibson and his aircrews. The pictures also revealed that, for some unknown reason, the Germans had weakened the Möhne Dam's antiaircraft defenses. The Eder had no antiaircraft defense at all. It seemed the Germans believed that the twisting approach between high hills that any British bomber would have to take rendered the dam impossible to attack. On May 14, the Chiefs of Staff gave Operation Chastise the official go-ahead. The Air Ministry ordered Bomber Command to execute it "at the first suitable opportunity."

Gibson had 19 Lancasters ready to undertake the mission. He and eight other aircraft made up the first wave, their target being the Möhne Dam. If that dam was breached successfully, any Lancaster whose bomb had not been dropped was to fly on to attack the Eder

▼ This Lancaster is test-dropping Wallis's "bouncing bomb" at Reculver in Kent. The Vickers Armstrong designer had to overcome high-level opposition before being allowed to create his revolutionary new weapon. Sir Arthur Harris described Upkeep, as the bomb was codenamed, as "just about the maddest proposition we have yet to come across," concluding "I am prepared to bet that the bomb will not work when we have got it." He was gentleman enough to apologize to Wallis for his skepticism after the successful attack.

Dam. The second wave consisted of five Lancasters led by Flight Lieutenant John McCarthy. He and his Lancasters were to take off first and fly singly to the Sorpe Dam. A third wave of five Lancasters was to take off two hours later and act as a flying reserve to support the other bombers in the event that their attacks on the Möhne and Sorpe dams proved unsuccessful. If they were not needed for this, they were ordered to attack the smaller Diemel, Ennepe, and Lister dams.

Shortly before 9:30 p.m. on the evening of May 16, the first flight of Lancasters took off from Scampton and started the long journey across the North Sea, over Occupied Holland and on into western Germany and the Ruhr. Two aircraft were forced to return early and five more were shot down by antiaircraft fire or crashed on their way to the target. This left just 12 Lancasters available to bomb the dams.

At the Möhne, Gibson was the first to attack. He dropped his Upkeep successfully, but it failed to breach the dam. Three more attempts also failed. After the fourth one, the dam started to crumble. Then it burst. As millions of gallons of water poured through the vast breach Upkeep had created, Gibson's wireless operator signalled the one word "Nigger." There was pandemonium in Scampton's Operations Room when the great news was received. Harris, who had journeyed north to witness the attack himself, turned to Wallis and shook him warmly by the hand. "Wallis," he exclaimed, "I didn't believe a word you said when you came to see me. But now you could sell me a pink elephant!"

Gibson than flew to the Eder to see if his remaining aircrews could repeat the feat. It took 10 attempts before the dam was spectacularly breached by an Upkeep dropped by Pilot Officer Les Knight's Lancaster. The Sorpe, too, was bombed, but this time without success. Gibson ordered the Lancasters to turn for home. One had been unable to find its target and returned to base without dropping its bomb. Three others were shot down after making their attacks.

A MILE-WIDE FLOOD

It was only an hour after the last Lancaster had touched down successfully at Scampton that Flying Officer Gerry Frey took off from RAF Benson. His mission was to fly the 300 miles (482km) to the Ruhr, confirm that the dams had been breached, and photograph them and the extent of the destruction. He was the pilot of one of the three Spitfires Benson dispatched to photograph the results of the raid that morning. He started his flight before the others because he had flown a reconnaissance over the dams only two days previously.

Frey flew to the Möhne Dam first. About 150 miles (241km) from his target, he spotted the industrial haze over the Ruhr and then what looked like a bank of thick cloud just to the east. As he drew closer, he realized that the cloud was in fact the sun shining on the flood waters filling the valley below the dam. "I was looking into the deep valley, which had seemed so peaceful before," he recalled, "and now it was a torrent with the sun shining on it." He reckoned that the flood was about a mile wide. Flying up the valley toward the dam, he could see water still gushing from the breach and the reservoir rapidly emptying.

Frey flew on to the Eder, where the destruction was even more spectacular. The long, snaking lake behind the dam had almost completely drained and the floodwaters beneath were stretching as far as Kassel. Villages were flooded, bridges swept away, and power stations destroyed, while rail lines and roads had completely vanished. As he turned to make a second pass over the devastation, he spotted two Luftwaffe aircraft approaching. He turned for home. As he landed, he saw the station commander waiting. "Have they hit them?" he called. Frey replied instantly, "Yes, they've pranged two of them properly. The floods are spreading for miles."

Frey and the Luftwaffe pilots were not the only men in the air that morning. Albert Speer, Hitler's

The Möhne Dam stands in all its pre-war glory (*below*). It was hailed as a masterpiece of structural engineering. The contrast with the aerial photograph of the breach in the dam taken just hours after the Dam Busters' raid by the Lancasters of 617 Squadron could not be more striking. The force of the water pouring through the breach was overwhelming. The resulting tidal wave was like a tsunami, sweeping before it practically everything in its path. It was little wonder that, after the raid, 617 Squadron adopted the French phrase *Après Nous Le Deluge* as its official motto.

After destroying the Möhne Dam, 617 Squadron's Lancasters flew on with its remaining bombs to breach the Eder Dam. It was a more difficult target as skillful maneuvering was required to get a Lancaster into an attack position, but the results were equally spectacular. However, 617 Squadron failed to inflict more than superficial damage on the Sorpe Dam, probably because its inner earth core resisted the impact of Wallis's bomb successfully, and so failed to totally disrupt the Ruhr's most important water supplies.

Armaments Minister, was making his own aerial assessment of the destruction. It certainly was immense. Homes and buildings in the Möhne Valley had been destroyed for up to 45 miles (72km) away; the Eder floods had reached the Fulda River. In the Ruhr Valley itself, power stations had been damaged, coal mines and steel works flooded, and rail links severed.

For the Germans, it was an unmitigated catastrophe. "The attacks of the British bombers on the dams in our valleys were very successful," noted Goebbels in his diary. "The Fuehrer is exceedingly impatient and angry about the lack of preparedness of our Luftwaffe." It took months to make the damage good, though, after the war, it became clear that the effects of the dams raid on the Ruhr's industry were not as dire as had been thought at the time.

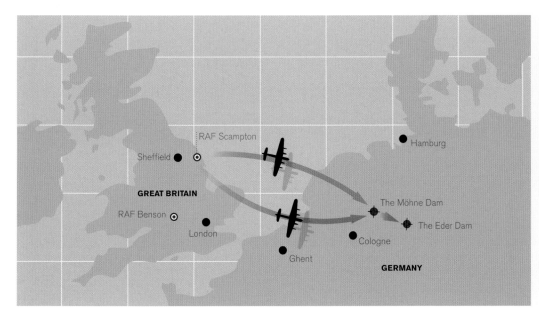

OPERATION CHASTISE

617 Squadron's Lancasters were organized into two formations, each of which flew by a different route. Formation 2 took the longer, more northerly route (marked in green) and Formation 1 followed the southern one (blue). Both were planned to avoid known concentrations of antiaircraft flak and were timed to cross the coast of mainland Europe simultaneously. The three aircraft still carrying bombs after the Möhne attack then flew on to the Eder Dam. Though he had already dropped his bomb on the Möhne Dam, Wing Commander Guy Gibson, the commander of 617 Squadron, flew with them so that, in the case of meeting antiaircraft fire, his plane could act as a diversion.

THE BATTLE OVER HAMBURG

Air Chief Marshal Sir Arthur Harris called it Operation Gomorrah. On four nights between July 24 and August 2, 1943, he dispatched huge formations of heavy bombers to blitz Hamburg, Germany's largest seaport and a leading ship-building and industrial center, from end to end. Bomber Command had never mounted such a destructive and continuous attack before. By the time it was over, around 10,000 tons of bombs had been dropped on the stricken city and more than 45,000 of its inhabitants had been killed.

HARRIS'S SECRET WEAPON

In theory, Hamburg was well-defended. General Josef Kammhuber, whom Goering had put in charge of the Reich's air defenses, had built up a sophisticated chain of overlapping radar "boxes" running the length of the coast from northern Germany to Belgium and around the country's most important cities. Hamburg had no fewer than 15 of them, plus nine night fighter bases in its immediate vicinity. It was also plentifully protected by searchlights and batteries of the latest radar-controlled antiaircraft guns. Previous raids had shown the RAF that these defenses could inflict heavy casualties on any attacking force.

Each of Kammhuber's "boxes" was equipped with Freya long-distance radar to provide early warning of the bombers' approach. As the Luftwaffe's night fighters scrambled to intercept them, the shorter-range Würzburgs took over. Each "box" had two of them, one to track a bomber more accurately and the other the intercepting night fighter, which orbited around a beacon until it was called in to attack. The ground controller guided the night fighter toward its target until its own Lichtenstein airborne radar could take over. The system had its drawbacks. The Würzburgs could only track one bomber and one night fighter at a time and the system could be swamped if a big enough stream of bombers was directed to fly through a single sector of it. Nevertheless, it proved extremely effective.

Harris, however, had a new weapon at his disposal, which he now employed for the first time. It was hoped that it would paralyze the German radar network on the ground and hopelessly confuse the night fighters by jamming their Lichtenstein radars. The weapon, codenamed "Window," was simple enough. It consisted of clouds of aluminum foil strips, which the attacking bombers would drop as they neared the enemy coast. The false images the strips produced would blind German radar. There were no immediate countermeasures that could be taken to neutralize the effect.

Window did exactly what was expected of it. When Harris's bombers attacked for the first time on the night of July 24, dropping bundles of the strips at one-minute intervals as they approached the city from the north, Hamburg's defenses were quickly thrown into confusion. The searchlights wandered aimlessly across the sky as the city's 56 heavy and 36 light antiaircraft batteries fired desperate blind box barrages, helpless because of their inability to use radar to track the bombers flying into the attack above them. None of the small number of night fighters that got into the air managed to make contact with the bomber stream. The result spoke for itself. Out of the 728 RAF aircraft which claimed to have attacked the city, only 12 were lost.

THE BOMBING BEGINS

The attack itself had been planned down to the last detail. Just before zero hour at 1:00 a.m., 20 Pathfinder aircraft dropped yellow target indicators on the city, using H2S, a revolutionary new airborne radar system, to get a clear picture of the ground below. Eight more Pathfinders then dropped red target indicators followed by a further 53 dropping their green ones. The main force then dropped 2,396 tons of bombs on their clearly marked target. Johann Johannsen, who was manning an antiaircraft battery in the city, recalled the moment the markers started to fall and what happened next.

TOP This Messerschmitt Me 110G night fighter is equipped with Lichtenstein airborne radar. The Lichtenstein "antlers" (antennae) were fitted to the nose of the plane. At first, the system was unpopular with Luftwaffe night fighter crews because the drag caused by the "antlers" reduced the Messerschmitt's speed by a crucial 25mph (40km/h). Lichtenstein also proved temperamental, at least initially. Many sets had to be returned to Telefunken for repairs, while the Luftwaffe also had to contend with a shortage of spares, particularly valves. Nevertheless, by the beginning of May 1943, nearly 82 percent of night fighters had been equipped with the system.

BOTTOM LEFT H2S airborne radar sets were standard Bomber Command target-locating equipment from the turn of 1942–43 onward. This one is fitted inside the cockpit of a Lancaster. H2S was the first airborne radar able to provide its operator with a shadowy image of the ground below. It was temperamental, working best near water, but soon proved its worth in improving bombing accuracy.

BOTTOM RIGHT H2S operated on a narrow waveband that could not be jammed by enemy defenses. In 1944, however, the Luftwaffe came up with Naxos, a night fighter radar system that could home in on the telltale H2S transmissions. As casualties among the bombers shot up, the Air Ministry was forced to order H2S to be used only in short bursts when flying over enemy territory.

"High above us, we could hear the drone of the enemy machines," he wrote. "Suddenly countless flares fell above us so that the whole city was lit up in a magically bright light... With incredible swiftness, the disaster was suddenly upon us. Before and behind our battery, heavy chunks of metal were striking. Howling and hissing fire and iron were falling from the sky. The entire city was lit up in a sea of flame."

The whole raid was over within just under an hour and the results were impressive: 306 of Harris's bombers dropped their bombs within three miles (4.8km) of their aiming points. There was to be no letup. The following afternoon, 123 Flying Fortresses from the 1st Bombardment Wing of the US 8th Army Air Force attacked Hamburg in broad daylight; 121 of them returned the next morning. The Fortresses badly damaged their main targets—the Blohm & Voss shipyards and the Klöckner aero-engine factory. The second attack also knocked out the Neuhof power station, putting it out of action for a month.

FIRESTORM

Harris renewed his assault the following night, when 735 of his bombers attacked the city from the east, using much the same tactics they had previously employed. There was one difference. The Halifaxes and Sterlings participating in the attack were carrying a greater number of incendiaries. The result was the creation of a vast firestorm, which raged through the working-class areas of the city.

The fires the bombers had started swiftly merged into one great conflagration, which sucked the air out of the surrounding area at hurricane force and spread inexorably outward. The howling spark-filled wind turned people caught on the streets into human torches. In the cellars and basements, in which many had taken shelter, thousands were killed either by carbon monoxide poisoning or suffocation as the collapsing buildings around them blocked exits and air

vents. Hamburg also had the misfortune to possess many old wooden dwellings, which, at the height of a hot dry summer, were tinder for the flames. "We came out into a thundering, blazing hell," wrote one eyewitness. "The streets were burning, the trees were burning and the tops of them were bent right down to the street. Burning horses out of the Hertz hauling business ran past us, the air was burning, simply everything was burning."

Many survived through sheer good fortune. Others were not so lucky. "There were people," one 19-year-old survivor recalled, "on the roadway, some already dead, some still lying alive but stuck in the asphalt... they were on their hands and knees screaming." After the firestorm finally burned itself out once all combustible material had been consumed, many corpses were found black and shrivelled. Some were lying in pools of coagulated body fat. More than 40,000 people died; thousands of others desperately sought emergency medical aid.

Harris had not finished with Hamburg yet. On July 29, 777 aircraft raided the still-burning city. The RAF lost 30 of the attacking aircraft. The fourth and final mass raid took place on the night of August 2 when Bomber Command dispatched 740 aircraft to the city. They flew into a huge electrical storm as they approached. One Lancaster pilot recorded in his diary what it was like flying through it. "There were huge luminous rings around the propellers, blue flames out of the wing-tips, gun muzzles, and also everywhere else on the aircraft where its surface was pointed. For instance, the de-icing tube in front of my window had a blue flame around it. Electrical flowers were dancing on the windows all the time until they got iced up, when the flowers disappeared. The wireless operator told me afterwards that sparks were shooting across his equipment all the time and that his aerials were luminous throughout their length. I didn't feel a bit happy and tried to go down below the clouds."

Hamburg under intensive Bomber Command attack; one of the attacking Lancasters is clearly silhouetted in this photograph taken from a bomber flying above it. The mass air raids on the city started on July 24, 1943. By the time the last one came to an end three nights later, RAF and US 8th Army Air Force bombers had dropped thousands of tons of bombs on the stricken city. Goebbels called the raids "the greatest crisis of the war" for Germany as thousands of evacuees fled the ruins to seek safety.

The intention had been for one wave of bombers—498 of them preceded by 54 Pathfinders—to attack the wealthy areas west of the Alster, Hamburg's central lake, while 245 bombers and 27 Pathfinders targeted the industrial area to the south. The appalling weather broke up both attacks. Many bombers dropped their bombs on small towns and villages in the countryside or turned back before they reached the actual city. Thirty-five of them were shot down by night fighters and antiaircraft fire. The Luftwaffe had speedily adopted its tactics to cope with Window. It now allowed its interceptors—day fighters as well as the Junkers Ju 88s and Messerschmitt Me 110s that were the mainstays of the night-fighting force—a free rein in the night skies, guiding them into the bomber streams by a continuous radio commentary from the ground.

CONSEQUENCES

The battle of Hamburg was over. For the RAF and the USAAF, it had been an unmitigated success. In one week, Bomber Command had killed more people than the Luftwaffe had managed to do during the eight months of the blitz. In total, 45,000 people had lost their lives and a further 125,000 required medical treatment, many of them for the severe burns they had received: 40,345 houses, 275,000 flats, 580 factories, 2,632 shops, 277 schools, 24 hospitals, 58 churches, 83 banks, 12 bridges, 76 public buildings, and the city's zoo had been obliterated. Starting directly after the first raid, more than a million refugees fled from the city in despair to seek shelter in other parts of the Reich.

Morale throughout Germany plummeted. Even the Nazi leadership was shaken by the devastation. Goebbels said that it was "a catastrophe, the extent of which simply staggers the imagination." Field Marshal Milch warned: "If we get just five or six more attacks like Hamburg, the German people will lay down their tools, however great their willpower. What the Home Front is suffering cannot be endured for very much longer." Albert Speer, the Minister for Armaments, was as blunt, if not blunter. "If air raids continue on this scale," he prophesied, "three months will see us relieved of many problems. Things will glide downhill smoothly, irrevocably, and comparatively fast." Speaking after the war to Allied interrogators, he declared that the effects of the raids could only be compared to those of a major earthquake and that more attacks on the same scale against six more cities would have brought the Third Reich to its knees.

Speer, however, underestimated German resilience. Even while the ruins of Hamburg were still smouldering, 14,000 firemen, 12,000 soldiers, and 8,000 technical experts were laboring night and day to deal with the fires and repair the worst damage caused by the attacks. The National Socialist People's Welfare Organization ferried in fresh water supplies and field kitchens to provide survivors with food and drink. Karl Kaufmann, Hamburg's Gauleiter, organized 625 special trains to evacuate more than 750,000 of the homeless to safety. He, like other Gauleiters, was also empowered to raise ration allocations, distribute extra food supplies, and issue emergency ration cards to those who had lost theirs. The National Socialist Women's League was also playing its part by caring for bombed-out families with children.

By the end of 1943, the recovery was well under way. The city's aircraft factories were operating at 91 percent efficiency; the shipyards had returned to near pre-bombing capability within two months. Why Harris did not bomb Hamburg again is unclear. Possibly, he was worried that, without the benefit of Window, the Luftwaffe would inflict unsustainable losses on his bombers. In any event, Bomber Command and the 8th Army Air Force were both poised to move on to new targets and even more destructive attacks.

B-17s from the US 457th Bombardment Group on their way to Hamburg on June 20, 1944. The second photograph shows them making their bomb run over the stricken city. As the Luftwaffe's fighting strength dwindled, Allied bomber losses dropped dramatically, thanks largely to the coming of the P-51 Mustang long-range escort fighter. After the war, Goering said that when he saw some Mustangs flying with importunity over Berlin, he knew that "the game was up."

"EUROPE'S SOFT UNDERBELLY"

Following their triumph in Tunisia in May 1943, when the remnants of the Afrika Korps and the Italian army in North Africa capitulated, the Allies prepared for their next move. At the Casablanca Conference earlier that year, President Roosevelt and Churchill agreed to launch their first thrust into what the British premier had christened "the soft underbelly of Europe." Churchill enthusiastically embraced the idea. Roosevelt, who would have preferred the Allies to launch the long-awaited Second Front in northern France, somewhat reluctantly went along with the plan.

There were various strategic possibilities open to the Allied planners. One was to attack Sardinia and Corsica as stepping-stones for an invasion of southern France. However, it was Operation Husky, the invasion of Sicily, that became the preferred option. On January 23, General Dwight D. Eisenhower was tasked with planning the attack on the island "with the target date as the period of the favorable July moon." General Sir Harold Alexander, Eisenhower's deputy, would be in overall command of all Allied land forces during the operation.

PREPARING FOR "HUSKY"

Air power was an essential constituent of the invasion equation. Allied aerial dominance had been a major factor in bringing about the Axis defeat in North Africa. Not only had it driven the Luftwaffe and the Regia Aeronautica practically out of the sky, but, by constantly harassing Axis shipping, it had also come close to severing Rommel's vital supply lines. As for the two Axis air forces, they were in dire straits. The Allies were soon raiding mainland and offshore Italy. Between May 16 and July 9, they flew 42,147 sorties over the western Mediterranean, destroying 325 Luftwaffe aircraft in the air and 122 on the ground for the loss of 250 of their own planes. For its part, the Regia Aeronautica had lost 2,190 aircraft between November 2, 1942 and June 30, 1943. When the Allies landed on

Sicily on July 10, the Luftwaffe had only 282 fighters and fighter-bombers stationed on the island to oppose them—and of these barely half were serviceable. The Regia Aeronautica could put a notional 387 fighters and 233 bombers into the air, but the vast majority of them were obsolescent or obsolete. By contrast, the Allies fielded 3,400 aircraft. It was clear that they would possess air supremacy from the start.

If such an operation was to succeed, advance aerial reconnaissance was vital, especially as there was little photographic cover of the island in existence. Air Marshal Sir Arthur Tedder, head of Mediterranean Air Command, ordered his photo-reconnaissance Mosquitoes from North Africa and his Spitfires from Malta to reconnoiter the island. Their first task was to obtain the extensive vertical photography required for large-scale mapping. The second was to take oblique pictures of any major defenses. The third was to monitor enemy activity on the ground. The flights quickly proved their worth. One of them brought back photographs showing a group of Sicilian women

An airfield in Sicily photographed from the air shortly after its capture by Allied invading forces during Operation Husky. The Luftwaffe and Regia Aeronautica were forced off the island to operate from the mainland after their bases were blasted by Allied bombers or captured. Allied fighters were soon operating from them. There would be no question of providing Axis troops on the ground with daylight air support.

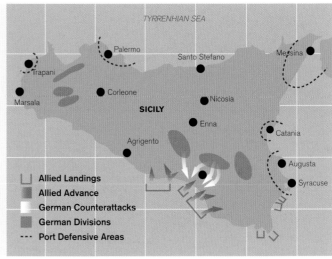

OPERATION HUSKY

The largest amphibious operation yet attempted by the Allies, the invasion of Sicily got off to a sticky start, largely because of disagreement between Generals Montgomery and Patton about whose army should be leading the exploitation of the initial attack. Nevertheless, by July 12, 1943, when Field Marshal Albert Kesselring flew into the island, he was forced to use a flying boat because most of Sicily's airfields had been captured by the Allies or bombed out of action. His aim was to contain the Allied advance for "as long as possible" before being forced to evacuate the island.

TYRRHENIAN SEA

Palermo
Santo Stefano
Messina
Trapani
Corleone
Nicosia
Marsala
SICILY
Enna
Catania
Agrigento
Augusta
Syracuse

- Allied Landings
- Allied Advance
- German Counterattacks
- German Divisions
- --- Port Defensive Areas

28.4.-1800 (E 3/8.10800)151 CASTELVETRO

disporting themselves in the surf on one of the designated invasion beaches. Obviously, as the photographic interpreters quickly pointed out, this meant that the beach could not have been mined. The quality of the low-level obliques was particularly praised. General George S. Patton, commander of the US 7th Army, said that the ones supplied to his landing forces had been "essential to the success of the operation."

Allied intelligence was hard at work as well, trying to convince Hitler that Sicily was not the target for attack and that the invasion would take place elsewhere in the Mediterranean. They succeeded. Operation Mincemeat, an elaborate deception scheme, confirmed the Fuehrer in his intuition that the attack would fall on Greece. Rather than reinforce Sicily, he raised the number of Wehrmacht divisions in the Balkans from eight to 18 and those in Greece from one to eight. By the time he was persuaded to send two more divisions to Sicily, it was too little and too late.

Nor were the Axis commanders on the spot in agreement about how best to defend the island. Field Marshal Albert Kesselring, now in overall command of all German forces in the Mediterranean, overruled General Alfredo Guzzoni's urgings to concentrate all his forces in the southeastern corner of Sicily, where the Italian commander believed the Allied landings were most likely to take place. Though he agreed to assign the Hermann Goering Division and the Napoli Division to the southeastern sector, the Livorno, the best Italian division in the island, was positioned around Agrigento and Gela to guard against an invasion on the south coast. The Aosta and Assietta Divisions, plus the 15th Panzer Grenadiers, were watching the western tip of the island behind Marsala, Trapani, and Palermo. He also decided to split his German divisions into four battle groups to reinforce the Italians, rather than keeping them as a mobile reserve ready to counterattack the Allied invasion beaches while they were vulnerable. He told his subordinates not to wait for Italian orders in the event of an Allied landing. This hardly made for a good working relationship between the defenders.

INVADING SICILY

The invasion began on the night of July 9, with Allied airborne troops going into action in advance of the main landings, which took place just after dawn the next day. The airborne operation was a failure, only a dozen gliders landing safely anywhere near their designated targets. The others were either blown off course by the gale-force wind, or released too soon by the aircraft towing them. Over 70 ditched in the sea. The paratroops fared little better; 27 of the aircraft carrying them were shot down by friendly fire before they reached their dropping zones.

Fortunately for the Allies, the actual landings went according to plan. Kesselring wrote bluntly that "the Italian coastal divisions were an utter failure." Most of the Napoli Division ran away after just a few shots had been exchanged, while the commander of the fortress at Augusta surrendered even before he was attacked. The only place where the defenders put up serious resistance was Gela, where the US 1st Infantry Division found itself up against the Littorio Division and elements of the Hermann Goering Division. A determined counterattack by them on July 11 almost succeeded, but by nightfall that day the beachhead was secure.

Somewhat surprisingly, it took the Allies five weeks to defeat their Axis opponents. The rivalry between Patton and General Sir Bernard Montgomery, commander of the British 8th Army, was much to blame, as the two disputed whose attack should be given priority. Alexander and Eisenhower failed to impose their authority over their prima donna generals and so let Kesselring off the hook. He was given the time he needed to organize a spirited defense. By the time Patton entered Messina to accept Sicily's formal

The Liberty ship *Robert Rowan* explodes after being hit by a string of bombs dropped by a Junkers Ju 88 off Gela on July 11, 1943. It was one of the Luftwaffe's few successes during the crucial opening of the invasion campaign. By July 22—the day Palermo, Sicily's capital, fell to the Allies—it had lost 273 aircraft and the Italians 115. The Allies were flying 1,100 fighter sorties a day to provide air cover for their advancing forces. Even the arrival of bombers equipped with the revolutionary Fritz-X air-to-ship guided missiles could not turn the tide in the Luftwaffe's favor.

surrender, 55,000 Germans and 70,000 Italians had been evacuated safely to the mainland, together with almost 10,000 vehicles, 163 guns, and 51 tanks.

ONWARD TO ITALY

What the Allied success brought about was the complete collapse of Italian morale. By the time the island surrendered, Mussolini had already fallen from power—arrested on the orders of Victor Emmanuel III after the Duce's own Grand Council had voted to oust him. Though Marshal Pietro Badoglio, the former Italian Chief of Staff whom the king appointed Prime Minister to take Mussolini's place, assured Hitler that the Italians would fight on, the Fuehrer did not believe him. By September 9, when Italy finally surrendered, he had shifted a total of 14 divisions into the peninsula.

The Allied invasion of Italy had begun six days earlier on September 3, when Montgomery crossed the Straits of Messina to land in Reggio di Calabria. A second landing by the US 5th Army, commanded by General Mark Clark, followed at Salerno and Paestum south of Naples on September 9. Kesselring, who had anticipated the attack, ordered the crack 16th Panzers to put up the fiercest possible resistance.

The panzers did more than Kesselring had asked of them. Such was the ferocity of their defense that the Americans on the spot planned an emergency evacuation. By September 14, though the German counterattacks were being contained, the situation was still critical. Some German tanks had penetrated to within five miles (8km) of the beaches before their advance was checked. The American success was largely attributable to air power. With the capture of the airfield at Paestum, US fighters were able to blunt the Luftwaffe's attempts to attack the invasion fleet and the beachhead. The Spitfires and Lightning P-38s constantly patrolling over the battlefield provided a shield that the Luftwaffe found impossible to dent. A US paratroop drop put paid to a last ground

counterattack. On September 17, Kesselring ordered his troops to pull back.

THE GUSTAV LINE

The Allies advanced laboriously up the Italian peninsula, meeting determined resistance every step of the way. With the terrain and the weather both favoring the defense, they relied increasingly on air power and artillery to help them to punch their way forward. By mid-November, they got as far as the

These juxtaposed photographs show Monte Cassino before and after the massive Allied aerial assault on February 15, 1942, when wave after wave of B-17s reduced Cassino town and the medieval abbey on the mountain above it to ruins. The intensive bombardment turned Cassino into a mini-Stalingrad, where the opposing ground forces fought inch by inch for the advantage through the rubble. The battle lasted for months until the Allied breakthrough toward Rome in May/June 1944.

Gustav Line, a string of seemingly impregnable fortified positions stretching across Italy from just north of where the Garigliano River flowed into the Tyrrhenian Sea across the Apennines to the mouth of the Sangro River on the Adriatic coast. The center of the line, where it blocked the main road to Rome, was anchored around the mountains behind the town of Cassino. Monte Cassino, which dominated the entrance to the Liri Valley, was the lynchpin of the position.

BLITZING MONTE CASSINO

Over the following months, Cassino degenerated into a miniature Stalingrad. Waves of British, Indian, and New Zealand attackers battled its defenders desperately for the advantage amid the rubble.

Though the attempt to outflank the Monte Cassino defenses by a landing at Anzio in January 1944 came close to failure, Kesselring's efforts to force the landing forces back into the sea withered in the face of Allied aerial superiority. Then, the Allied bombers turned on Cassino itself—in particular the ancient Benedictine monastery which stood near the top of the mountain. The Allies suspected the monastery was being used by the Germans as a military headquarters.

On February 15 142 heavy and 112 medium bombers dropped 576 tons of high explosive on the monastery, reducing its historic buildings to rubble. Allied ground forces still failed to break through. On March 15, they tried again. This time the plan was to deploy sufficient air power to literally blast a way through the German lines: 275 B-17s and B-24s and 200 B-25s and B-26s flattened what was left of the hapless town. The subsequent attack bogged down. Though by March 23 two-thirds of Cassino was finally in Allied hands, the Germans still held Monastery Hill, rising 1,700ft (518m) above the town.

The Allied High Command decided on a different air strategy. Operation Strangle was launched. By cutting off Kesselring's supply lines, the German commander would be forced to give ground. In the meantime, Alexander ordered up substantial reinforcements. By May 11, his forces—now 14 divisions strong with the 6th South African Armored Division in reserve—were ready to attack. It took some time, but finally the 8th Army spearheaded the breakthrough. On May 18, Monte Cassino fell at last.

FROM THE RUHR TO BERLIN

By March 1943, Sir Arthur Harris was finally ready to launch his master plan to bomb the Reich into submission. He and his squadrons were ready to launch the first of the three great battles that made the year to come the most celebrated and at the same time bloodiest of the entire area bombing offensive. The Ruhr, Hamburg, and finally Berlin were to suffer the full weight of British bombing.

The RAF was better equipped than ever before to deliver what Harris was certain would prove a killer blow. His Pathfinder squadrons would mark the targets for the main force of bombers. H2S airborne radar would enable the latter to hit their objectives more accurately. Oboe would provide them with an invaluable directional aid. Gradually, too, the Sterlings and Halifaxes would be phased out in favor of Lancasters, the best strategic bombers produced by either side during the course of the entire war.

THE GERMAN RESPONSE

The bombers needed all the help they could get, for German air defenses were being transformed. Up until now, the Luftwaffe had prioritized antiaircraft guns and searchlights as the main defense against air assault. Night fighters were given a subordinate role. Now, the tactics changed. Getting the night fighters into action became the priority, though, with an average strength of rarely more than 350, there were never quite enough of them to establish a clear-cut aerial superiority.

So-called "Tame Boars"—Messerschmitt Me 110s and Junkers Ju 88s—were scrambled to orbit visual beacons once the approximate course of the attacking bombers had been established by radar and ground observers. As the bombers penetrated into Germany, Luftwaffe ground controllers operating from what were christened Battle Opera Houses, vectored the "Tame Boars" into the bomber streams by means of a continuous radio commentary. The commentary

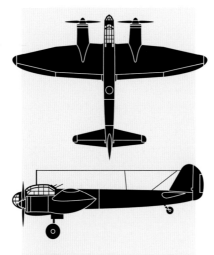

JUNKERS JU 88

Type Medium bomber/Dive-bomber/Night fighter/Torpedo bomber/Reconnaissance aircraft/Heavy fighter

Crew 4/3

Length 47.¼ft (14.4m)

Wingspan 65.⅔ft (20.0m)

Speed 280mph (450km/h)

Range 1,606 miles (2,370km)

The Ju 88 was one of the most versatile aircraft the Luftwaffe flew during World War II. After initial production hiccups, its adaptability earned it the affectionate soubriquet of "maid of all work" because of the dozens of tasks it was asked to perform. Produced in excess of 60 variants, the aircraft was flown successfully as a conventional bomber, dive-bomber, night fighter, torpedo bomber, reconnaissance aircraft, heavy fighter, and even as a flying bomb during the closing stages of hostilities.

continued until the night fighters established visual contact or, on moonless nights, switched to radar to guide them into their interception.

From the fall onward, many German night fighters were also equipped with a deadly new weapon to help them bring the bombers down. Called *Schräge Musik* (Jazz Music), it consisted of two upward-firing cannon mounted behind a night fighter's cockpit. It was designed to enable a night fighter to take advantage of the blind spot immediately below a bomber's fuselage. It became the standard Luftwaffe attack tactic to try to side-slip beneath a bomber and then open fire. A short burst of *Schräge Musik* almost invariably proved fatal.

Nor were the Germans backward in providing their night fighters with other aids to attack. While Harris's Pathfinders were striving to place their target markers accurately, Luftwaffe aircraft flying above them were dropping streams of flares of their own to illuminate the bombers flying below for night fighter attack. On the ground, the searchlight batteries arched their beams upward on moonless nights, aiming to light up the clouds so that the bombers were silhouetted for the intercepting fighters. To fool H2S, the Germans tried to altar the radar profile of the countryside around key targets—they laid vast carpets of metal strips on rafts on the lakes around Berlin, for instance. They also devised Naxos, a new airborne radar system which homed in on H2S transmissions. As bomber losses mounted, the RAF was eventually forced to limit H2S's use over enemy territory.

BOMBING THE RUHR

What Harris called the Battle of the Ruhr began on March 5, 1943. It ended on July 12. Night after night Bomber Command's aircrews flew against some of the most heavily defended targets in Germany. Not for nothing did they sardonically christen the Ruhr "Happy Valley." By the time Harris called a halt to the battle on July 12, 43 major attacks later, 872 aircraft had been

By the time this photograph of a Messerschmitt Me 110 flying over France was taken, the aircraft was obsolete. Nevertheless, its production continued because of the failure of its chosen successor—the Messerschmitt Me 210—to live up to expectations. The plane had been rushed into production before the massive problems revealed when prototypes had been test-flown had been resolved. Test models went into flat spins, side-slips, or suffered undercarriage collapses on landing. Eventually, in April 1942, Field Marshal Erhard Milch ordered the cancellation of the entire program. It was not until 1943 that a replacement aircraft—the Messerschmitt Me 410—was ready for squadron service.

lost. The average loss rate was 4.7 percent; a further 16 percent returned damaged. On some nights, though, 30 percent of the aircraft Bomber Command dispatched came home heavily damaged or failed to return at all. All in all, Harris's aircrews dropped 58,000 tons of bombs and razed an estimated 26,000 acres (10,521ha) of urban Germany to the ground.

The first attack was launched against Essen. On the moonless night of March 5, 455 bombers struck at the city. Led by eight Mosquito Pathfinders, the Halifaxes were the first to bomb. Wellingtons and Stirlings followed with the Lancasters bombing last. They carried mixed bomb loads—one-third of high explosive bombs to two-thirds incendiaries. This was a carefully calculated switch, since previous raids had shown that setting fire to towns was a much more effective way of destroying them than relying on blast. Bomber Command hailed the raid as an outstanding success; an estimated 160 acres (64ha) of Essen had been laid waste for the loss of only 14 aircraft.

All through the spring and early summer, Harris's squadrons blasted city after city. Duisberg, Dortmund, Krefeld, Gelsenkirchen, Aachen, and Cologne were repeatedly attacked. The force Harris employed was never less than 500 strong. More often than not, 600 or more bombers were involved, as on May 27 when 719 of them blitzed Wuppertal as it had never been blitzed before. Though the rate of loss was high, it was considered supportable. Before the battle started, Harris had a frontline strength of 593 aircraft. By August this had risen to 787, despite the casualties the Germans had inflicted on the bombers while they were attacking the Ruhr.

BLITZING THE "BIG CITY"

By comparison, Hamburg (*see pp. 128–133*) was a shorter-lived affair. Harris limited the campaign to four devastating night attacks between July 24 and August 2. The USAAF weighed in with two daylight raids.

Harris had his eye on even bigger game. "It is my firm belief," he wrote to Sir Charles Portal, the Chief of Air Staff, on August 12, "that we are on the verge of a final showdown in the bombing war, and that the next few months will be vital. Opportunities do not knock repeatedly and continuously. I am certain that given average weather and concentration on the main job, we can push Germany over by bombing this year."

Harris did not stop there. On November 3, he appealed over Portal's head to the Prime Minister

BOMBING ESSEN

The schematic diagram shown here was created using information gleaned from the photographic montage of Essen (*right*). The photographs were taken after 443 RAF bombers pounded the city on March 5, 1943. The analysis showed that 153 of the aircraft involved had bombed within three miles (4.8km) of their aiming point. Some 160 acres (64km) of the city, one of the best defended of the entire Ruhr, were laid waste for the loss of only 14 aircraft. Precision marking of the target by eight Pathfinder Mosquitoes, employing Oboe, were a major factor in the success of the attack. A subsequent raid, bombing on estimated time of arrival through ten-tenths cloud on May 27, was less successful, but, by spring 1944, Krupps had lost a total of three months armaments production as a result of these and other attacks.

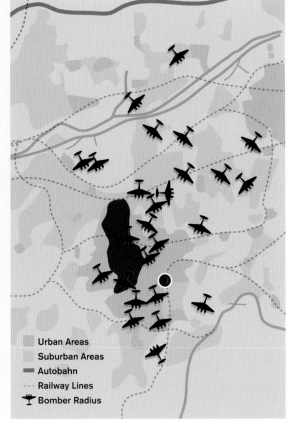

Urban Areas
Suburban Areas
Autobahn
Railway Lines
Bomber Radius

Photographic montages, like the one of Essen shown here, were indispensable aids when it came to assessing the success of Bomber Command's massive night raids on key industrial targets. What they could not reveal, however, was the speed at which the German war economy was able to recover from even the heaviest assault. Plants and factories which the RAF believed it had totally destroyed were often back in action within weeks of being attacked.

himself. In a minute to Churchill, he listed 19 German cities which he claimed Bomber Command had "virtually destroyed," adding that they were now "a liability to the total German war effort vastly in excess of any assets remaining." The list was certainly imposing. Harris went on to name a further 19 cities, which, in Bomber Command's view, had been "seriously damaged." He ended with a promise. "We can wreck Berlin from end to end if the USAAF will come in on it," he wrote. "It will cost between 400–500 aircraft. It will cost Germany the war."

It was an eloquent appeal, but it failed in its main purpose. Neither Portal nor Churchill was prepared to press the Americans to abandon their daylight bombing strategy to join in with the RAF assault on Berlin. Nevertheless, Harris was given sufficient encouragement for him to decide to proceed. On November 18, 1943, Bomber Command launched the Battle of Berlin. It lasted until March 30, 1944, during which time the RAF launched 16 major raids on the German capital.

Berlin—the "Big City" as Harris's aircrews christened it—was no easy nut to crack. Even before the battle proper began, many of them came to fear and loathe their target. "This was our first raid on Berlin," Ferris Newton, a Flight Engineer from 76 Squadron, wrote in his diary. "As we had all heard such stories about the place, we were not at all happy about going. Everyone sat around the kite waiting for start-up time and no one spoke a word."

Newton continued: "We were first wave in. Berlin's 35-mile area was dotted with light, so that it was hard to distinguish the burst of antiaircraft shells below from the colored markers dropped by the Pathfinders. First thing we have to do is to fly through a wall of searchlights—hundreds of them in cones and clusters. Behind all that is an even fiercer light. It's glowing red, green, and blue, and over that there are myriads of flares hanging in the sky. There is flak coming up at us

now. All we see is a quick red glow from the ground—then up it comes on a level—a blinding flash."

"There is one comfort, and it's been a comfort to me all the time we have been going over, and that is it is quite soundless. The roar of your engines drowns everything else. It's like running into the most gigantic display of soundless fireworks in the world. The searchlights are coming nearer now all the time...We start weaving, George puts the nose down and we are pelting away at a furious rate. As we are coming out of the searchlight belt, more flak is coming up from the inner defenses."

Having dropped its bombs, Newton's aircraft began to weave again before its pilot set course for home. "We are out of it," Newton concluded, "and now we are through I turn and get a glimpse of that furious glowing carpet of light and explosions, that's all I can see of Berlin."

AN UNEQUAL BATTLE

When the battle started for real, conditions were even tougher. The Sterlings' inadequate ceiling forced Harris to pull them out of the attack after only two raids; most of his Halifaxes were similarly withdrawn a few weeks later. This left the Lancasters to bear the brunt of the battle. Night after night, the heavily laden bombers struggled through the rain and sometimes snow to make the 1,500-mile (2,414km) round trip to the Big City. It was hardly surprising that many aircrews started dumping part of their bomb loads in the North Sea to increase height and flying speed. As they penetrated German airspace, they came up against the cream of the Luftwaffe's night fighter force, flying at the peak of its wartime efficiency.

When they finally reached Berlin, the bombers often found it shrouded in thick, impenetrable cloud. The unfortunate Lancaster aircrews were told to bomb on the ground markers if they could see them, or fall back on the sky markers if they could not. Many bombed

An extremely unusual aerial photograph, taken from a B-17, shows one of its bombs striking the Flying Fortress below during a daylight raid on Berlin. By striking and breaking off the port elevator, the bomb caused the flight control gust lock to engage, which, in turn, locked the remaining elevator in the full nose-down position. The mortally wounded aircraft power-dived to the ground before any of its crew could attempt to bale out. All of them were killed. Such accidents happened less frequently than might be expected, given the sheer number of aircraft involved in any given attack, though there were frequent near misses. Training accidents were another matter. In the RAF, some courses lost as many as a quarter of their trainees in the three to four months before they were posted to frontline squadrons.

blind without catching a glimpse of the markers or target. Nor was it often possible for photo-reconnaissance flights to confirm how much damage the bombers actually were inflicting. After one December raid, for instance, it took 18 flights to produce a single useable damage assessment photograph.

Harris remained convinced he was hitting the Germans hard. The truth was different. Berlin was just too big to be razed to the ground. Goebbels noted in his diary: "The British are greatly overestimating the damage done to Berlin. Naturally it is terrible, but there is no question of 25 percent of the capital no longer existing. The English naturally want to furnish their public with a propaganda morsel. I have every reason to want them to believe this and therefore forbid any denial. The sooner London is convinced there is nothing left of Berlin, the sooner they will stop their air offensive against the Reich capital."

As his losses mounted, Harris faced increasing pressure from above to change tactics and abandon the area-bombing offensive. On the last raid of the battle—paradoxically directed against Nuremberg, rather than Berlin—on March 30, 1944, 96 out of the 795 aircraft Harris dispatched failed to return. This was a loss rate of 11.8 percent, which was clearly insupportable. With D-Day looming, Harris was told to switch targets. From April 14, he and the other "bomber barons" would be taking their orders from General Eisenhower.

PRECISION BOMBING

Like the RAF, the USAAF had its own "bomber barons"—commanders who had convinced themselves that the strategic bombing of Germany would win the Allies the war. Where they differed from their Bomber Command counterparts was how best to carry it out. They dismissed area bombing, the tactic that Sir Arthur Harris, commander-in-chief of Bomber Command, favored, as wrong-headed. They believed that the daylight precision bombing of a carefully selected list of key industrial targets would dislocate the German war effort to such an extent that the Reich eventually would become incapable of putting up any further resistance on the battlefield.

As early as 1942, Major Alexander Seversky, one of the USAAF's leading military theorists, dismissed what he described as the "haphazard destruction of cities—sheer blows at morale" as "costly and wasteful in relation to the tactical results achieved." Instead, he argued that bombing should "increasingly be concentrated on military rather than on random human targets. Unplanned vandalism from the air," he continued, "must give way, more and more, to planned, predetermined destruction." He concluded: "More than ever, the principal objectives will be the critical aggregates of electric power, aviation industries, dock facilities, essential public utilities, and the like." It was an eloquent and convincing outline of the case for precision bombing.

EAKER AND SPAATZ

General Ira Eaker, in command of the US 8th Army Air Force, and General Carl Spaatz, his predecessor who, after a spell in the Mediterranean theater, became overall commander of US Strategic Air Forces in Europe in January 1944, both shared Seversky's beliefs. Precision bombing of key enemy targets, Eaker believed, would "completely dislocate German industry and commerce and bring about a speedy enemy collapse." In any event, he also argued, US bombers

BOEING B-17

Type	Heavy bomber
Crew	10
Length	74ft 4 in (22.66km)
Wingspan	103ft 9in (31.62m)
Speed	287mph (462k/h), 182mph (293Km/h) cruising
Range	2,000 miles (3,219km)

Boeing's B-17 Flying Fortress, which, with the Liberator, became the standard USAAF heavy bomber of World War II, was aptly nicknamed. The aircraft, which progressed from drawing board to first test flight in less than 12 months, bristled with defensive armament, carrying up to 12 machine guns. It cemented the USAAF's belief that, even flying in daylight, boxed formations of B-17s would be able to fight off attacking fighters and power their way through enemy skies to precision-bomb their carefully selected targets.

were not equipped and their aircrews not trained to carry out the kind of night raids that Bomber Command favored.

Spaatz completely concurred with Eaker's views. Both men argued that 8th Army Air Force and Bomber Command should continue to pursue their operations independently, the Americans flying by day while the British continued to strike at night. Churchill, for one, was convinced by the American argument. "How fortuitous it would be," he commented, having read a paper in which Eaker uncompromisingly set out his views, "if we could as you say bomb the devils around the clock and give them no rest."

After the Casablanca Conference of January 1943, Eaker was given the chance to put his ideas into practice. Like Harris, he was boundlessly optimistic about what he thought the 8th Army Air Force could achieve. Provided that it could be built up to a frontline strength of 1,746 aircraft by January 1, 1944 rising to 2,702 three months later, he promised that U-boat construction would be cut by 89 percent, Luftwaffe fighter and bomber production by 43 percent and 65 percent respectively, ball-bearing manufacture by 76 percent, and synthetic rubber production by 50 percent. "These figures," he wrote, "are conservative and can be absolutely relied on."

THE INITIAL ATTACKS

All this, of course, was for the future. In the meantime, Eaker had to make do with what was available. Though the 8th Army Air Force flew its first raid against targets in Occupied France on August 17, 1942 and completed another 26 missions by the end of the year, its objectives were strictly limited. Not a single mission had taken its B-17s into German air space. Moreover, despite the American belief that their B-17s were more than capable off fighting off Luftwaffe fighters on their own, all their missions had been escorted by RAF Spitfires.

The B-17 Flying Fortress "Memphis Belle," pictured here in flight, became famous as being among the first US heavy bombers to complete an entire tour of operations successfully. This involved flying 25 missions over enemy territory. The aircraft was then flown back to the USA, where she and her crew were sent on a war-bond-selling tour, visiting 32 cities. Her commander, Captain Robert E. Morgan, named his plane after Margaret Polk, his girlfriend and a resident of Memphis; the artwork decorating the Boeing's nose was inspired by a pinup in a 1941 issue of *Esquire* magazine.

Even more to the point, the buildup of fighting strength that Eaker had been counting on was constantly delayed. As fast as new bomber groups reached Britain, they were being transferred to support Allied operations in North Africa. By January 1943, Eaker had barely 90 B-17s at his disposal. Nevertheless, he pressed ahead. On January 27, he launched his first attack on Germany proper, dispatching 91 bombers to attack the U-boat bases at Wilhelmshaven. Fifty-three of his aircraft dropped their bomb-loads on target; only three B-17s were lost.

By April, Eaker, still convinced that his bombers possessed the ability to penetrate the German defenses by day and fight off the defending German fighters without escort, felt it was time to start tackling the target list the planners had promulgated after the Casablanca Conference. He now had 337 B-17s

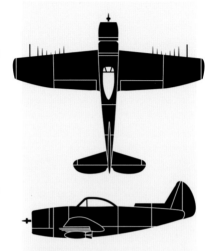

REPUBLIC P-47D THUNDERBOLT

Type Fighter

Crew 1

Length 36ft 1in (11.0m)

Wingspan 40ft 9 in (12.42m)

Speed 433mph (697km/h)

Range 900 miles (1,290km)

Dubbed the "Jug" by its pilots, the P-47 was either loved or loathed by those who flew it. Many of the latter likened flying it to trying to pilot a bathtub around the sky because of its poor rate of climb and lack of maneuverability, though, in a power dive, it out-flew many of its contemporaries. Later, improved versions of the aircraft overcame the problems. The resulting plane excelled as an escort fighter and, when equipped with bombs or rockets, in a ground-attack role.

available, although only 153 of them, on average, were operational at any one time.

On June 11, Eaker dispatched 168 B-17s to strike at Wilhelmshaven again. He lost eight aircraft. Missions to Bremen and Kiel two days later were far less successful. The Americans lost 26 of the 122 bombers that flew on the first attack and 26 out of 60 on the second. This translated into a loss rate of 21 percent and 43 percent respectively. Worse was to come when the decision was made to switch targets. The destruction of the aircraft industry rather than the U-boats now became the 8th Army Air Force's top priority.

Accordingly on July 28, the 8th Army Air Force embarked on its deepest penetration yet into German airspace, when 39 of its B-17s attacked the AGO Flugzeugwerk at Oschersleben. The objective was to halt the factory's production of Focke-Wulf Fw 190 fighters. It was a costly attack—15 B-17s failed to return—but it set a precedent for the future. As the surviving bombers flew home, they were met by 105 Republic P-47 Thunderbolt fighters flying 260 miles (418km) out from the coast. This extension of the fighters' range, though by only 30 miles (48km) or so, caught the Luftwaffe off guard. Out of the 60 German fighters surprised while trying to down the B-17s, nine were shot down and the rest put to flight. Just one P-47 was lost.

The presence of the P-47s was made possible by the fitting of improvised 250-gallon drop tanks to the aircraft. These, however, were unsuitable for use at heights above 22,000ft (6,705m). Work proceeded apace to perfect a pressurized droppable fuel tank that would extend fighter range by 340 miles (547km) or more. In the meantime, the B-17s were forced to continue to fly unescorted.

THE SCHWEINFURT RAIDS

On August 17, the 8th Army Air Force commemorated the first anniversary of the start of its bombing operations in Europe by launching its deepest

▼ The Republic P-47 Thunderbolt fighter, seen here in flight, was extremely powerful, being fitted with a 2,000 hp Pratt & Whitney Double Wasp XR−2800−21 turbocharged engine. It was also extremely heavy, weighing twice as much as a Spitfire or Messerschmitt Me 109. The aircraft first went into action in Europe in November 1942. It soon proved its worth as a high-altitude escort fighter, though its limited range meant that, until the Allied invasion of Europe, it could not penetrate into German skies to any great extent.

A section of a vertical aerial reconnaissance photograph taken over Wilhelmshaven in early 1943, prior to a daylight attack by B-17s from the US 8th Army Air Force on January 27 and a night raid by RAF Bomber Command the following month. The naval munitions depot at Mariensel can be seen clearly in the center right of the picture. So, too, can the Kriegsmarine's U-boat pens. It was the first raid the Americans had flown over German soil. Their commander, General Ira Eaker, had predicted that, providing his bombing force could be built up to a strength of 2,702 machines by April 1944, he could cut U-boat construction by 89 percent.

penetration into Germany to date. Eaker dispatched 367 B-17s in two waves against two critical targets—the Schweinfurt ball-bearing plants, where more than 40 percent of the Reich's ball-bearings were manufactured, and the Messerschmitt aircraft factory at Regensburg: 230 B-17s were to strike at the first target and 146 at the second. It was the biggest raid the Americans had launched against Germany yet.

The striking force consisted of the 3rd Air Division, led by Colonel Curtis LeMay, and the 1st Air Division, commanded by Brigadier-General Robert B Williams. The plan was for LeMay's aircraft to take off for Regensburg first, followed by Williams and his B-17s nine minutes later. They would both fly the same route until they were just beyond Frankfurt, when the 1st Division would swing toward Schweinfurt. Both divisions aimed to reach their targets at much the same time. The bombs would start falling on Schweinfurt at 10:12 a.m. and on Regensburg a minute later.

There would be no fighter escort for most of the way. RAF Spitfires could provide air cover only as far as Antwerp; the P-47 Thunderbolts would be forced to turn back at Eupen, 10 miles (16km) short of the German frontier. After that, the B-17s would be on their own. Nevertheless, Eager was confident that such a large force would be able to "operate without fighter cover against material objectives anywhere in Germany without excessive losses." He was soon proved wrong.

Though heavily armed with no fewer than 12 .50 calibre machine guns, arranged to provide overlapping cones of fire from the gun positions in the waist and from top, belly, and tail turrets, most of Eaker's B-17s lacked nose turrets. This left them open to frontal attack—a fact of which the Luftwaffe was well aware. Also, the Luftwaffe's best day fighters were no longer concentrated in a so-called fighter belt close to the coast as the Americans thought. Luftwaffe High Command had recently decided to switch to a strategy of defense in depth. Fresh squadrons of Messerschmitt Me 109s

FOCKE-WULF FW 190 D-9

Type Fighter/Ground-attack aircraft

Crew 1

Length 33ft 5in (10.2m)

Wingspan 34ft 5in (10.5m)

Speed 440mph (710km/h), 426mph (685km/h) cruising

Range 519 miles (853km)

Many pilots considered Kurt Tank's FW 190 to be the best fighter produced by either side during World War II. Early models of the aircraft were plagued by mechanical problems—notably engine overheating—and inferior performance at high altitude, while flyers complained of a lack of firepower. The first two problems were overcome by substituting a Junkers Jumo 213A supercharged engine for the original one. The FW's armament was improved as well; the D-9, which came into service in 1944, was fitted with two 20mm cannon—one in each wing—and two M9 machine guns.

and Focke-Wulf Fw 190s accordingly had been transferred from the Eastern Front to defend southern Germany against air attack.

DOGGED BY MISFORTUNE

Things started to go wrong right from the start. Dense fog in East Anglia forced takeoff to be delayed for around an hour-and-a-half. It was 7:15 a.m. before the first of LeMay's B-17s was airborne. It was only because LeMay had drilled his aircrews in instrument flying so thoroughly that they were able to get into the air when they did. Williams's aircrews, who had not enjoyed the benefit of such intensive training, waited stuck on the ground until the fog started to clear. They finally took off five hours behind schedule and more than four hours behind LeMay who had almost got to Regensburg before the first of Williams's B-17s left the ground. LeMay's force had been supposed to be the decoy to lure the German fighters away from Schweinfurt, so giving Williams the chance to strike his target really hard. Now he would have to face concerted attack by the entire Luftwaffe day fighter force defending the southern part of the Reich.

From the moment his escorting Thunderbolts turned back at Eupen, LeMay's B-17s came under relentless fighter attack. Nevertheless, they fought their way to their target. As they started their bomb runs, they had a relatively clear approach. Lieutenant-Colonel Beirne Lay Jr., a copilot of one of the B-17s, noted how after the last of "at least 200 individual fighter attacks, the pressure eased off, although hostiles were nearby."

B-17s from the US 8th Army Air Force power through German skies in defensive box formation on their way to attack the ball-bearing plants in the Bavarian town of Schweinfurt on August 17, 1943. A second wave of bombers was heading simultaneously to strike at the Messerschmitt aircraft factories at Regensburg. The 8th Army Air Force commanders believed that the Schweinfurt raid was especially crucial; if, they argued, the B-17s could obliterate the ball-bearing facilities there, it would "sever Germany's jugular vein."

50120 A.C.

LeMay's B-17s bombed accurately. They not only hit the main factory buildings, but also destroyed 37 brand-new Messerschmitt Me 109s lined up neatly on the tarmac just off the assembly lines. They also wrecked the building turning out the jigs for the top-secret Messerschmitt Me 262 jet fighter. Turning south after completing their bombing runs, the aircraft set course for the Alps, the Mediterranean, and the bases at which they were to land in French North Africa. LeMay lost a total of 24 bombers.

It was now Williams's turn to face whatever the Luftwaffe chose to throw at him. As he approached his target, he decided to change the plan of attack. The original intention had been for the B-17s to overfly Schweinfurt, turn and attack from the east, so that the mid-morning sun would be at their back not in their face. Because they were arriving so late, Williams decided that sticking to the plan would mean spending 17 more dangerous minutes flying over the target before his B-17s could bomb for no appreciable gain. He told his aircrews to switch direction and bomb from west to east, rather than east to west.

The B-17s reached their target at 2:59 p.m., but their bombing was not as accurate as had been hoped. Some of the aircrews were confused by the last-minute change in direction of approach and many of their bombs fell wide. Nevertheless, according to Albert Speer, Hitler's Armaments Minister, the raid led to a 38 percent drop—albeit only a temporary fall—in Schweinfurt's ball-bearing productivity.

Williams now had to fight his way back through the German defenses, harried mercilessly by the Luftwaffe's day fighters for much of the way. He lost a total of 36 aircraft, while more than a hundred B-17s were so badly damaged that, even though they made it home, they never flew again. The B-17 air gunners—Williams himself had manned a machine gun in a cheek blister and fired it until the barrel burned out—optimistically claimed to have shot down 288 German

As the B-17s hit the Schweinfurt factories, an alert photographer captured this shot of bombs from a high-flying B-17 plummeting past his aircraft. Some of the smoke seen in the picture comes from the smoke generators the Germans had installed to help to protect the facilities. As a result of the attack, Albert Speer, Hitler's Armaments Minister, estimated that ball-bearing production fell by 38 percent, but the loss was only temporary. Tactically, both raids were a costly disaster. Luftwaffe day fighters harried the B-17 formations almost constantly from the time they entered German air space; the Americans lost 60 of the 376 aircraft they dispatched. 600 flyers failed to return. The surviving aircrews christened the day of the raid "Black Thursday."

fighters during the course of both raids. The actual figure was no more than 35.

THE SECOND RAID

Eaker needed time to recover. There were no more major raids launched against Germany until September 6, when 407 B-17s were dispatched to bomb the ball-bearing and aircraft factories at Stuttgart. Bad weather again hampered the bombers, but 262 succeeded in reaching and bombing their target. Unfortunately for them, despite an early morning reconnaissance report from an RAF Mosquito indicating that the skies over the city were clear, the bombers arrived to find their targets obscured by dense cloud. They circled three times over Stuttgart, hoping for a break in the cloud cover, before deciding to bomb. The delay proved costly. Forty-five B-17s were shot down in flames, 18 percent of the attacking force.

Over the next few days, raids on Bremen, Anklam, Marienburg, and Münster followed. The 8th Army Air Force lost 30 bombers over Bremen, 28 attacking Anklam-Marienburg, and 30 over Münster, loss rates of eight percent, eight percent, and 13 percent respectively. The figures, though still too high for comfort, were an improvement on the ones before. Encouraged by this, Eaker ordered another strike against Schweinfurt on October 14. The day went down as "Black Thursday" in the annals of the 8th Army Air Force. After it, all unescorted daylight bombing over the Reich ceased.

This time, the striking force consisted of two waves of bombers, one led by Colonel Budd J. Peaslee and the other by Colonel Archie J. Old Jr. The bombers began taking off shortly after 10:00 a.m. Though 317 started the raid, some returned to their bases before they reached the Dutch coast. This left 291 of them in total. Their escorting Thunderbolts turned back between Aachen and Düren, just across the German border. Almost immediately, the Luftwaffe's fighters swarmed into the attack, coming at the B-17s seemingly from every direction. They were still attacking the B-17s as Schweinfurt finally came into view at around 2:30 p.m. The B-17s bombed more accurately this time, plastering Schweinfurt's three largest ball-bearing facilities with their bombs. Speer estimated that 67 percent of Schweinfurt's production capability had been destroyed.

Unfortunately, the B-17s paid an extremely high price for their success. The official Army Air Forces history described the Luftwaffe's response to the attack as "unprecedented in its magnitude" and in "the severity with which it was executed." Of the 291 B-17s involved in the raid, a staggering 60 were shot down, a loss rate of more than 20 percent.

What this meant in human terms was starkly simple. If the Germans continued to shoot down B-17s at anything like this rate, Eaker's aircrews would be lucky

NORTH AMERICAN
P-51D MUSTANG

Type Fighter/Escort fighter/ Ground-attack aircraft

Crew 1

Length 32ft 3in (9.83m)

Wingspan 37ft (11.28m)

Speed 437mph (703km/h), 362mph (580km/h) cruising

Range 1,650 miles (2,755km) with external drop tanks

Though an American aircraft, the Mustang was actually designed to meet a 1940 British specification for a long-range fighter. The RAF, however, was disappointed by the aircraft's inferior performance at altitude. Substituting its Allison engine with a Rolls-Royce Merlin engine transformed the plane. The Mustang excelled as an escort fighter and as a ground-attack aircraft. Its superb flying ability soon won it aerial supremacy over the Luftwaffe.

if they managed to fly five missions safely. The chances of them completing the 25 missions needed to complete a full combat tour were practically zero. Aircrew morale plummeted. The USAAF leaders admitted that such losses were too great to be borne. They concluded that they were incapable of launching more deep penetration daylight raids into Germany unescorted by their own fighters. With no suitable long-range escort fighter immediately available, Eaker reluctantly abandoned unescorted daylight attacks.

"BIG WEEK"

The search for a new long-range escort fighter was now top priority. A small number of Lockheed P-38 Lightnings and Thunderbolts were fitted with 75-gallon pressurized wing tanks, but though these extended both aircraft's operational radius to 520 miles (836.8km), they were not the real answer to the problem. The solution turned out to be the North American P-51 Mustang. Originally intended for the RAF, its underpowered Allison V-1710 engine meant that its performance was disappointing. When the RAF replaced the Allison with a Rolls-Royce Merlin V-1650, however, the Mustang was transformed. With a range of 1,800 miles (2,896km), which meant it could fly all the way to Berlin and get back with fuel to spare, and a maximum speed of 437mph (703km/h), it was the answer to the bombers' prayers.

The results spoke for themselves. On January 11, 1944, the 8th Army Air Force's B-17s, joined by its B-24s, ventured into German airspace for the first time since the previous October. Their targets were the aircraft factories in Brunswick, Oschersleben, and Halberstadt. The difference was that this time they were not flying alone. They were escorted by 13 fighter groups of Lightnings and Mustangs all the way to their targets and back again. When the Luftwaffe's fighters closed to intercept the bombers, they were taken by surprise by the American fighter presence. Over Brunswick, for instance, the 44 Mustangs of the 354th Fighter Group shot down 15 enemy aircraft without a single loss. Major James Howard, the Group's commander, dived on a Messerschmitt Me 110 formation about to descend on the B-17s and broke up the German attack.

The next step was to launch an all-out assault on the German aircraft industry. Moreover, the Germans would be forced to commit their entire day fighter force to try to defend it. The Luftwaffe's fighters would be destroyed en masse in the air by the Mustangs and Lightnings escorting the bombers.

"Big Week" was mounted by the 8th Army Air Force, operating from its airfields in East Anglia, and the newly formed 15th Air Force, flying from its Italian bases. Between them, the two air forces mustered 1,160 B-17 and B-24 bombers plus 676 P-47, P-38, and P-51 fighters for the attacks. Against them, the Germans fielded 350 Focke-Wulf Fw 190s and Messerschmitt Me 109s, 100 Me 110s, 210s and 410s, and 50 night fighters. The attacks started on February 19. The assault lasted until February 25, when bad weather ended it.

In total, the Americans dropped 6,000 tons of bombs on their targets. The RAF, which joined in the operation by bombing the same industrial centers by night, made the total tonnage dropped 19,177 tons. Two hundred and twenty six US bombers were shot down, a loss rate of six percent per mission. The Americans lost 28 fighters. The Messerschmitt plants at Regensburg, Leipzig, Augsburg, and Gotha and the Focke-Wulf

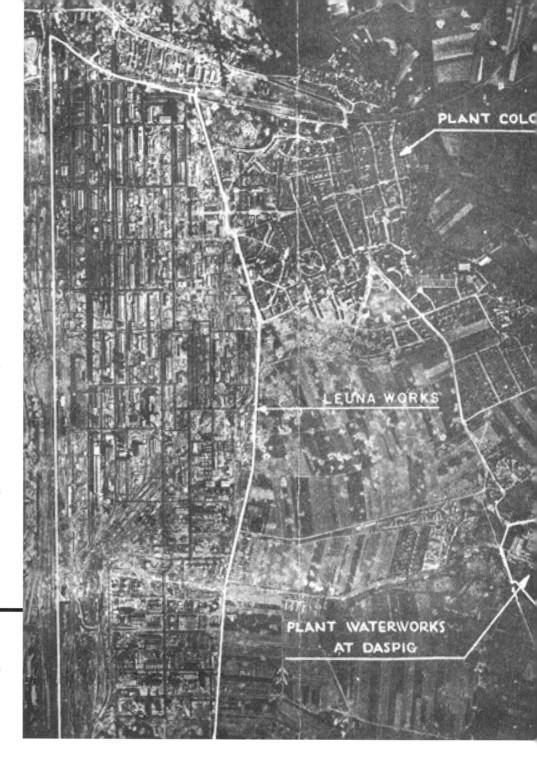

An aerial photograph of the Ammoniakwerk Merseburg at Leuna has been marked up by the photographic interpreters to highlight major points of interest. In fact, the picture was taken by the Luftwaffe in August 1944; it later fell into Allied hands. The Leuna complex was the principal target in General Carl Spaatz's Oil Plan in which he targeted the Reich's synthetic oil refineries in the belief that destroying them would bring the entire Wehrmacht to a grinding halt. The first US raid, on May 12, 1944, was carried out by 935 US bombers; it was the first of 22 attacks on the Leuna plants. The results were dramatic. By late summer 1944, the Luftwaffe had been starved of the fuel it needed to fly anything like its available order of battle.

PLANT COLO

LEUNA WORKS

PLANT WATERWORKS AT DASPIG

factories at Kreising, Tutow, and Posen were all savaged. The Americans also pounded the ball-bearing facilities at Steyr, Stuttgart, and Schweinfurt. The Germans lost about 700 fighters in production and another 232 awaiting dispatch.

The real disaster for the Luftwaffe, though, was the punishment the Americans inflicted on the day fighter force. At least 282 Luftwaffe fighters were shot down.

▼ The Ploesti oil fields, 30 miles (48km) north of Bucharest, the capital of Romania, were also one of Spaatz's targets. Here, storage tanks are seen blazing at the Columbia Aquila refinery after an air raid carried out by B-24 Liberator bombers flying from airfields around Benghazi on August 1, 1943. Out of the 178 aircraft taking part, 53 were lost in the attack. The day went down in USAAF annals as "Black Sunday." It was thanks to the Soviet Army's summer offensive in the east and Romania's consequent decision to change sides and desert the Axis that finally deprived Hitler of his sole remaining source of crude oil. By September 1944, German oil production was near to the point of collapse. It was only the onset of winter weather that postponed its complete destruction.

Even more critically, many of the Luftwaffe's most experienced pilots—the "Old Hares" as they were referred to in Luftwaffe parlance—were killed in action. By May, the number of fighter pilots the Luftwaffe had lost rose to 1,684. Another 440 fighters had been shot down in air-to-air combat, while close to 900 had been destroyed on the ground.

THE OIL CAMPAIGN

Now the back of the Luftwaffe had been broken, the USAAF switched its attention to Germany's synthetic oil plants, which the Luftwaffe relied on for its supplies of aviation fuel. There were 13 of them in all, mostly situated in the heart of the Reich. Raids on them started in May 1944 and their impact became apparent almost immediately. "The assaults on the oil industry," said Speer, "caused the first serious shortages of indispensable basic products and produced the greatest anxiety for the future conduct of the war."

Speer was right to be concerned. On May 12, 935 US bombers bombed the synthetic oil refineries at Leuna and Politz; on June 20, 1,500 of them, escorted by 1,000 fighters, blitzed the vital refineries again. The results were immediate and dramatic. The amount of aviation fuel supplied to the Luftwaffe fell from 180,000 tons in April to 54,000 tons in June, 17,000 tons in August, and a derisory 10,000 tons in September. From that point onward, the Allied strategic-bombing forces were free to attack Germany day and night on an unprecedented scale—and, as far as the Luftwaffe was concerned, virtually unopposed.

THE END OF THE WAR

Allied and Axis leaders alike recognized that what happened during 1944 would decide the course of the war. On November 3, 1943, Hitler warned that the final crisis was at hand. "The threat from the East remains," he wrote, "but an even greater danger looms in the West: the Anglo-American landing! If the enemy here succeeds in penetrating our defenses on a wide front, consequences of staggering proportions will follow within a short time." For once Hitler was correct. The success of Operation Overlord marked the beginning of the end in the West. Even the belated deployment of Hitler's vaunted V-weapon failed to buy time for the Nazis. In the east, Operation Bagration, the Soviet summer offensive in which Russian ground forces were supported by over 10,000 aircraft, led to the breakthrough that eventually took the Soviets to Berlin. In the Far East, the Japanese, too, were on the defensive. As island after island in their outer defensive ring fell to the Americans, they faced the prospect of an all-out US air assault on their sacred Home Islands.

OVERLORD AND AFTER

When the Allies hit the D-Day beaches on June 6, 1944, their superiority in the air proved vital in enabling them to establish firm footholds in Normandy quickly. Between them, the Allied air forces fielded 2,434 fighters and fighter-bombers plus around 700 light and medium bombers to directly support the Normandy landings. There were thousands more in reserve. By contrast, the Luftwaffe, which had only 300 combat-ready aircraft stationed west of the Seine, was unready and outclassed. It managed to fly only 295 sorties on the day of the landings as opposed to the Allies' 12,351.

Fighters continuously circled the skies above the invasion fleet, keeping the troop transports safe from air attack, while the fighter-bombers and bombers ranged inland. The fighter-bombers, operating at low altitude, concentrated on attacking vehicles and troops on the roads or in the fields. The bombers struck at towns and rail centers to hamper German resupply efforts and to slow down reinforcements desperately trying to move forward toward the fighting front.

By contrast, only a single Luftwaffe sortie, flown by Colonel Josef "Pips" Priller, commander of JG 26, and Heinz Wodarczyk, his wingman, managed to get as far as the invasion beaches on June 6. The Junkers 88s heading for Gold Beach were intercepted by an Allied fighter wing and shot down. The two German pilots made one swift pass over Sword Beach before turning for the safety of their home airfield at Lille 200 miles (321.8km) away. "The Luftwaffe," Priller commented to Wodarczyk sardonically, "has had its moment." The writing was on the wall for Hitler's much-vaunted Thousand-Year Reich.

PROTRACTED RECONNAISSANCE

All this, of course, was in the future. Two years before the invasion was launched, preparations for it started. These involved launching a major photo-reconnaissance effort over the European mainland. It began in May 1942, when a small team of Army photographic interpreters were spirited away from RAF Medmenham, where they had been stationed, to Norfolk House, the headquarters of Home Forces Army Intelligence, in London. There they were tasked with working on a top-secret project—identifying possible landing beaches for the invasion of Europe when it was launched.

The photographic interpreters were given a head start. Based at Mount Farm in Oxfordshire, a satellite of RAF Benson, 140 Squadron had been photographing all the coastal defenses and beaches between Calais and Cherbourg ever since the fall of France in 1940. The search was now broadened to cover the entire coastal area from Den Helder in Holland to the Spanish frontier. Gradually, elaborate aerial mosaics were put together of the most likely landing areas. These were of inestimable help to the planners when it came to selecting the most suitable beaches for the invasion.

It was not until August 1943, however, that, after the Quebec Conference held between Roosevelt, Churchill, and the Allied Chiefs of Staff, Operation Overlord was given the final go-ahead. Rather than land in the Pas de Calais, which was heavily defended, the planners

Allied ground troops supported by their assault vehicles storm ashore onto one of the Normandy beaches. The British and Canadians met with surprisngly little resistance and quickly began moving inland. The Americans on Utah were pinned down on the beach for most of the opening day of the invasion, taking heavy casualties. It took them almost until nightfall to find a way off Utah and start to break through the stout German defenses.

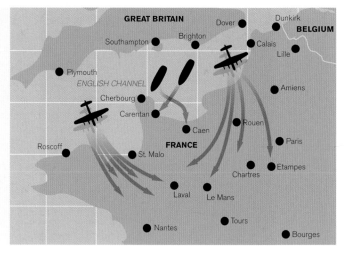

D-DAY

After one postponement due to bad weather, the D-Day landings went ahead on June 6, 1944. The outcome of the ensuing battle would depend on how quickly the Allies could move off the beaches and consolidate their bridgeheads. The one thing they could be sure of was total air superiority. By the time of the invasion, Luftflotte 3 had only 200 aircraft west of the Seine ready for action.

opted for the Normandy beaches between Cherbourg and Le Havre as providing better landing places. Months of detailed photo-reconnaissance followed. The aim was to pinpoint German gun positions and other strongpoints as well as producing a photographic mosaic so that the photographic interpreters could assess and monitor the state of the actual beach defenses.

The beaches were photographed at high and low tide to build up a complete picture of them and the nature and state of their defenses. The low-level oblique coverage the photo-reconnaissance pilots brought back was incredibly detailed. By closely examining the pebbles on each beach, for instance, the geologists among the photographic interpreters could determine whether the shingle would support the weight of Allied tanks driving forward over the beach once they had been landed.

As the date set for the invasion grew closer, Allied air activity was stepped up accordingly. German radar stations were singled out for special attention—starting on May 22, rocket-firing Typhoons and Spitfires put 80 percent of them out of action in a series of daring low-level attacks. The potential invasion beaches were being continuously monitored as well, though right up to the last minute no one outside the highest levels of Allied supreme command knew which ones had been actually chosen. US photo-reconnaissance Lightnings from 10th Group flew practically constant low-level sorties over them—so low that the American fliers called them "dicing" missions, as in dicing with death.

Meanwhile, RAF Medmenham was working flat out, producing thousands of detailed photographic maps and master-models of the Normandy coastline, stretching inland for around 12 miles (19km). Nothing was being left to chance. Even the rows of obstacles on the foreshore were modeled.

THE ATLANTIC WALL

The invasion planners had two major concerns. One was to keep the identity of the beaches they had selected secret, which meant that photo-reconnaissance had to be maintained along the entire length of Hitler's much-vaunted Atlantic Wall. The second was the Atlantic Wall itself. Was it as impregnable to attack as the Nazi propaganda machine claimed?

To counter any Allied threat, the Germans busied themselves constructing powerful chains of fortifications along the coasts of Western Europe. The idea was to stop an invasion at the tide line on the beaches, so forcing the invaders to re-embark or face being driven into the sea. Work on the Atlantic Wall began in March 1942; that September, Hitler upgraded it by ordering the construction of no fewer than 15,000 concrete strongpoints along it. These were to be garrisoned by an army of 300,000 men.

▼ Laborers are seen hard at work on the Atlantic Wall fortifications. Thousands of French conscripts were drafted in by the Organization Todt in an arrangement with the government of Vichy France; French building firms were also contracted to work on the Atlantic Wall's construction. Hitler had ordered work on the wall to begin in March 1942, but, by the time of the invasion just over two years later, it was still far from complete. In France, the most impressive fortifications were in the Pas de Calais. By comparison, Normandy, where the Allies intended to land, was comparatively lightly fortified.

THE ATLANTIC WALL

Hitler intended his famed Atlantic Wall (marked in red) to stretch along the coast of Nazi-occupied Western Europe from Norway to the Spanish border. Building it involved the construction of 15,000 strongpoints, the employment of 450,000 laborers, and the use of 11 million tons of concrete and a million tons of steel. Hitler claimed that what he christened "Fortress Europe" was impregnable; in fact, despite the image its German propaganda sought to project, the wall that had been built was never intended to be a continuous structure.

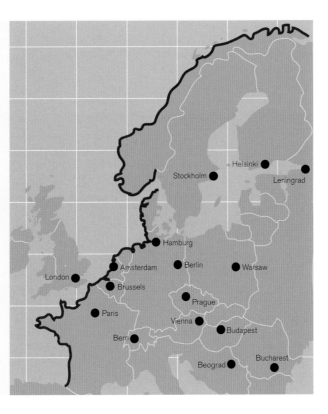

The Fuehrer also decreed that construction work was to be finished by the following May, even though the Todt Organization responsible for building the Atlantic Wall protested that only 40 percent of it at most could be completed by that time. In fact, the figure fell far below this estimate. That fall, Field Marshal Gerd von Rundstedt, the commander-in-chief in the West since spring 1942, warned Hitler that the defenses were still far from complete. Field Marshal Erwin Rommel, in command of Army Group B and responsible for the defense of the Channel coast from the Pas de Calais to Normandy and Brittany, was even more scathing about the overall lack of preparedness.

RACE AGAINST TIME

Rommel embarked on a detailed inspection of the Atlantic Wall in December 1943, shortly after his appointment. What he discovered shocked him to the core. Rather than being impregnable, as Hitler was boasting, the wall was "an enormous bluff, more for the German people than the enemy." Most of the defenses were incomplete and in some places had not been started at all. It was, he concluded, "a figment of Hitler's *Wolkenkuckucksheim* (cloud cuckoo land)." He estimated that he had less than six months to rectify the situation before the Allies attacked. His task was to transform the Atlantic Wall into a reality.

Taking the defenses he had created at El Alamein as his model, Rommel ordered belts of new fortifications to be constructed in depth to slow the Allies down and make them more vulnerable to counterattack. If the invading forces made it onto the beaches, they immediately would be faced by pillboxes, concrete bunkers, flame throwers, and machine gun nests, all with overlapping fields of fire. Just beyond the beaches "heavy antitank guns, self-propelled guns, and antiaircraft combat troops" would be standing ready for action in the forward part of the defense zone.

Even before they got on shore, the Allies would be subject to attack. Four "rows of obstacles, mined or otherwise" were to be erected in the sea below the high-water line to blow up the landing craft or tear the bottoms out of them as they neared the beaches. The beaches themselves were to be festooned with barbed wire and other obstacles. According to Army Group B's War Diary, 517,000 of the latter were in position by May 13, 1944. Rommel also ordered 20 million more mines to be laid. By the end of the month, more than four million mines of various types were in place all along the Channel coast.

It seemed that Rommel had thought of everything. Aware that the Allies were likely to deploy airborne troops to assist the main landing forces, he ordered 10ft

(3m) high poles to be planted at 100ft (30.4m) intervals in any likely spot where gliders might land. The poles were christened "Rommel's asparagus."

PARATROOPS AND GLIDERS

Rommel was right in his assessment, since airborne landings were an integral part of the Allied invasion plan. Minutes after midnight on D-Day, paratroopers from the US 101st and 82nd and the British 6th Airborne Divisions began dropping out of the skies over Normandy. Glider-borne troops swiftly followed.

The British got into action first, their targets being the bridges across the Caen Canal at Ronville and the River Orne at Benouville. The aim was to seize control of the bridges, so blocking German access to the left flank of the amphibious landings and, at the same time, opening up the way for the British to attack Caen itself. Other bridges over the River Dives were to be blown up using the demolition charges the Germans had placed obligingly under them. The task was given to two companies of the Oxfordshire and Buckinghamshire Light Infantry, commanded by Major John Howard, who had been training his men for months for the job. His orders were simple—to capture the two bridges intact and "hold until relieved."

Just after midnight, two groups of three Halifax bombers, each bomber towing a Horsa glider, headed for the Caen area. At 12:16 a.m. precisely, the first glider touched down in a field just west of the Orne River and south of the main road, crushing the wire entanglements the Germans had erected on the field with its nose. Moments later, the men on board were pouring over the bridge at Ranville. The other gliders landed safely as well and the paratroopers on board them went straight into action. It took Howard less than 10 minutes to take both his objectives.

With the bridges secured, Howard and his troops prepared to defend their positions until they were relieved. They expected paratroops from the 5th

Parachute Brigade, which had begun landing just after Howard's gliders touched down, to reach them first. Forces advancing from the invasion beaches were expected to arrive by noon.

In the event, the task of relieving Howard fell to the 1st Special Services Brigade, commanded by the flamboyant Lord Lovat. Accompanied by his personal piper, who played "Blue Bonnets" and other Highland bagpipe music to encourage the commandos as they marched, Lovat and his men fought their way through slight German resistance to relieve Howard at 2:00 p.m.

It was perhaps not surprising that the troops from the 5th Parachute Brigade were delayed since the 6th Airborne, of which they were a part, had another equally important task to fulfill. Air reconnaissance had revealed that the Germans had built a new artillery battery at Merville. It was thought to be equipped with 150mm howitzers with a range of 14,000yd (12,802m). This put the British beaches within easy range of the guns. If they were allowed to get into action, the result would be havoc.

The position was a formidable one. The howitzers were housed in four concrete casemates, each containing a single gun. The casemates themselves were concealed by a covering of soil and the concrete of which they were constructed was 6ft 6in (2m) thick. Stout steel doors protected the entrance to each casemate, while the northern approach was guarded by a 140-feet-wide (42.7m) and 300-yards-long (274m) antitank ditch, festooned with two concertinas of barbed wire with mines in the gap between the concertinas. Around 160 men were believed to be holding the position, which was lavishly equipped with machine- and antiaircraft guns as well as the four howitzers.

Lieutenant-Colonel Terence Otway, commander of the 9th Parachute Battalion, devised a daring plan of attack. It would start with 100 Lancasters bombing the battery before he and his men dropped from the skies

These Airspeed Horsa 1 gliders, seen under tow, were painted in 1944 by the British war artist Roy Nockolds. Paratroopers from the US 82nd and 101st Airborne Divisions, the British 6th Airborne Division, and the 1st Canadian Parachute Battalion spearheaded the airborne assault on D-Day, being dropped or landed by glider on the Cotentin Peninsula five hours before the seaborne landings took place. They were reinforced a few hours later by glider-borne infantry. Each Horsa could carry up to 30 soldiers; 500 of them took part in the D-Day operation.

US paratroopers drop from the C-47s carrying them into action in Normandy on D-Day. The assault did not succeed in its immediate objective, thanks to the excessive scattering of the parachute drops. Many of the paratroopers over- or undershot their designated drop zones, only 25 percent of one unit dropping within a mile of their target. After 24 hours, only 2,500 of the 6,000 men in the 101st Airborne Division were under the control of their headquarters. The rest were either bottled up in isolated pockets or roaming lost behind enemy lines.

ready to begin their assault. Once his paratroops had been dropped, an advance party would cut through the protective wire and clear a path through the minefield. Finally, while the rest of his battalion waited, 60 paratroopers would be landed by glider right on top of the battery. The attack would then begin.

At the start, nothing went according to plan. The bombers missed their target completely and the C-47s carrying Otway's paratroops were scattered by antiaircraft fire. They dropped the paratroops over an area of around 50 sq. miles (129.5km²), with the result that most of them never made it to the rendezvous point. Nevertheless, Otway decided to press ahead with the 150 men he had at his disposal. His troops blasted a way through the wire with their Bangalore torpedoes, stormed the battery, forced its garrison to surrender, and blew up the guns.

MIXED FORTUNES FOR THE AMERICANS

Howard and his men had been fortunate, but the US paratroops from the 101st and 82nd Airborne Divisions were not as lucky. As the C-47s carrying them in a 300-mile-long (482km) formation crossed the French coast, the aircraft ran into heavy cloud. All of the pilots instinctively banked, turned, climbed, dived, and dodged attempting to avoid a mid-air collision. By the time they had emerged from the cloud, their flying formation had fallen apart.

Worse was to follow. As heavy German antiaircraft fire commenced, many pilots reacted by increasing their speed, diving, or climbing to lose or gain height and taking violent evasive action. The paratroops were tossed around inside the planes like ninepins. They anxiously awaited the signal to drop as the pilots— some of whom now hopelessly lost—searched for the markers that were supposed to mark the drop zones. They could see little or nothing. Flying virtually blind, they hit their dropping signals when they thought they were close to their targets. And then, once the

paratroops had tumbled out of their planes, they "took off for England, full bore, like a scalded dog" as one embittered paratrooper later put it.

As the paratroops jumped, they realized that their planes had been flying too fast and much too low. Many lost their leg bags, containing weapons, ammunition, and hard rations, as soon as their parachutes opened. Some swung just once in their chutes before hitting the ground; others never had the time to get their chutes open. Some dropped into the sea and drowned in the English Channel; others landed in the marshes that had been formed when the Germans flooded the Merderet River. The vast majority of them were hopelessly out of position and lost.

Given the confusion, it was scarcely surprising that the 82nd Airborne got off to a bad start. The division had been tasked with securing bridgeheads over the Merderet River and occupying and holding the town of St. Mère-Église. Even though one of its battalions succeeded in capturing the town at around 4:30 a.m. that morning and then defended it successfully through the day against German counterattack, most of 82nd Airborne's troops remained stalled on the west side of the Merderet River.

The 101st Airborne Division ran into much the same difficulties. Its tasks were to secure the western end of the four exists from Utah Beach, where the US VII Corps, consisting of the 4th, 90th, and 9th Infantry Divisions, would be landing. It also was to destroy the bridges spanning the Douve River, establish bridgeheads across it at Le Port, and capture the lock at La Barquette. In addition, it was ordered to take the coastal artillery battery at St. Martin-de-Varreville, though reconnaissance revealed that its gun positions had been destroyed by bombing and the fortification was deserted.

The two northern beach exists were secured quickly, but it took longer to reach the southern ones, largely because the paratroops assigned to the task had been

▲ US paratroopers stand in line to board a Douglas DC-4, the military variant of the Douglas DC-47 21-passenger aircraft. The DC-47, with its more powerful engines, utility seating for up to 35 soldiers, strengthened floor and rear fuselage, and large loading doors, became the Allies' most important transport plane of the entire war. It was used to carry troops, freight, air-drop supplies, and paratroops; tow gliders; and to evacuate battle casualties. Its rugged construction made it practically indestructible. In the USAAF it was dubbed the Skytrain; in the RAF it was called the Dakota.

dropped out of position. They reached the first exit around noon, capturing Pouppeville in the process, but by the time they got to the second one about an hour-and-a-half later, the amphibious troops had already secured it. Though other units from the division succeeded in getting across the bridges at Le Port and in digging in defensively on the east back of the river, enemy artillery fire soon made their position untenable. They pulled back to the west bank for the rest of the day.

The attempt to take the lock at Le Barquette started disastrously. Lieutenant-Colonel Robert G. Carroll, commander of the battalion of the 501st Parachute Infantry Regiment entrusted with the job, was killed, Major Philip S. Gage, the Executive Officer, was captured, and all the company commanders were missing. Luckily, Colonel Howard R. Johnson, the regimental commander, landed in the right place and was able to rally 150 men to take the lock and save the situation. However, attempts to destroy the Douve bridges west of St. Côme-du-Mont had to be abandoned after a reconnaissance patrol came under heavy German fire as it approached the target. Johnson concluded that his force was too small to blow

the bridges. He decided to hold the lock and wait for reinforcements.

Neither division succeeded in completing the whole of their missions. Nevertheless, by fulfilling the most important parts of their assignments, they made the landings on Utah and the subsequent movement inland relatively easy. They suffered heavy losses in the process, although not on the scale predicted by Air Marshal Sir Trafford Leigh-Mallory, the commander of the Tactical Air Force, when he tried to persuade Eisenhower to call off the drops. Leigh-Mallory predicted 70 percent losses among the glider-borne troops and up to 50 percent among the paratroops even before they could get into action on the ground. It would all end in a "futile slaughter of two fine divisions." In fact, the 82nd Airborne lost 1,259 men and the 101st Airborne 1,250 out of the roughly 6,600 men both divisions deployed on D-Day.

THE TRANSPORT PLAN

By refusing to cancel the airborne landings, Eisenhower showed that he was his own man. He had been equally opposed to attempts to abandon or water down what became known as the Transport Plan. Like all the other Allied ground commanders, he was convinced that achieving total air superiority was the key to winning the subsequent battle. When his son, a young second lieutenant, met his father a week after D-Day, he commented on the rows of US vehicles, parked bumper to bumper out in the open at Eisenhower's beachhead headquarters, waiting to get into combat. "You'd never get away with this if you didn't have air supremacy," he told his father. The general replied: "If I didn't have air supremacy, I wouldn't be here."

Air power was the key not only to getting onto the beaches in the first place, but also to stopping German efforts to get reinforcements into position to counterattack the invasion beachheads in strength. The Allied commanders probably had the example of the Anzio landings earlier that year in Italy at the back of their minds. There, after meeting only light initial resistance, the Allies were counterattacked by the reinforcements the Germans hastily rushed to the scene from as far away as Yugoslavia and southern France. They came perilously close to driving the Allies back into the sea.

What was needed was a strategical rethink to ensure that the Germans could not repeat that feat in Normandy. The key, Eisenhower and the other Allied ground commanders decided, was the French railway system. If they could bomb this to a standstill, they believed that the Germans, who were already short of fuel and motorized transport, would be forced onto the roads. This would leave them exposed and vulnerable to the hundreds of fighter-bombers that would rove the skies above the main highways, attacking anything and everything trying to move along them.

Opinion, however, was divided as to whether the Transport Plan, as it was termed, would work or not. Eisenhower, Air Marshal Air Arthur Tedder, the Deputy Supreme Commander, and Leigh-Mallory were in favor of it. Tedder argued that it was the only plan "offering a reasonable prospect of disorganizing enemy movement and supply... and of preparing the ground for imposing the tactical delays which can be vital once the land battle is joined." Harris and Spaatz, the two "bomber barons," opposed it.

Harris's opposition was overcome by his own airmen, who, at the insistence of Sir Charles Portal, Chief of the Air Staff, launched a series of experiment raids on the important marshalling yards at Trappes, Aulnoye, Le Mans, Amiens/Longueau, Courtrai, and Laon in March

This aerial reconnaissance photograph shows the scene near Vierville-sur-Mer in lower Normandy just over three weeks after D-Day. Note the DUKW amphibious trucks shuttling between the beach and the ships offshore, the vehicles heading off the breach, and the knocked-out German coastal defense position to the west of the port.

1944. The attacks were a complete success; French civilian casualties, too, were far lower than expected. Harris was left nonplussed. One of his main arguments against the Transport Plan was that his aircrews lacked the precision bombing skills to carry it out.

Spaatz persisted in his opposition. So, too, did Churchill because of the civilian casualties he still feared the plan might cause. Eventually, Eisenhower appealed to Roosevelt, telling him that he considered the plan indispensable if the Allies were to achieve success. "There is no other way in which this tremendous air force can help us, during the preparatory period, to get ashore and stay there," he wrote to the President. Roosevelt came down on Eisenhower's side.

THE PLAN IN ACTION

The attacks began in April and gradually intensified over the following weeks as bombers from the 9th and 12th Air Forces swung into action, joined later by the 15th Air Force and the heavy bombers of the 8th Army Air Force and Bomber Command. The Germans started to feel the effects immediately. By the end of the month, the Allies had dropped more than 30,000 tons of bombs on rail targets in France, Belgium, and western Germany. 1,000 trains—600 loaded with Wehrmacht supplies—were backed up all along the rail lines, unable to move forward or backward. It was the equivalent of a monster traffic jam.

In particular, the backlog of delayed trains scheduled for Normandy and Brittany rose from 30 on April 1 to 228 on May 1. Rundstedt was forced to order 18,000 men to stop working on the strengthening of the Atlantic Wall defenses to start repairing the damaged tracks. 10,000 more followed them in May, but to no avail. Military train capacity in the crucial northern region of France fell from around 58,000 tons a day to barely 25,000 tons. The number of miles of track in use dropped from about 236,000 miles (379,810km) to just over 62,000 miles (99,779km) by June 1.

The railway yards at Aulnoye, around 100 miles (160km) northeast of Paris, were photographed before and after 253 Lancasters from Bomber Command blitzed them on April 27, 1944. Air Chief Marshal Sir Arthur Harris had argued fervently that Bomber Command was incapable of carrying out the kind of precision attacks crippling the French transport system required, but his aircrews proved him wrong. Churchill, too, required persuading to get him to agree to such attacks. He was concerned about the number of French civilian casualties they might cause.

CLOSE TO PARALYSIS

This was as nothing compared to the chaos that overtook subsequent German troop movements in response to the Allied landings. What happened to the Panzer Lehr Division was typical. Early on June 6, it was in the Le Mans area, actually preparing to load its tanks onto rail transporters for the journey to Poland when the order was countermanded. Late the same afternoon, it got underway northward to confront the Allies and attack the Normandy bridgeheads. The next morning, it suffered its first air attack near Falaise. Blasted bridges and bombed road junctions slowed its progress to a crawl. By nightfall, it had lost more than 200 of its vehicles to Allied fighter-bomber attack.

The 7th Panzer Division suffered the same fate. Strikes by Typhoon and Mustang squadrons decimated its tanks and transport as it moved toward the Channel coast on June 7. The 2nd SS Panzer Division Das Reich was struck as well once it had crossed the Loire on its way from Toulouse to Normandy. Nowhere was safe from Allied air attack. "The worst thing," one exasperated German soldier wrote, "continues to be the planes, so everything has to be done at night. Those bastards strafe individuals with their onboard machine guns; we should have antiaircraft artillery and planes here, but they are nowhere in sight. You can imagine that this completely exhausts morale."

Rundstedt and General Leo Geyr von Schweppenburg, commander of Panzer Group West, were both taken aback by the ferocity of the Allied air attack. Rundstedt's last combat command had been against the Russians in 1941, when the Luftwaffe still ruled the skies. Schweppenburg was also an Eastern Front man, who had little idea of what enemy air supremacy could achieve. He was soon to find out for himself. On June 10, his poorly camouflaged headquarters were heavily bombed. Many of his staff were killed and his command put out of action for a crucial two weeks.

On the other hand, Rommel, the one-time "Desert Fox" who was in command of Army Group B, knew that the Luftwaffe was a spent force, totally incapable of protecting his armies from the hordes of Allied fighters and bombers that would be supporting the invasion. The Allies, he insisted, had to be defeated on the beaches or not at all. Therefore, all available reserves—especially the panzers—had to be positioned within striking distance of the coast to bring this about.

Rommel, however, had reckoned without Hitler. By keeping the bulk of the German panzers in reserve to deal with landings in the Pas-de-Calais that never took place, the self-proclaimed "greatest commander of all time" himself destroyed his best and only chance of success. Though the Germans held on grimly in the Normandy *bocage* for weeks, they were not able to muster sufficient reinforcements quickly enough to deliver a decisive counterattack before Allied numerical and material superiority began to tell.

THE ALLIED BREAKTHROUGH

The Allied plan to exploit their success and break out of Normandy was as follows. The British and Canadians would advance on Caen, so luring most of the German panzers to their part of the front. This would enable the Americans on the Allied right to envelop the weakened enemy there with a wheeling movement south and east. The Caen battle was codenamed Operation Goodwood; the American advance Operation Cobra.

Operation Goodwood began with a massive aerial bombardment; 1,900 bombers dropped 6,858 tons of bombs within a matter of minutes. Montgomery was relying on this overwhelming air support to redress the odds on the ground, which were against him. As the two sides battled ferociously, General Omar Bradley, commander of the US 12th Army Group, prepared to launch Operation Cobra. His Army Group, spearheaded by Patton's newly formed 3rd Army, broke through at Avranches and penetrated deep into Brittany.

By mid-August, the British and Canadian forces in the north and Patton's troops sweeping round to the south had encircled the Germans creating the so-called Falaise Gap. In three days of continual air attack, the armored divisions of the 5th and 7th Panzer Armies were practically annihilated. Of the 2,300 tanks with which the Germans had started the battle, all bar 120 were destroyed.

It was the beginning of the end for the Germans in France. There was no prospect now of an orderly retreat to the line of the Seine; instead, constantly harried from the air, the Wehrmacht fell back in disorder into Belgium and eventually to the German frontier. Paris was liberated—despite explicit orders from Hitler to burn the city to the ground, General Dietrich von Choltitz, its mlitary governor, surrendered it without putting up a fight. Brussels followed. Allied air power ruled the skies. Many confidently believed that the war in Europe would end in 1944 with Germany's capitulation. Rekindled German resistance, Arnhem, and the Ardennes offensive were to prove these hopes unfounded.

This vertical air reconnaissance photograph of Cagny, a small village southeast of Caen, was taken on July 18, shortly after aircraft from Bomber Command had blitzed German fortified positions there. Six-hundred-and-fifty tons of bombs were dropped on them in 10 minutes. The attack was part of Operation Goodwood, the British and Canadian armored thrust toward Caen. The German high command concentrated six-and-a-half panzer divisions to face Montgomery's attack, leaving only one-and-a-half to face the Americans in Brittany.

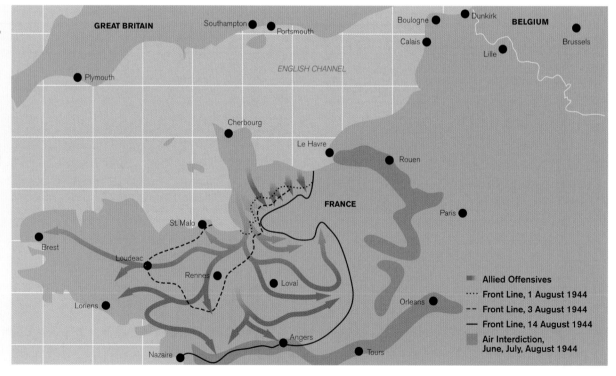

NORMANDY BREAKOUT

The Allied breakout from Normandy began on July 18, 1944, when the British and Canadians launched Operation Goodwood, their aim being to thrust forward with their armor to capture Caen. 2,000 bombers paved the way for them with a massive aerial bombardment. The city fell on July 20. Five days later, the Americans struck in Brittany; 2,251 US tanks faced just 190 German panzers. Avranches fell to US forces on July 30. By August 19, the German 5th and 7th panzer armies had been practically encircled at Falaise. When the encirclement was completed a few days later, the battle for Normandy was effectively over.

GREAT BRITAIN

Southampton
Portsmouth

Plymouth

ENGLISH CHANNEL

Boulogne Dunkirk   BELGIUM
Calais   Brussels
         Lille

Cherbourg

Le Havre
         Rouen

FRANCE

Paris

St. Malo

Brest

Loudeac

Rennes

Loriens

Loval

Orleans

Angers

Nazaire   Tours

■ Allied Offensives
···· Front Line, 1 August 1944
-- Front Line, 3 August 1944
— Front Line, 14 August 1944
■ Air Interdiction,
   June, July, August 1944

V-WEAPONS

It was RAF Medmenham's finest hour. Starting in 1943, Wing Commander Douglas Kendall's photographic interpreters led the hunt for Hitler's so-called "Vengeance Weapons," which the Fuehrer believed would turn the tide of war decisively in his favor. The search involved the taking of more than 1,200,000 reconnaissance photographs and months of patient air intelligence work before the full extent of German missile developments was revealed.

Despite Hitler's belief that his terrible new missiles would prove to be war-winners, this was not to be the case. By the time they were finally deployed, the Russians were in Poland and the Western Allies had landed in Normandy. Had the Germans started their bombardment six months earlier, as had originally been planned, the story might have been different, but, in the final analysis, the missiles were what Goebbels christened *Vergeltungswaffe*—"vengeance weapons." They were nothing more and nothing less.

ACCIDENT, NOT DESIGN

Though rumors that the Germans were engaged in experimental rocket research had been prevalent in intelligence circles since November 1939, the first hard evidence for it was obtained by accident, not design. On May 15, 1942, Flight Lieutenant Donald Steventon, piloting his Spitfire on a routine naval reconnaissance mission over the Baltic, noticed major construction work being carried out around an airfield on the northern tip of an island below him. Steventon decided to take a few photographs of the site. Once these reached RAF Medmenham, the photographic interpreters, though puzzled by what they saw, most notably three strange circular clearings carved into the forest, had the photographs filed for reference as showing nothing of immediate military significance.

The photographic interpreters could not have been more mistaken. What Steventon had stumbled across was the German rocket research establishment at Peenemünde, where Nazi scientists, technicians, and engineers were feverishly developing what they hoped would prove to be revolutionary new secret weapons.

PEENEMÜNDE

German fascination with rocketry began in the late 1920s. Many of the first enthusiasts were men of peace, but, from 1929 onward, the army became interested in it, primarily as a way of getting around the weapons restrictions imposed by the Treaty of Versailles. After Hitler came to power in 1933, the amount of government money made available to the early rocket scientists dramatically increased. In 1936, work began on the construction of a vast new rocket research center at Peenemünde, on an island off the Baltic coast. It became the hub for all subsequent missile development.

Peenemünde was the ideal place to site a rocket

▼ The Germans launched their first V2 successfully at Peenemünde on October 23, 1942. Rocket developments at the research facility there were one of the Third Reich's most closely guarded secrets. Though Flight Lieutenant Donald Steventon had photographed the site on May 15, 1942, no evidence of rocket activity was then detected. No one knew what the strange circular sites were intended for or was even prepared to hazard a guess. It was not until June 12, 1943 that an actual rocket lying horizontal on its side in a rail truck was spotted. Two more V2s on transporters were photographed by an RAF Mosquito just over a week later. The British response was immediate. Bomber Command was ordered to bomb Peenemünde.

A. EXPERIMENTAL STATION.
  1. Elliptical Earthwork.
  2-6. Experimental Sites.
B. ELECTROLYTIC HYDROGEN PEROXIDE PLANT.
  1. Production.
  2. Concentration.
  3. Loading Point.
C. POWER PLANT AREA.
  1. Steam and Power Plant.
  2. Electrolytic Hydrogen Plant.
D. ELECTROSTATIC HYDROGEN PEROXIDE PLANT.
E. EXPERIMENTAL ESTABLISHMENTS.
F. SLEEPING AND LIVING QUARTERS.
G. AIRFIELD.
  1. Experimental Site.
  2. Airfield Buildings.
  3. Test Houses.
  4. Launching Track.

Bomber Command launched Operation Hydra, its first massed strike against Peenemünde, on August 17, 1943. The aircrews taking part in the attack were not made aware of the significance of their target; they were merely told that if it was not damaged significantly, they would be sent back to do the job again. This detailed plan of the facility was produced by RAF Medmenham some time following the operation after a searching analysis of all available air-reconnaissance photographs. The raid, though not completely successful, forced the Germans to abandon plans to mass-produce V2s at Peenemünde and to manufacture it underground elsewhere. The enforced change delayed the deployment of the missile for crucial months.

firing range. Its remoteness made it easy to keep what was going on there secret; the fact that the island was densely forested made it easy to conceal workshops, laboratories, hangars, power plants, and test stands from prying eyes. Gradually, the number of scientists, engineers, and technicians working there grew. The initial figure was 30. By the middle of the war, this had increased to around 4,000 living on the island. Another 11,000 commuted forward and backward from the mainland via a specially constructed rail link each day.

Two teams worked independently at the facility. The Luftwaffe thought that Peenemünde was the best place for the development of new and revolutionary jet aircraft. The army team, under the technical direction

▲ A test stand at Peenemünde. After the RAF bombed the facility successfully, V2 testing was shifted to Blizna in southeastern Poland. The Germans were confident that their work would go undetected, but they were mistaken. Mosquitoes, flying from Italy, started photographing the site in April 1944. In July, the Polish Underground succeeded in recovering the remains of a crashed rocket and getting them flown safely out of the country.

V1 FLYING BOMB

Type Pilotless missile

Crew 0

Length 25ft 9in (7.89m)

Wingspan 17ft 3in (5.27m)

Speed 350/400mph (563/2km/h, 643.7km/h)

Range 150 miles (214.4km)

The first of Germany's "vengeance weapons" to be deployed, the V1 (also called the Fiesler F1 103), was a small, pilotless aircraft powered by a pulse-jet engine and fitted with a one-ton high-explosive warhead. Ramp-launched by a hydrogen peroxide-powered catapult, the missile could fly an average of 150 miles (241km) before its engine automatically cut out and it dived silently on its intended target.

of Wernher von Braun, a brilliant young scientist it had been funding since 1932, focused on rockets. The first two rockets von Braun and his colleagues designed— the A1 and A2—were small and relatively rudimentary. The 20-foot-long (6m) A3, which came next, was larger and more sophisticated, though its failings demonstrated that there were a host of technical problems the rocketeers still had to resolve. Nevertheless, impressed by the progress von Braun and his team had made, the army authorized the development of an even more advanced rocket. What was eventually to become the V2 had been born.

V1 AND V2

Fuelled by a mixture of liquid oxygen and alcohol, the A4 was to travel at three times the speed of sound 50 miles (80km) up into space and down onto its target, its one-ton warhead exploding before its victims could even hear the rocket coming. It was to have a minimum range of 200 miles (322km). Designing it, getting it to fly, and hitting its target would push German technological expertise to its limits. It was not until October 14, 1942 that the first A4 successfully took to the air. Up until then, Hitler had been skeptical about the chances of success. Now, after von Braun showed him a film of the successful test launch, he was convinced that the A4 would become "the decisive weapon of the war. Humanity will never be able to endure it."

By this time, the Luftwaffe had embarked on the development of its own "Vengeance Weapon"—the V1 flying bomb. It was the brainchild of Fritz Gosslar of the Argus engine works and Robert Lusser of the Fieseler aircraft company. Gosslar devised the pulse jet that would power the new weapon; Fieseler designed the airframe. The idea was to build a cheap, expendable pilotless aircraft with a one-ton warhead, capable of flying faster than the fastest enemy fighter. What emerged from the drawing board was a small, straight-

TOP The rocket-powered Messerschmitt Me 163B Komet interceptor was one of the most unusual aircraft produced by either side during World War II. Testing of the prototypes started in 1941, but the aircraft was not ready for operational use until July 1944. With a top speed of 596mph (959km/h), the plane was certainly fast with a phenomenal rate of climb, but its combat range was just 50 miles (80km) as its fuel, which was dangerously volatile, lasted for only 7.5 minutes.

BOTTOM The Messerschmitt Me 262 was the world's first turbojet fighter to go into action. Though it first flew as a pure jet in July 1942, its subsequent development was bedevilled by political infighting—Hitler insisted that the revolutionary new aircraft be deployed as a fast bomber and not a fighter—and it did not get into service until late summer 1944, far too late to regain air superiority for the Luftwaffe. While over 1,000 Me 262s were produced, only 200 to 250 made it to the frontline squadrons, due to shortages of fuel, pilots, and spare parts.

winged airplane with an Argus Tube, as Gosslar's pulse jet was christened, attached to the top of the tailplane. It would have a top speed of 440mph (708km/h) and a range of some 160 miles (257km).

The beauty of the V1 lay in the fact that its main fuselage was constructed of readily available thin steel plate, rather than costly and scarce aluminum, while its short, stubby wings were made of even cheaper plywood. The Argus Tube was fuelled by cheap kerosene, which was in plentiful supply, as opposed to the pure aviation fuel that powered conventional aircraft engines. Luftwaffe experts estimated that each missile would probably take no more than 550 man-hours to build as opposed to the 10,000 man-hours required to construct a Messerschmitt Me 109 fighter and would cost around 100 times less than an A4 rocket. The idea was to catapult it into the air at 200mph (322km/h) and then the Argus Tube would take over. Gyroscopes would keep the V1 stable so that its automatic pilot, linked to a magnetic compass, could keep it flying straight, level, and on course for its target. Once it got there, a counter driven by a vane anemometer on its nose would cut off the fuel supply to the pulse jet, so triggering the missile's final unpowered dive.

The logic was simple. Compared to a manned bomber and its crew, the V1 was quicker and cheaper to produce. Even if the majority of the missiles were to be shot down by the British defenses—an eventuality the Luftwaffe considered extremely unlikely—enough of them would get through to wreak havoc on their targets below. The V1 prototype made its first powered test flight in December 1942, only 15 months after its development started; the Luftwaffe optimistically planned mass production to start early the following year.

MEDMENHAM ON THE ALERT

Across the English Channel, British Intelligence was becoming concerned by reports it was receiving from its agents in the field about various secret weapons the Germans supposedly were developing. In March 1943, it received more tangible evidence that something was indeed afoot. Generals von Thoma and Crüwell, whom the British had taken prisoner in North Africa, were secretly bugged talking about a top-secret weapons program. Thoma told Crüwell that he had actually witnessed an experimental rocket launch and been told to "wait until next year and the fun will start."

The conversation was the catalyst that prompted British Intelligence to take further action. RAF Medmenham was alerted to be on the watch for "any suspicious erections of rails or scaffolding" along the French coast, the presence of which would be an indication that the Germans were beginning to construct possible missile-launching sites. The photographic interpreters were also given Intelligence's best guess as to the weight and length of the missile and of its range, which was thought to be around 130 miles (209km). "The obvious target for such a weapon," the Intelligence report concluded, "is London."

THE SEARCH BEGINS

The response to these warnings was to step up photo-reconnaissance over the Baltic and to start a search of every square mile of the French coast from Cherbourg to the Belgian border to try to identify possible launch sites. On April 15, Churchill was alerted to the possible danger. His response was to set up an investigatory committee, chaired by Duncan Sandys, a junior minister at the Ministry of Supply and also the premier's son-in-law, to investigate the threat.

A Flying Fortress, seen from above, makes its bomb run over a V2 launching site. The pockmarked craters littering the site are a clear indication of the success of this and previous attacks. Raids like this one forced the Germans to abandon massive fixed sites. Instead, they fired their rockets from mobile transporters, which were easy to conceal and so hard to detect.

Sandys and his committee went to Medmenham and examined all the photographs of Peenemünde that had been taken over the previous months. They concluded that the site was "probably an experimental station" but that "the whole area is not in full use" and that "a heavy long-range rocket is not yet an immediate menace." It was an accurate summary of the position as it existed at the time, but took no account of the speed at which the Germans were working. Both the Peenemünde teams were under constant pressure from above to get their weapons into action. There was also substantial rivalry between them to win the race.

The trouble was that neither Sandys, his committee, the photographic interpreters at Medmenham, or the reconnaissance pilots knew exactly what they should be looking for. They had no idea, for instance, that the Germans were developing two missiles, not just one. The Air Ministry speculated that the target was "a long-range gun… or rocket aircraft… or some sort of tube located in a disused mine out of which a rocket could be squirted." It was thought possible, too, that the rockets, if indeed they existed, would be launched horizontally from a cave or quarry, rather than vertically from a rocket stand.

The scientific community itself was divided about exactly what the Germans were up to. Lord Cherwell, Churchill's closest scientific adviser, argued that the Germans were incapable of developing a rocket with sufficient propulsive power to fly as far as 130 miles (209km). If, however, they tried, the rocket would be too heavy to ever get off the ground. Physicist Dr. R.V. Jones, the scientist working with the Secret Intelligence Service who had solved the mystery of the Luftwaffe's direction-finding radio beams, disagreed. He was convinced the Germans were developing an extremely powerful rocket that could possibly weigh as much as 80 tons. If, as Jones speculated, it was able to carry a 10-ton warhead, just one of the rockets might kill up to 4,000 people if it landed in a city center.

V2 (A4) ROCKET

Type	Rocket missile
Length	45ft 11in (14m)
Wingspan	11ft 8in (3.56m)
Warhead	2,200lb (1,000kg)
Speed	3,580mph (5,760km/h)
Range	200 miles (320km)

Fuelled by a potent mixture of ethanol, water, and liquid oxygen (the latter acting as an oxidizer), the second of Hitler's "vengeance weapons" was undetectable and unstoppable once it had been launched. The first V2 was launched against Paris on September 8, 1944, followed by one aimed at London later the same day. Over the next months, at least 3,172 V2s were launched, with the Belgian port of Antwerp and London the principal targets.

THE V2 DISCOVERED

The one thing that was clear from the hundreds of photographs from the reconnaissance missions the RAF was now mounting from RAF Benson and the USAAF from Mount Farm on an almost daily basis was that activity at Peenemünde was constantly on the increase. The Medmenham photographic interpreters noticed, for instance, that giant crane-like structures had appeared at the center of the giant circular concreted clearings the Germans had carved out of the forest. Then, on June 12, there was a major breakthrough.

Photographs taken on that date showed a long object lying horizontal on its side on a trailer close to one of the circular emplacements. "The appearance presented by this object," the Medmenham report concluded cautiously, "is not incompatible with its being a cylinder tapered at one end and provided with three radial fins at the other," presumably waiting to be launched. Close by a number of what the photographic interpreters described as "columns" were standing upright. By measuring the shadows they cast, it was calculated they were about 40ft (12.1m) in length. When he saw the photographs six days later, Jones positively identified them as being rockets.

A follow-up reconnaissance flight on June 23 was even more revealing. Its photographs captured "two torpedo-like objects" lying horizontally on some form of transporter inside the elliptical earthworks north of what was thought to be the development area. The new objects were 38ft (11.5m) long and six ft (1.8m) wide with a tail of three 12ft (3.6m) wide fins. The photographic interpreters also spotted high-pressure containers on some nearby railway wagons. These, they thought, must contain liquid fuel for the objects they had seen. If this assessment was correct, it meant that whatever the Germans were testing could be smaller and lighter than previously had been assumed.

Sandys was convinced. On June 29, he chaired a top-level meeting in the Cabinet War Rooms to discuss

A V2 rockets skywards, photographed four seconds after lift-off into a Peenemünde test flight on June 21, 1943. The German Army pressed Hitler to make the mass production of the missile a top weapons priority. At first, the Fuehrer had been ambivalent about the missile program, but successes like this—and the ever-growing ferocity of British and American bomber attacks on Germany—changed his mind. He ignored the fact that the V2 was expensive to produce, that the liquid oxygen that was an essential part of its fuel was in short supply, and that it could carry only a one-ton high-explosive warhead.

the Medmenham findings and all the other intelligence that had been gathered about Peenemünde over the preceding months. Cherwell and Jones were both present. So was Churchill himself. Sandys said that all the evidence pointed to the rockets being a fact. The best countermeasure to them was for Bomber Command to launch a mass attack on Peenemünde, though that could not be mounted until the nights were long enough, which meant early August at the earliest. Cherwell vehemently disagreed. The whole thing was a hoax, he argued, devised to lure Bomber Command into a trap so that it could be decimated by the German night fighter force. Or it might have been planned to divert attention away from something else altogether, such as the development of a pilotless plane. If the photographs showed anything sinister at all, he concluded, the objects might well be giant torpedoes. The one thing they were not was rockets.

Jones supported Sandys. Churchill, having listened to all the arguments carefully, came down on his son-in-law's side. Peenemünde was to be blitzed. The RAF would activate Operation Hydra as soon as the conditions were right.

THE PEENEMÜNDE RAID

While Peenemünde itself won a temporary respite from air attack, photographic reconnaissance over France revealed another new and potentially terrifying development. Hitler personally had given the go-ahead for the construction of a massive rocket launching site, situated in what had been a gravel quarry at Watten, near St. Omer in the Pas-de-Calais.

The initial assumption was that what the Germans were building at Watten was a new command bunker as part of their Atlantic Wall defenses against Allied invasion, but the sheer size of the structure seemed to be far in excess of anything required for that purpose. The French Resistance reported that thousands of slave laborers had been brought in to work on the site night and day and that thousands of tons of steel and concrete were being used to make whatever it was the Germans were building impregnable to air attack. Sandys added it to the list of targets he felt must be bombed at the first opportunity.

Meanwhile, the first priority remained the attack on Peenemünde. On August 17, Bomber Command finally bombed it: 596 Lancasters and Halifaxes, loaded down with 281 tons of incendiaries and nearly 1,600 tons of high-explosive bombs, set out that night for the Baltic. It was what Bomber Command termed "maximum effort." The aircrews taking part in the attack were briefed that their target was "a radar development station that promises to improve greatly the German night defense organization." The briefing ended with a chilling warning: "If the attack fails... it will be repeated the next night and on ensuing nights regardless of loss."

It was a clear moonlit night and flying conditions were excellent. The plan was for the bombers to attack in three waves, each wave making a timed run from an offshore island to the target at a height of no more than 7,000ft (2,133m) to help them to bomb as accurately as possible. The priority target was the scientists' living quarters, followed by Peenemünde's workshops and laboratories. The raid caught the antiaircraft defenses off guard. Nor, distracted by a dummy Mosquito raid on Berlin, did the German night fighters arrive on the scene until after most of the attacking aircraft had bombed and turned for home. Forty of the bombers were shot down.

Post-raid photo-reconnaissance the following day indicated that the attack had been a complete success. The Medmenham photographic interpreters reported as follows. "There is a large concentration of craters in and around the target area and many buildings are still on fire. In the north manufacturing area some 27 buildings of medium size have been completely destroyed; at least four buildings are still seen

Watten, in the Pas-de-Calais, was chosen as the most suitable site for the first giant V2 launching bunker in December 1942; the Todt Organization began building the bunker the following spring. The Germans were not left undisturbed for long. In May 1943, RAF aerial photographic reconnaissance detected the construction work. On August 27, 187 B-17 Flying Fortresses from the US 8th Army Air Force targeted the site, bombing it in the late evening. As the photograph here demonstrates, the northern part of the bunker was devastated. Eventually, attempts to deal with the damage having failed, the entire site was abandoned in favor of mobile V2 launch operations.

burning." In fact, the pilot production works had escaped serious damage, while many bombs had fallen in the surrounding forest and done no damage at all. Though the living area had been blitzed, what had suffered the most was the camp housing Peenemünde's foreign forced labor force, 790 of whom had been killed.

Nevertheless, the damage was sufficient to put Peenemünde out of action for two crucial months. Dr. Walter Thiel, in charge of developing the A4's rocket engine, was killed. The raid also indirectly claimed another scalp. The morning after it, Hitler and Goering berated General Hans Jeschonnek, the Luftwaffe's Chief of Staff, for the air force's failure to defend Peenemünde effectively. Jeschonnek went back to his office and shot himself. The suicide note he left behind him concluded: "It is impossible to work with Goering any longer. Long live the Fuehrer! Heil Hitler!"

Watten was the next target: 224 Flying Fortresses from the US 8th Army Air Force blitzed the construction site 10 days after the raid on Peenemünde. The American aircrews were told they were attacking an "aeronautical facilities station." US aircraft losses were light and the damage inflicted severe. Fortuitously, the Germans had just laid tons of concrete at the site, which was still wet when the bombs came raining down. It hardened over the twisted mass of iron and steel girders the bombers had left behind them.

Another American raid on September 7 was even more destructive. The Medmenham photographic interpreters described what was left of Watten after this second raid as "a desolate heap." Sir Malcolm McAlpine, a leading British construction specialist, was also asked to examine the post-raid reconnaissance photographs. Having studied them carefully, he opined that the Germans would find it easier to start all over again elsewhere rather than to waste time trying to repair such extensive damage. McAlpine was correct in his assessment. Work at Watten was abandoned for good.

SKI SITES AND V1S

Though the Medmenham photographic interpreters had managed to confirm that the Germans were developing and testing a rocket at their top-secret Baltic base, it was suspected that Peenemünde had not yet yielded up all its secrets. The suspicion was confirmed when a secret agent in France reported to British Intelligence that the Germans had started building unfamiliar new structures at eight sites near Abbeville in northern France. At the beginning of November 1943, reconnaissance aircraft from RAF Benson photographed them from the air. The photographs were immediately handed over to Medmenham and Douglas Kendall for photographic interpretation.

On close examination, the photographs revealed that all eight sites shared features in common. At the center

▼ A V1 launching ramp hidden in woodland on the road to Abbeville near Amiens is examined by Allied troops after being abandoned and partly demolished by the retreating Germans. At the peak of the V1 offensive, sites like this were firing 300 missiles a day at Britain, targeted mainly at London. More than 6,000 Londoners were killed and 18,000 wounded. For some reason, the Germans decided not to target the invasion supply ports for attack. If they had, a protracted V1 bombardment would have caused real chaos.

A V1 ground crew manhandles a flying bomb toward its launch ramp, from which it will be catapulted into the air. After their original launch sites had been detected, heavily bombed, and put out of action before a single V1 could be launched from them, the Germans came up with a much simpler concept. All the buildings were prefabricated, which meant that they could be assembled at the last minute, while the V1s themselves were brought onto the site ready to launch as and when required. Rather than concentrate on bombing the sites, which were hard to find, the Allies focused on destroying the bombs' storage depots.

of each site, large buildings were being constructed that, from the air, looked like giant skis lying on their sides. Other similarly shaped structures were dotted around them, including the foundations of what Kendall and his team thought could be long, narrow launching ramps. One ominous fact was also clear. Every one of the ramps was pointing directly toward London.

Constant aerial reconnaissance soon detected another 26 sites. Within the space of a few weeks, the number had risen to 96. What did the Germans intend to use them for? The scientific experts doubted that they could be employed to launch rockets as these would require heavy handling gear and there was no evidence of this being installed. Nor were they situated near railway lines, which the experts believed would be needed to deliver rockets to their firing sites. They concluded it was more likely than not the Germans were developing some sort of pilotless bomb to be launched against London either before or in conjunction with a rocket offensive. The scientists' view confirmed intelligence that had reached London on July 25 from what was guardedly described as "a diplomatic source." This stated explicitly that two weapons—a rocket and a pilotless plane—were under development at Peenemünde.

UNMASKING THE V1
Kendell asked Constance Babington Smith, one of Medmenham's most skillful photographic interpreters, to re-examine all the photographs the RAF had taken of Peenemünde to see if she could spot anything that looked like a very small airplane—possibly even smaller than the experimental Messerschmitt Me 163 rocket fighter she had already discovered parked neatly on the tarmac of Peenemünde's airfield. Toward the end of November she struck gold.

Armed solely with her stereo viewing frame and jeweler's Leitz magnifying glass, Babington Smith noticed something outside a building in which she assumed some sort of engine was being tested. It was a small cruciform object less than a millimeter in length on the photograph she was studying and only just visible thanks to its white reflective outline and the shadow it was casting on the tarmac. Babington Smith had found a flying bomb.

Now the photographic interpreters knew what they were looking out for, progress was swift. They found similar midget planes on other Peenemünde photographs. Then, following another photo-reconnaissance mission on November 26, they detected ski sites similar to the ones being built in France being erected at Zinnowitz, a few miles away from Peenemünde along the Baltic coast. The sites featured what looked like a steel ramp pointing out toward the sea. Using their stereo viewers to make three-dimensional measurements, the photographic interpreters calculated that the ramp was angled upward at an angle of around 10° and was 125ft (38m) long.

Similar ramps were soon spotted at Peenemünde itself. To cap it all, Babington Smith spotted a tiny airplane in position at the bottom of one of the ramps. It was a V1 about to be launched on a test flight. The jigsaw was complete.

Everyone from Churchill and Sandys down appreciated that Medmenham's efforts had been invaluable. Support for its findings came from a somewhat unexpected source. On August 22, a mysterious object fell out of the sky into a cabbage field on the island of Bornholm in occupied Denmark. Superintendant Hansen, a senior Danish policeman, and Lieutenant-Commander Christiansen of the Danish Navy, set off to investigate and got to the scene before the Germans. Christiansen photographed the wreckage. It appeared to be that of a miniature aircraft with no cockpit and a mysterious tube strapped underneath the fuselage. A cylinder that seemed to have been the aircraft's power plant lay nearby. It was still "very warm an hour after the crash."

In these remarkable photographs taken from a USAAF F-5 on July 4, 1944, a Hawker Tempest fighter is captured in hot pursuit of a flying bomb across the English countryside: the photographs were probably taken over Kent. Only a few Allied aircraft, such as the Tempest, possessed the speed to catch up with and destroy the V1s in midair. Nevertheless, once the V1s were within range of the British defenses, more than one-tenth of them were shot down into the sea by fighters. Once the remaining missiles had crossed the Channel, more than half of them were brought down over land by fighters, antiaircraft fire, or balloon barrages. London's 880 antiaircraft guns were shifted nearer to the south coast, so that they could bring down the V1s relatively safely over open country rather than over the capital.

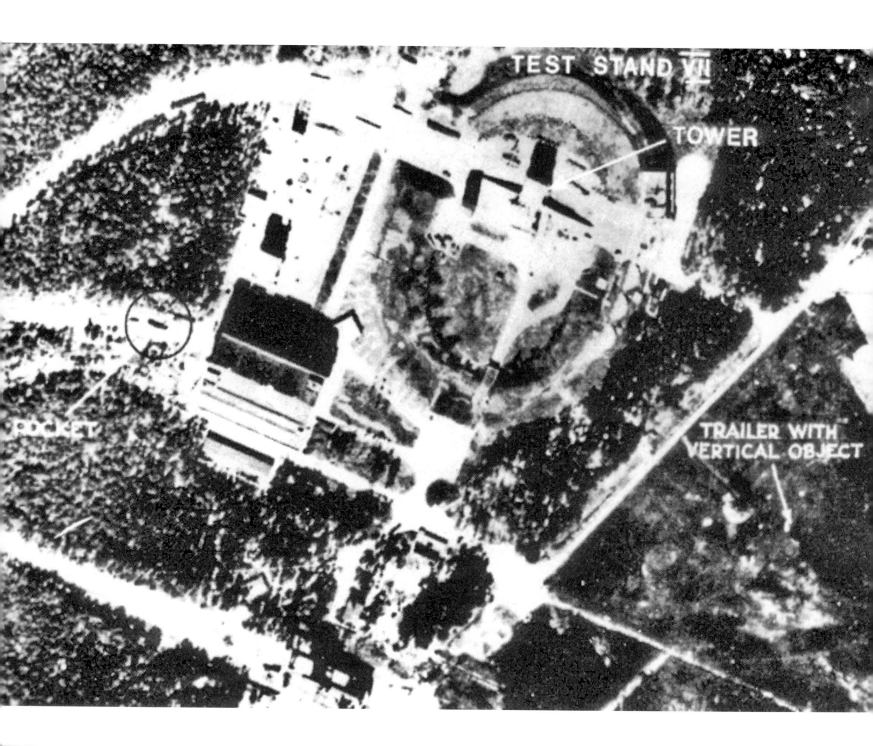

TEST STAND VII

TOWER

ROCKET

TRAILER WITH VERTICAL OBJECT

This annotated aerial reconnaissance photograph of V2 rockets poised on Test Stands I and VII at Peenemünde in June 1943 shows the quality of the material the photographic interpreters at RAF Medmenham had to work with. Coming up with a convincing overview of what the Germans were up to was taxing in the extreme. It was, said Constance Babington Smith, as if "two or three jigsaw puzzles had been jumbled together."

Inside the airframe, there were some curious wire-wrapped spheres and what seemed to be some sort of guidance mechanism "operating valves with compressed air which in turn operate the rudder." The Danes smuggled the photographs to Copenhagen and then to neutral Sweden, where they were passed to the British Embassy in Sweden for onward transmission to London and, via the Secret Intelligence Service, to Sandys and his committee.

PRODUCTION DELAYS

Not much could be done to attack V-weapons manufacture directly. Following the Peenemünde raid, the Germans shifted A4 rocket development to a new site at Blizna in Poland, well out of Allied bombing range, though this did not stop partisans from the Polish Home Army locating a missile that had gone off course and crashed without exploding. The Poles managed to conceal the rocket from the German patrols searching for it. They then dismantled it. In July 1944, the RAF sent a Dakota to collect the pieces, which were then flown to Brindisi and then back to Britain for expert examination.

Months earlier, it had been decided to site the mass production of the A4 in a vast underground factory complex the Germans were constructing deep beneath Kohnstein Mountain, near Nordhausen in central Germany. Himmler, who on Hitler's orders had taken over responsibility for A4 manufacture, put Hans Kammler, an SS Brigadier-General, in charge. Thousands of concentration camp inmates, most of them Polish, Russian, and French, were employed as forced labor to tunnel under the site. "Pay no attention to the human cost," Kammler told his SS overseers. "The work must go ahead, and in the shortest possible time." Even if RAF or USAAF air reconnaissance had managed to locate it, the complex would have been impervious to bombing.

V1 production went unbombed until June 20, 1944, when 137 B-17s raided the missile's assembly plant in the Volkswagen works at Fallersleben (Volkswagen had been selected for mass-production purposes because Fiesler was incapable of making the number of flying bombs the Luftwaffe required). The attack was repeated by a force of B-24s nine days later with great success.

Unbeknownst to the Allies, however, the Luftwaffe had already been its own worst enemy. It decided to rush its wonder-weapon into mass production without waiting for the prototypes to complete all their trials. The results were disastrous from the German point of view. Design flaws meant that the first 2,000 V1s churned out by the Volkswagen works had to be scrapped. It took months to iron out the faults and get the flying bomb back into production.

OPERATION CROSSBOW

What the Allies could destroy were the ski sites in France. The plan to attack them was christened Operation Crossbow. The first raid was launched on December 16, 1943, by which time Medmenham had managed to build up a comprehensive picture of what particular roles the various buildings on each site had been given. The long, low ski-shaped ones were for bomb storage; the curve was intended to serve as antiblast protection in the event of an accidental explosion. The square buildings were for bomb assembly. When the Germans were ready, the completed V1 would be hauled onto its firing ramp. A powerful rocket booster would catapult it up the ramp and into the air, when the bomb's pulse jet would take over and the V1 would set course for its target.

The aim was to time the bombing raids so that they were launched when most of the construction work had been completed, but before the sites were ready for action. This meant mounting regular photo-reconnaissance flights to monitor them. Medmenham allocated points to each construction element as it was completed—10 for each ski building, five for the sunken control bunker, 10 for the square assembly workshop,

10 for the launching ramp, and so on. Half those numbers of points were given to buildings that appeared to be half-complete. When 90 points had been awarded, the site was made a bombing priority.

The first raid, carried out by 470 RAF bombers, targeted the ski sites around Abbeville. On Christmas Eve, 722 B-17s and B-24s from the US 8th Army Air Force's 1st, 2nd, and 3rd Bombardment Wings struck at the sites in the Pas de Calais with devastating results. The attack spread to newly discovered sites around Cherbourg early in the New Year, the heavy bombers being joined by medium bombers and fighter-bombers from the RAF's 2nd Tactical Air Force and the US 9th Air Force as winter started to turn into spring. The results were certainly impressive. By the end of March 1944—the Luftwaffe had originally planned to launch the flying bomb offensive by bombarding London on April 20 to celebrate Hitler's birthday—all 96 sites had been bombed and 88 of them put permanently out of action.

THE V1 OFFENSIVE

The Germans, however, were by no means beaten yet. They designed far less complex launching sites, many of which were adapted from existing farm buildings, or built to resemble such buildings if spotted from the air. Some were concealed in woods so as to be practically invisible. All the permanent building required was the concrete foundations for the launch ramps. There was no bomb storage on sight; the completed V1s were brought in ready-assembled as required. One square building was prefabricated and so could be erected quickly at the last minute prior to launch. It was estimated that it would take just 48 hours to get the sites ready for action.

By the beginning of June, 68 new sites had been located; the total rose to 133 by the end of the month. Photographic reconnaissance clearly indicated that the Germans were in the last stages of getting them ready for action. On June 11, Medmenham signalled the code

HAWKER TEMPEST V

Type Fighter

Crew 1

Length 33ft 8in (10.26m)

Wingspan 41ft (12.49m)

Speed 432mph (695km/h)

Range 740 miles (1,190km), 1,530 miles (2,462km) with drop tanks

Logically, the Tempest was Hawker's obvious fighter development after the Typhoon. The aircraft combined a new semielliptical wing with the Typhoon airframe and a Sabre IIA engine. First deliveries of Tempests to British fighter squadrons began in January 1944; they showed themselves to be the fastest low- to medium-altitude fighter in RAF service. Between June 1944, when the first V1s were launched to the beginning of September, Tempest pilots were responsible for the destruction of 638 of them.

word "Diver" to the Allied Chiefs of Staff. This warned them that an attack could be expected imminently. The photographic interpreters were right again. In the early hours of June 13, the first 10 flying bombs took to the air. It was hardly the mass attack that the Luftwaffe had promised Hitler it would make. Five V1s crashed shortly after launch and one went missing completely. It probably went down somewhere over the English Channel. Three made it as far as Kent and Sussex. Only one reached London. It hit a railway bridge in Bethnal Green, killing six people in the nearby houses and making 200 more homeless. It was a grim foretaste of what was to come.

Two days later, the flying bomb offensive finally began in earnest. More than 200 V1s were successfully launched. Over the next months, the number rose inexorably. As the campaign reached its climax, 100 V1s were dropping in London minute by minute, hour by hour, and day by day. However, it could have been worse. Originally, the Germans had calculated that they could launch 2,000 V1s every 24 hours. Now, the most they could manage was 300. Nor did all of them get through to their target. The RAF's fastest fighters—notably the new Hawker Tempests—tried every trick in the book to shoot them down in mid-flight, either over the Channel or the open countryside in Sussex and Kent. On the ground, General Sir Frederick Pile, the head of Antiaircraft Command, masterminded a massive reorganization of London's antiaircraft defenses, moving them south to the strip of coast running from Beach Head to Dover. After the move was completed on July 19, he had 412 heavy and 572 light antiaircraft guns, 168 Bofors guns, and 246 20mm guns in position ready to open fire. By the end of the second week of August, they were responsible for nearly 40 percent of the V1s that were shot down in flight.

All in all, 2,340 V1s hit London. More than 6,000 civilians were killed, 18,000 wounded, and 750,000 homes were damaged or destroyed. But, though civilian morale was dented by the strangely impersonal nature of the constant attack, it did not break. Also, as the invading Allied armies pushed farther and farther into France after the breakout from their Normandy beachheads, Londoners could see an end in sight. By the end of September, most of the V1 launch sites had been overrun and the offensive slowly came to an end. The Flying Bombs did not possess the range to reach Britain once France had been liberated. The Germans switched targets to Antwerp and later to Liège. Though some attempts were made to launch V1s from Heinkel III bombers flying over the North Sea, these were few and far between.

NO DEFENSE

The Germans had one last trick up their sleeves. On September 8, the first A4 rocket—now renamed the V2—was fired against London. It landed in Chiswick, killing three people and wounding another 17, some of them severely. There was no conceivable defense against V2 attacks. The only way of stopping them was to capture the V2s' launch sites, but these proved almost impossible to find. The V2 was highly mobile and could be fired from practically anywhere. It did not need a permanent launching site—a handy road or clearing in a wood would suffice. It did not have to be moved by rail either. It traveled on a motorized transporter that could easily be concealed until just before the rocket was fired. The best air intelligence could do was to establish that the V2 was being launched from Holland, most likely in or near The Hague. Only once, on February 26, 1945, did three photo-reconnaissance Mosquitoes fortuitously catch sight of a V2 ready for launch, its fuel tanker, transporter, and other support vehicles standing close to hand.

A grand total of 2,115 V2s were launched against Britain, the last one falling on Orpington in Kent on March 27, 1945. Half of the rockets the Germans managed to fire landed in the London area, killing 2,054 people and seriously injuring a further 7,000. Around one in three V2s exploded in flight, probably because Himmler had ordered their deployment before the rocket's test program had been completed. The Germans were also short of the specialist fuels the rocket required, which cut down the number that could be fired. Nevertheless, its deployment marked the start of a revolution in warfare as future events were to show.

A Tempest V Series II is photographed during a test flight from the Hawker factory at Langley, outside Slough, on November 25, 1944. Test pilot William "Bill" Humble is in the cockpit and at the joystick. By this time, the Tempest's main purpose had been redefined. It was to carry out "armed reconnaissance" operations deep behind enemy lines. The aircraft proved supremely successful. That December alone, Tempest pilots shot down 52 Luftwaffe fighters and destroyed 89 trains.

SETTING TOKYO ABLAZE

On March 9, 1945, 363 Boeing B-29 Superfortresses carried out the single deadliest air raid of the entire war when they rained ton after ton of incendiary bombs on Tokyo, the Japanese capital. It was a low-level attack—the Superfortresses bombed from around 5,000ft (1,524m)—and, from the American point of view, it proved immensely successful. The raid triggered a firestorm that killed upward of 100,000 people, left more than a million homeless, and razed a quarter of the city to the ground. The death toll was higher than the one that resulted from the dropping of atomic bombs on Hiroshima and Nagasaki six months later.

Codenamed Operation Meetinghouse, the assault marked the start of an aerial onslaught which proved so destructive that, at the end of July, the US air force high command concluded that there were no more cities worth attacking remaining on the Japanese Home Islands. The B-29s had gone on to launch strike after strike against Japan's other large cities. Nagoya, Osaka, and Kobe were blitzed particularly heavily, Nagoya being hit twice within the space of a single week. US planes blanketed the few cities that remained unscarred with leaflets warning their inhabitants to flee before the inevitable attack. By the time the war ended in August, more than 60 Japanese cities had been laid waste. Only Kyoto, the ancient imperial capital, and four other cities were spared.

ISLAND HOPPING AND SUPERFORTRESSES

After the Doolittle Raid in 1942 (*see pp. 108–111*), there were no more air attacks on Japan itself for just over two years. The reason for the hiatus was simple. The B-17 Flying Fortress, the US Army Air Force's main strategic bomber, could not get there and back carrying a full bomb load without running out of fuel on the return flight. As US forces advanced step-by-step across the central Pacific—a strategy aptly termed "island hopping"—one of their aims was to open up the Japanese Home Islands to aerial assault.

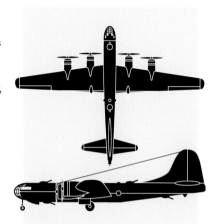

BOEING B-29 SUPERFORTRESS

Type Long-range strategic bomber

Crew 11

Length 99ft (30.18m)

Wingspan 141ft 3in (43.06m)

Speed 357mph (574km/h), 220mph (350km/h) cruising

Range 3,250 miles (5,230km)

One of the most advanced aircraft of its day, the Superfortress featured a pressurized cabin for its aircrew, an electronic fire-control system, remote-controlled machine gun turrets, and many other technological innovations. Boeing built 2,766 of the giant planes, which served primarily in the Pacific theater of war. With more than 1,000 of them taking to the air at a time, they were at the forefront of American air attacks on the Japanese Home Islands from late 1944 onward.

With the liberation of the Marianas group of islands in the late summer of 1944, this aim was achieved. Rather than fly from mainland China, which the Americans had started doing that June, the bombers would now be shifted to the massive new airbases being constructed on Guam, Saipan, and Tinian. They were only 1,500 miles (2,414km) south of Tokyo, meaning that the Home Islands were now well within bombing range.

The bomber the Americans would rely on for their aerial assault had already been chosen. It was the giant B-29 Superfortress, the biggest, heaviest, and most expensive bomber the US aircraft industry had produced to date. Its development, however, had been fraught with problems, largely because it pushed existing military aviation technology to its limits. The complicated airframe was unlike anything Boeing had ever built before. The four radial engines—giant Wright R-3550 Duplex-Cyclones—were initially unreliable, prone to overheating and catching fire in the air. Their propellers proved almost equally troublesome. Then there was the revolutionary cabin pressurization system, larger and more sophisticated than anything that ever had been attempted before. It was essential if the B-29 was to fly at its planned service ceiling of 40,000ft (12,192m). Even the machine guns it relied on as its defensive armament were automated, so they could be fired by remote control. It meant that a single gunner could operate several gun turrets simultaneously from sighting positions in the nose, tail, and the Perspex blisters in the central fuselage.

The prototype B-29 first flew in August 1942. Mass production started in July 1943. Six months later,

A B-29 Superfortress cruises over Osaka, Japan, on 1 June 1945. It was the second great US air raid on the city; subsequent attacks were launched on 6, 7, 15 and 26 June, 15 and 24 July and on 14 August, the last day of the war. The first US air raid, on 13 March, set the pattern for what was to follow. About 8.1/10 sq. miles (21kmÇ) of Osaka was destroyed. The damage was done by clusters of M-69 incendiary bombs. The B-29s carried just over 1,400 of them per plane.

however, only 97 B-29s had actually been delivered and just 16 of these were considered fit to fly. The problem stemmed from the immense pressure Boeing was under to get the bombers into action. There were so many design changes that special plants had to be set up to modify the B-29s coming off the assembly lines. It took precious months for all the problems that had been detected to be finally sorted out.

OPERATION MEETINGHOUSE

The B-29s assigned to attack Tokyo were further modified for their task. General Curtis LeMay, in command of the operation, had decided on a radical change of tactics. Rather than continuing to fly at high altitude in daylight to deliver precision attacks on specific Japanese targets, his bombers would now fly by night to launch low-level area assaults. His objective was to set fire to the closely packed wooden houses and buildings characteristic of Japanese cities, creating a raging inferno that ultimately would turn into a devastating firestorm.

Because Japanese air defenses were virtually nonexistent by this stage of the war, the Boeings were stripped of their defensive armament, with the exception of the tail turrets, and the number of aircrew was cut back to the minimum required to fly the planes. This meant an increase of 65 percent in bomb capacity; each Superfortress was now able to carry more than seven tons of bombs. These included deadly white phosphorus and napalm incendiaries. Napalm was a new gasoline-based fuel-gel cocktail recently developed by scientists at Harvard University. It was to prove chillingly effective. LeMay, now commander of the 20th Army Air Force, told the aircrews who were to fly the

FIRE BOMBING

This map composite, produced by the USAAF, shows the most important Japanese cities attacked by General Curtis LeMay's B-29s at the start of their 1945 fire-bombing campaign. The red indicates the areas of each city that were leveled as a result of the raids. LeMay, in command of the 20th Army Air Force decided on this new tactic because high-level precision bombing of specific Japanese targets was proving a failure. He believed that area bombing entire cities from heights ranging from 5,000–8,000ft (1,524–2,438m) would be the answer. The first raids, launched against Tokyo, Kobe, Osaka, and Nagoya proved LeMay right. Large areas of each city were burned to the ground.

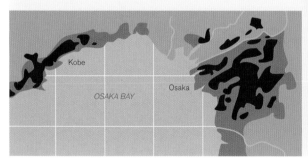

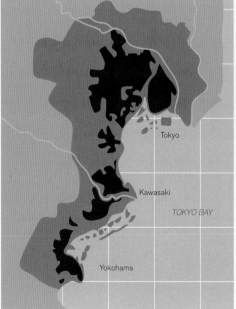

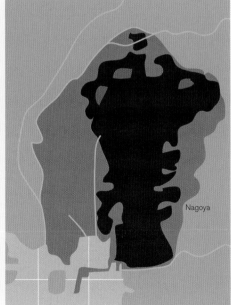

Tokyo photographed from the air before and after the first fire-bombing raid on the city, carried out on March 10, 1945: 334 B-29s took part in the raid, striking late at night so they could take advantage of daylight when flying back to their bases in the Marianas Islands. A quarter of the city was destroyed, more than 100,000 of its citizens killed, and over a million Japanese left homeless. It was the single deadliest air raid of the entire war, greater in its impact than Hamburg, Dresden, Hiroshima, or Nagasaki.

mission that they were "going to deliver the biggest firecracker the Japanese have ever seen."

The lead attackers acted as pathfinders, arriving over Tokyo around midnight. Their job was to mark the target area—downtown Shitamachi—with a flaming "X" to guide the main waves of bombers, flying at around 6,000ft (1,828.8m), in to bomb. The raid proper which followed lasted for three hours with roughly 2,000 tons of incendiaries being dropped on the hapless city. As the second wave of B-29s approached, they could see the flames rising into the sky from 150 miles (241km) away.

"SOWING THE SKY WITH FIRE"

The Japanese on the ground never stood a chance. Tokyo's fire brigades, understrength, poorly trained and inadequately equipped, were totally overwhelmed. With most men of fighting age conscripted into the armed forces, women, children, and the elderly struggled in vain to battle the flames. The B-29s quickly kindled a giant bonfire that, fanned by a 30-knot wind, spread across the entire city. By dawn, 16 sq. miles (41.4km²) of it were in ashes.

Masses of panicking civilians scrambled to escape the inferno. Most of them were unsuccessful. Walls of fire blocked tens of thousands fleeing for their lives. The heat of the firestorm was so intense that it boiled the water in Tokyo's rivers and canals. "In the black Sumida River," wrote a doctor, "countless bodies were floating, clothed bodies, naked bodies, all black as charcoal. It was unreal." In some places, the temperature rose to as much as 3,272°F.

Police cameraman Koyo Ishikaw was another eyewitness. He described the scene on the streets as "flaming pieces of furniture exploded in the heat while the people themselves blazed like matchsticks and their wood-and-paper homes exploded in flames. Thanks to the wind, immense incandescent vortices rose in a number of places, swirling, flattening, and sucking whole blocks of houses into their maelstrom of fire." Even the American bomber crews were affected. Aircrews of the B-29s coming in to bomb toward the end of the raid reported that they were able to smell the stench of charred human flesh as they flew over the burning capital. Many put on their oxygen masks to avoid being made physically sick by the smell.

Robert Guillain was a French news reporter, who had been in Japan since 1938 and remained there throughout the war. He compiled a vivid record of the great attack, starting at the moment when the sound of the city's air-raid sirens pierced the night as the first B-29s prepared to bomb.

"They set to work at once sowing the sky with fire," he wrote. "Bursts of light flashed everywhere in the darkness, like Christmas trees lifting their decorations of flame high into the night, then fell back to earth in whistling bouquets of jagged flame. Barely a quarter of an hour after the raid started, the fire, whipped by the wind, began to scythe its way through the density of the wooden city."

Guillain's district was not singled out for direct attack. He decided not to seek shelter. "There was no question in such a raid of huddling blindly underground," he opined. "You could be roasted alive before you knew what was happening." Instead, he tried his best to observe what was going on. He watched as the waves of B-29s powered in, seemingly impervious to the increasingly desperate Japanese antiaircraft fire.

"The bright light dispelled the night and B-29s were visible here and there in the sky. They flew low or middling high in staggered levels. Their long, glinting wings, sharp as blades, could be seen through the oblique columns of smoke rising from the city, suddenly reflecting the fire from the furnace below, black silhouettes gliding through the fiery sky to reappear farther on, shining golden against the dark roof of heaven or glittering blue, like meteors, in the searchlight beams spraying the vault from horizon to horizon. All the Japanese in the gardens near mine were out of doors or peering out of their holes, uttering cries of admiration—this was typically Japanese—at this grandiose, almost theatrical spectacle."

AFTERMATH

The Japanese bearing the brunt of the bombing were in no mood to admire anything. "Hundreds of people gave up trying to escape and crawled into the holes that served as shelters. Their charred bodies were found after the raids," Guillain recorded. "Wherever there was

a canal, people hurled themselves into the water... thousands of them were later found dead, not drowned but asphyxiated by the burning air and smoke. In other places, the water got so hot that the luckless bathers were boiled alive."

"In Asakusa and Honjo," Guillain continued, "people crowded onto the bridges, but the spans were made of steel that gradually heated; human clusters clinging to the white-hot railings finally let go, fell into the water, and were carried off on the current. Thousands jammed the parks and gardens that lined both banks of the Sumida. As panic brought ever fresh waves of people pressing into these narrow strips of land, those in front were pushed irresistibly toward the river; whole waves of screaming humanity toppled over and disappeared in the deep water." They all drowned.

The raid finally came to an end, though the fires the bombers had started continued to burn for four days afterward. "The sirens sounded the all-clear at around 5:00 a.m.," Guillain concluded. "I talked to someone who had inspected the scene...What was most awful, my informant told me, was having to get off his bicycle every couple of feet to pass over the countless bodies strewn through the streets. There was still a light wind blowing, and some of the bodies, reduced to ashes, were simply scattering like sand. In many sectors, passage was blocked by whole incinerated crowds."

It was not over. On May 23, 520 Superfortresses dropped a further 4,500 tons of bombs on Tokyo, obliterating the city's commercial center, the railway yards, and the Guiza entertainment district. Two days later, 502 B-29s dropped another 4,000 tons of bombs. LeMay boasted that the American bombers were "driving [the Japanese] back to the Stone Age." The city was bombed for the last time on 10 August, four days after the dropping of the first atomic bomb on Hiroshima and less than a week before the Japanese surrender. By that time, 50 percent of Tokyo had been reduced to rubble.

Tokyo photographed from the air while the city was being bombed by LeMay's B-29s on the night of May 26, 1945. The target for the 520 Superfortresses taking part in the raid was the area immediately south of the imperial palace. The planes dropped between 3,500 and 4,000 tons of incendiaries between them, turning the city below them into what one B-29 pilot described as "one horrendous area of fire."

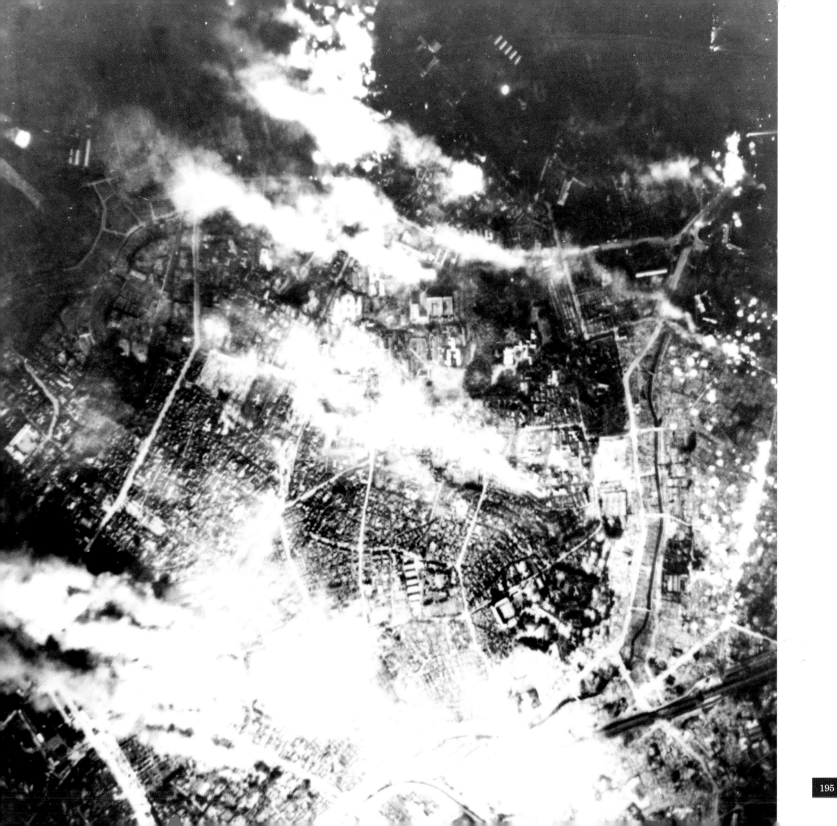

HIROSHIMA AND NAGASAKI

On August 6, 1945, the world changed forever. An American B-29 Superfortress dropped the first atomic bomb to be deployed in warfare over the city of Hiroshima in Japan. The resulting explosion wiped out 80 percent of the city and killed an estimated 80,000 of its inhabitants outright. Tens of thousands would die later as the result of their exposure to nuclear radiation.

The age of atomic warfare had begun. Three days later, another B-29 dropped a second atomic bomb on Nagasaki. The bomb was almost 10 times more powerful than the one dropped on Hiroshima. This time, almost the entire industrial area of the city was destroyed and nearly 74,000 Japanese were killed. Ironically, Nagasaki had not been the mission's original target. The American intention had been to bomb Kokura, but, when the B-29 reached it, it found that the city was shrouded in smoke from the firebombing of nearby Yawata the previous day.

FLIGHT OF THE ENOLA GAY

The mission to Hiroshima began at 2:45 a.m. when a B-29 took off from Tinian, an island in the Marianas group in the North Pacific 1,500 miles (2,414km) south of Japan. It carried just one bomb, weighing about 9,000lb (4,082kg). "Little Boy" as the bomb had been codenamed, was 28in (71cm) in diameter and 10ft (3m) long. Colonel Paul W. Tibbets, the bomber's commander, had nicknamed his aircraft "Enola Gay" after his mother. Shortly before takeoff, he had the name painted onto its fuselage just below the cockpit.

Though four hours into the flight, Tibbets finally was able to tell his aircrew exactly what type of bomb they were carrying, he was burdened with another secret he was unable to share. Before boarding his aircraft, he had been handed a dozen cyanide capsules to distribute to his crew. They were to kill themselves in the event of the B-29 being shot down. Tibbets was ordered to shoot anyone refusing to swallow his capsule—the Japanese could not be allowed to capture anyone alive.

Fortunately, the flight went smoothly for Tibbets and his crew. He later described it as a "milk run." Enola Gay rendezvoused successfully with its two escorting planes over Iwo Jima and, having received radio confirmation from a reconnaissance flight that the weather over Hiroshima was clear, the three aircraft flew on toward their target. The B-29 arrived over Hiroshima only 17 seconds behind schedule. Major Thomas W. Ferebee, the plane's bombardier, spotted his target—the distinctive T-shaped Aioi Bridge in the downtown part of the city. As Tibbets held the Enola Gay steady at 31,600ft (9,632m), Ferebee released the bomb. Watching it through the Plexiglas window right in the nose of the plane, he saw it hover momentarily and then pick up speed. It exploded 57 seconds later at a height of 1,890ft (576m) just a few hundred feet off target.

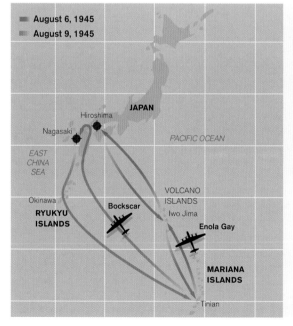

August 6, 1945
August 9, 1945

JAPAN

Hiroshima

Nagasaki

PACIFIC OCEAN

EAST CHINA SEA

Okinawa

RYUKYU ISLANDS

Bockscar

VOLCANO ISLANDS

Iwo Jima

Enola Gay

MARIANA ISLANDS

Tinian

Hiroshima photographed from the air by one of the two B-29s accompanying Tibbets prior to and shortly after the first atomic bomb was dropped on the city. Visibility was perfect over the target as Tibbets flew over it to drop his bomb. It detonated 57 seconds later at its prescribed height over a medical center; the original aiming point was the Aioa Bridge, but the wind blew the bomb off course. "A bright light filled the plane," Tibbets recalled. "The first shock wave hit us. We were eleven-and-a-half miles (18.5km) slant range from the atomic explosion, but the whole airplane cracked and crinkled from the blast."

HIROSHIMA AND NAGASAKI FLIGHT PLANS

The B-29 Superfortress was the only US warplane capable of carrying the first atomic bombs to Hiroshima and Nagasaki. Commanded by Colonel Paul Tibbets of the 509th Composite Bombardment Group, Enola Gay carried out the Hiroshima attack; Bockscar, commanded by Major Charles Sweeney of the 393rd Squadron, attacked Nagasaki. Because of poor visibility, Sweeney bombed the city in preference to Kokura, the original choice of target.

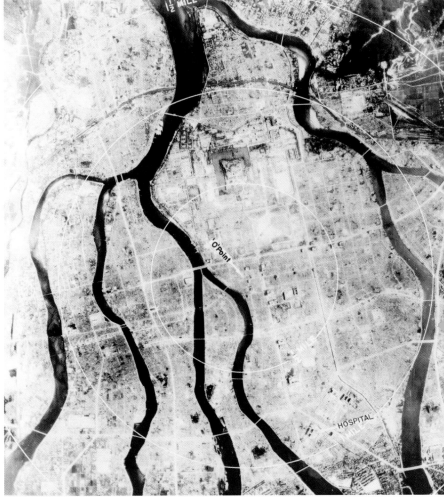

"LITTLE BOY" EXPLODES

As soon as Ferebee released the bomb, the B-29 lurched suddenly upward. Tibbets threw it into a tight turn, dropped 1,700ft (518m) in height and flew away from the target area as quickly as he could to minimize the risk of Enola Gay being damaged by the shock waves caused by the bomb's detonation. He was nine miles (14.5km) away by the time "Little Boy" exploded. Even so, the B-29 was still tossed around in the air like confetti; one of the aircrew said that it felt "as if a giant was smashing the plane with a telegraph pole." Even though they had been told to put on protective dark glasses before dropping the bomb, the explosion was so bright that some of the crew feared they had been blinded. Ferebee recalled: "There are no words to describe how bright the flash was. The sun doesn't compare at all." Tibbets told his crew: "Fellows, you have just dropped the first atomic bomb in history."

Only Staff Sergeant Bob Caron, seated in his rear gun turret, actually saw the bomb explode. The others

In milliseconds after the explosion a plasma fireball began to form and then a dense cloud started to rise up high into the air. Around 70,000 to 80,000 Japanese in the city were killed instantly by the initial blast and an area of the city one mile (1.6km) in radius reduced to total ruin. Fires broke out through much of the remainder of Hiroshima. Tibbets wrote how "the city was hidden by that awful cloud, mushrooming terrible and incredibly tall."

had to wait until Tibbets had completed his evasive maneuvers before they could see its effects. Caron described what he saw as "a peep into hell." He continued: "A column of smoke is rising fast. It has a fiery red core... Fires are springing up everywhere, like flames shooting out of a huge bed of coals. I'm starting to count the fires. One, two, three, four, five six, 14, 15—it's impossible. There are too many to count."

Caron continued: "Here it comes, the mushroom shape... It's coming this way. It's like a mass of bubbling molasses. The mushroom is spreading out. It's maybe a mile or two wide and half a mile high. It's growing up and up. It's nearly level with us and climbing. It's very black, but there is a purplish tint to the cloud. The base of the mushroom looks like a heavy undercast shot through with flames. The city must be below that. The flames and smoke are billowing out, whirling out into the hills. The hills are disappearing under the smoke."

Tibbets concurred. In his biography, *The Tibbets Story*, he wrote: "The giant purple mushroom... had already risen to a height of 40,000ft (12,192m), three miles (4.8km) above our own altitude, and was still boiling upward like something terribly alive. Even more fearsome was the sight on the ground below. Fires were springing up everywhere amid a turbulent mass of smoke that had the appearance of boiling tar."

THE SCENE ON THE GROUND

Tibbets and his aircrew could see little or nothing of what was happening on the ground. Captain Robert Lewis, the B-29s copilot, recorded: "Where we had seen a clear city two minutes before, we could not see the city. We could see smoke and fires creeping up the side of the mountains." Hidden from view, what remained of Hiroshima was burning. Two-thirds of the city had been destroyed; within three miles (4.8km) of the bomb's detonation point, 60,000 out of 90,000 buildings had been demolished.

The unsuspecting people caught by the explosion

"LITTLE BOY" BOMB

Type Nuclear weapon

Weight 9,700lb (4,400kg)

Length 16ft (3m)

Diameter 28in (71cm)

Filling Uranium 235

Yield 16 kilotons

"Little Boy" was the codename for the nuclear device dropped on Hiroshima on August 6, 1945. It was the first atomic bomb to be deployed as a weapon. The Los Alamos scientists and engineers produced two other atomic bomb designs—"Fat Man" and "Thin Man." "Fat Man," a plutonium bomb, was dropped on Nagasaki on August 9. "Thin Man" was a failure.

suffered equally. Michihiko Hachiya, a Japanese doctor who survived the bombing, wrote at length about his experience:

"Suddenly a strong flash of light startled me—and then another. So well does one recall little things that I remember vividly how a stone lantern in the garden became brilliantly lit and I debated whether this light was caused by a magnesium flare or sparks from a passing trolley.

"Garden shadows disappeared. The view which a moment before had been so bright and sunny was now dark and hazy. Through swirling dust I could barely discern a wooden column that had supported a corner of my house. It was leaning crazily and the roof sagged dangerously.

"Moving instinctively, I tried to escape, but rubble and fallen timbers barred the way. By picking my way cautiously, I managed to reach the *roka* and stepped down into my garden. A profound weakness overcame me, so I stopped to regain my strength. To my surprise, I discovered I was completely naked. How odd! Where were my drawers and undershirt?

"All over the right side of my body, I was cut and bleeding. A large splinter was protruding from a mangled wound in my thigh and something warm trickled into my mouth. My cheek was torn, I discovered as I felt it gingerly, with the lower lip laid wide open. Embedded in my neck was a sizable fragment of glass, which I matter-of-factly dislodged, and, with the detachment of one stunned and shocked studied it and my bloodstained hand."

Hachiya's next thoughts were of his wife. "Suddenly, thoroughly alarmed, I began to yell for her. 'Yaeko-san, where are you?' Pale and frightened, her clothes torn and bloodstained, she emerged from the ruins of our house holding her elbow. Seeing her, I was reassured. My own panic assuaged, I tried to reassure her. 'We'll be all right,' I exclaimed. 'Only let's get out of here as fast as we can.'"

"She nodded and I motioned her to follow me."

Hachiya and his wife were lucky. Tens of thousands were not as fortunate. An unnamed survivor described the carnage elsewhere in the city. "The appearance of people was... they all had skin blackened by burns... They had no hair because the hair was burned, and at a glance you couldn't tell whether you were looking at them from in front or in back... They held their arms bent forward....and their skin—not only on their hands, but on their faces and bodies too—hung down... If there had been only one or two such people, perhaps I would not have had such a strong impression... But wherever I walked I met these people... Many of them died along the road—I can still picture them in my mind—like walking ghosts."

THE SECOND BOMB

By this time, Enola Gay had turned for home. Its aircrew ate their sandwiches. No one spoke—it was, said one of them later, as if they were stunned by the enormity of what they had done. They landed to be greeted by cheering crowds of soldiers lining the runway and, said another crew member, "more generals and admirals than I had ever seen in my life."

Everyone was convinced that the successful bombing of Hiroshima would trigger a Japanese surrender, but there was complete silence from Tokyo. On August 9, another B-29 took to the air and headed toward Japan. It carried "Fat Man," the second atomic bomb. The flight was captained by Charles W. Sweeney, who had piloted one of the two other Superfortresses that had accompanied Tibbets to Hiroshima.

Sweeney dropped "Fat Man" 1,650ft (502m) above Nagasaki precisely at 11:02 a.m. Approximately 40 percent of the city was destroyed. Around 70,000 people died, either in the explosion or of radiation sickness by the end of the year. Fujie Urata Matsumoto was a survivor. She recalled: "The pumpkin field in front of the house was blown clean. Nothing was left of the

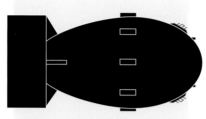

"FAT MAN" BOMB

Type Nuclear weapon	
Weight 10,300lb (4,670kg)	
Length 128in (3.3m)	
Diameter 60in (1.5m)	
Filling Plutonium Yield	
Yield 21 kilotons	

Filled with plutonium as opposed to the uranium 235 used in "Little Boy," "Fat Man" was a more powerful and sophisticated nuclear weapon—it was ten times more efficient than "Little Boy." Many of the physicists involved in the Manhattan Project believed that the device could not be made to work; only Seth Neddermeyer's faith in it kept it alive.

entire thick crop, except that in place of the pumpkins there was a woman's head... It was a woman of about 40... A gold tooth gleamed in her wide-open mouth. A handful of singed hair hung down from the left temple over her cheek, dangling in her mouth. Her eyelids were drawn up, showing black holes where her eyes had been burned out... She had probably looked square into the flash and got her eyeballs burned."

Preparations got underway for the dropping of a third atomic bomb, but this proved unnecessary. On August 14, the Japanese surrendered. Before this, however, the decision to drop the bomb on Japan was already provoking considerable high-level controversy. Some of the physicists involved in the Manhattan Project to build the bomb, opposed it, arguing that, at the least, the Japanese leadership should have been given the chance to witness a demonstration of the bomb's awesome power before a city was targeted. Others argued that, given the Japanese refusal to consider peace terms and the 500,000 to 1,000,000 casualties it was predicted the USA would incur if it was forced to mount an invasion of the Japanese Home Islands, there was no alternative.

Eventually, the buck stopped with President Harry S. Truman, who, as Vice-President of the USA, had succeeded to the presidency after Roosevelt's death earlier in the year. He decided that there was no other course of action open to him other than to authorize the atomic bombing of Japan to go ahead. After the bombing of Nagasaki, he told the American people he had ordered the bomb's use "to shorten the agony of war, to save the lives of hundreds and thousands of young Americans." He believed this until his own death.

A fully formed mushroom cloud towers over Nagasaki, following the city's atomic bombing. Sweeney dropped his bomb through a break in the cloud over the Urakami Valley, which meant that much of the main part of Nagasaki was shielded from blast damage. Nevertheless, between 40,000 and 70,000 of the city's inhabitants were killed instantly. The heat generated by the explosion reached a temperature of 7,052°F (3,900°C); the blast generated winds that gusted at up to 600mph (965km/h). Sweeney turned for home, but, thanks to the time it had taken him to switch targets, he was forced to land on Okinawa as his B-29 was running out of fuel.

5838

BIBLIOGRAPHY/FURTHER READING

In an overall survey like this, the problem is to decide what to put in and what can be omitted. Readers should regard at least some of the information here as a taster to encourage them to probe into specific subjects more deeply. This bibliography has been devised with this purpose in mind, as well as crediting key reference works used in the compilation of this title. For reasons of space, it has been impossible to acknowledge the Internet resources that have been consulted.

Babington Smith, Constance
Evidence in Camera
Sutton Publishing

Ralph Barker and Sidney Cotton
Aviator Extraordinary
Chatto & Windus

Bishop, Patrick
Bomber Boys: Fighting Back
Harper Perennial

Bishop, Patrick
Fighter Boys: Saving Britain
Harper Perennial

Clarke, Nigel C.
Adolf's British Holiday Snaps
Fonthill

Cumins, Keith
Cataclysm: The War on the Eastern Front
Helion

Dorr, Robert F.
Fighting Hitler's Jets
Zenith Press

Dorr, Robert F.
Hell Hawks!
Zenith Press

Dorr, Robert F.
Mission to Berlin
Zenith Press

Dorr, Robert F.
Mission to Tokyo
Zenith Press

Downing, Taylor
Spies in the Sky
Little, Brown

Evans, Sir Richard
The Third Reich at War
Penguin

Glines, Carrol V.
The Doolittle Raid
Schiffer

Hastings, Sir Max
Bomber Command
Zenith Military Classics

Hastings, Sir Max
Nemesis: The Battle of Japan
Harper Perennial

Hersey, John
Hiroshima
Vintage

Holland, James
Dam Busters
Atlantic Monthly Press

Holland, James
Fortress Malta: An Island under Siege
Phoenix

Holland, James
The Battle of Britain
St. Martin's Griffin

Hooton, E. R.
The Luftwaffe
Classic Publications

Horne, Alastair
To Lose a Battle: France 1940
Penguin

Jones, R. V.
Most Secret War
Penguin

Irons, Roy
Hitler's Terror Weapons
Harper

Irons, Roy
The Relentless Offensive
Pen & Sword Aviation

Irving, David
Goering
William Morrow

Irving, David
The Rise and Fall of the Luftwaffe
Little, Brown

Irving, David
Nuremberg: The Last Battle
World War II Books

Kerr, E. Bartlett
Flames over Tokyo
Dutton

Miller, Donald
Masters of the Air
Simon and Schuster

Middlebrook, Martin
The Berlin Raids
Cassell

Middlebrook, Martin
Firestorm Hamburg
Pen & Sword

Middlebrook, Martin
The Nuremberg Raid
Pen & Sword

Middlebrook, Martin
The Peenemünde Raid
Bobbs-Merrill

Middlebrook, Martin
The Schweinfurt-Regensburg Mission
Pen & Sword

Middlebrook, Martin
The Sinking of the Prince of Wales and Repulse
Leo Cooper

Nesbit, Roy Conyers
Eyes of the RAF
Sutton

Overy, Richard
The Bombing War: Europe 1939–45
Allen Lane

Overy, Richard
The Bombers and the Bombed
Viking

Porch, Douglas
Hitler's Mediterranean Gamble
Cassell

Price, Alfred
Targeting the Reich
Greenhill Books

Roosevelt, Elliott
As He Saw It
Greenwood Press

Shores, Christopher
Great Air Battles of World War II
Grub Street

Speer, Albert
Inside the Third Reich
Simon & Schuster

Staerck, Chris (ed)
Allied Photo Reconnaissance of World War II
Thunder Bay Press

Stanley, Colonel Roy M.
World War II Photo Intelligence
Scribner

Stanley, Colonel Roy M.
V Weapons Hunt: Defeating German Secret Weapons
Pen & Sword

Thomas, Geoffrey J.
Eyes for the Phoenix
Hikoki Publications

Wilson, Kevin
Bomber Boys: The Ruhr, the Dambusters and Bloody Berlin
Phoenix

INDEX

Page numbers in **bold** include maps.
Ship names are shown in *italics*.

PHOTO CREDITS

4 © Corbis/ AP/Association Press Images

7 © Hulton-Deutsch Collection/Corbis/ AP/Association Press Images

17 © Imperial War Museum

18 © Imperial War Museum

21 © Australian War Museum B02226

25 Bottom © German Federal Archives

27 © Mick Gladwin – www.airrecce.co.uk

29 © Charles Cotton, with thanks to Jeffery Watson

41 © RCAHMS. NCAP/ncap.org.uk

44 Crown Copyright, reproduced by Courtesy of the Medmenham Collection

47 © IWM via Getty Images

49 © AP/Association Press Images

55 Top & bottom © AP/Association Press Images

57 © RCAHMS. NCAP/ncap.org.uk

59 © Australian War Museum P01528.005

63 © German Federal Archives

72 Bottom, Crown Copyright, reproduced by Courtesy of the Medmenham Collection

75 © RCAHMS. NCAP/ncap.org.uk

79 © www.bismarck-class.dk – John Asmussen

87 © German Federal Archives

105 Crown Copyright, reproduced by Courtesy of the Medmenham Collection

110 © Australian War Museum P02018.086

112 © Australian War Museum P00913.002

113 © Australian War Museum P02018.117

116 © Australian War Museum P02028.076

117 © Australian War Museum P02028.075

119 © (Seine Departmental Archives) Archives départementales des Hauts-de-Seine – 1J545/14

120 Crown Copyright, reproduced by Courtesy of the Medmenham Collection

149 © Imperial War Museum

159 Top © AP/Association Press Images

163 © The National Archives (UK)

164 © Hulton-Deutsch Collection/Corbis

167 © RCAHMS. NCAP/ncap.org.uk

174 © German Federal Archives

177 © AP/Association Press Images

181 © RCAHMS. NCAP/ncap.org.uk

182 © Australian War Museum

183 © German Federal Archives

185 Left & right © The National Archives (UK)

All images listed below are public domain: 12, 13, 14, 16, 20 with thanks to the Canadian Air Force, 22 & 60 & 107 & 147 & 175 bottom with thanks to the National Museum of the US Air Force, 23, 25 top, 26, 28, 31, 32 & 109 & 193 left & right with thanks to Maxwell Air Force Base, 33, 36 with thanks to the San Diego Air and Space Museum, 37, 38, 43 top & bottom, 50 left & right, 51, 53, 56, 61 & 89 with thanks to www.wwii-photos-maps.com, 67, 68, 69, 71, 72 top, 76, 77, 81, 83, 84, 85, 90, 91 top & bottom, 93, 95, 96, 99 top & bottom, 103, 106, 115, 121, 123, 124 & 125 & 168 top & bottom & 189 with thanks to the Royal Air Force, 126, 129 top, 129 bottom left & bottom right Crown copyright photos taken by the Telecommunications Research Establishment at Malvern. Provided with thanks to the Defford Airfield Heritage Group, 131, 133 top & bottom, 135 with thanks to Maxwell Air Force Base and forgottenairfields.com, 137, 138, 139, 141, 143 with thanks to the department for Geoinformation, Measurement and Land Registry, Essen, 145, 148, 151 & 152 reprinted permission of Air Force Magazine published by the Air Force Association, 154, 155, 160, 166, 171, 172, 173, 175 top, 179, 186, 191, 195, 197 left & right, 198, 201.

Every effort has been made to credit the copyright holders of the images used in this book. We apologize for any unintentional omissions or errors and will insert the appropriate acknowledgment to any companies or individuals in subsequent editions of the work.